SO-BBR-287

America since World War II
Warren F. Kimball, Editor

Holding the Line

Eisenhower and John Foster Dulles conferring on the mounting Suez crisis, October 30, 1956. PHOTO COURTESY NATIONAL PARK SERVICE.

Holding the Line

THE
EISENHOWER ERA
1952-1961

Charles C. Alexander

INDIANA UNIVERSITY PRESS

Bloomington & London

Published in Canada by Fitzhenry & Whiteside Limited,
Don Mills, Ontario
Manufactured in the United States of America

Library of Congress Cataloging in Publication Data

Alexander, Charles C.
Holding the line.

(America since World War II)

Bibliography
Includes index.

1. United States—Politics and government—1953–
1961.   2. United States—Foreign relations—1953–
1961.   I. Title.

E835.A645   320.9′73′0921   74-11714

ISBN 0-253-32840-3

To the memory of
C. C. Alexander
(1903-1961)

Contents

Foreword

"How come we never get past World War II?" Teachers of United States history must hear that refrain a hundred times a year, and in all too many cases the complaint is valid. Having lived through the 1950s and 60s, many of us find it hard to think of those years as textbook-type history, and we have often failed to take the time to sit back and make the historical judgments that must precede any attempt to teach about those years. An even greater problem is posed by the scarcity of solid, fully researched syntheses dealing with the more immediate past. That gap is precisely what the series America since World War II is designed to fill.

Some will quarrel with the decision to construct the series along the traditional lines of presidential administrations. Granted, such an organization does tend to disguise the broader social, political, and economic trends which developed and/or continued after 1945 without regard for what Winston Churchill called America's "quadrennial madness." Yet, in each volume, the authors have consciously examined such trends, and, when read as a whole, the series provides an overview of the entire postwar period. Periodization is not only a useful teaching device, but has a validity all its own. As will quickly become clear to the reader, each of these administrations possessed a personality that, while reflecting the broader ideals and attitudes of the American nation, nonetheless remained unique and identifiable. Nor have the authors merely summarized the political history of the period. Rather, each has carefully examined the cultural, social, and economic history which make an era much more than just dates and names.

The series provides, in a relatively brief and readable fashion, a synthesis for use by teachers and students studying American history since the Second World War. In keeping with that purpose, the decision was made to dispense with all but a few necessary informational footnotes. Much more than a mere survey, each

volume is a scholarly interpretation based on extensive research
and thought. The extensive bibliographical essays, which are useful contributions by themselves, give an indication of the author-
itative scholarship that underpins each book.

Charles C. Alexander's *Holding the Line: The Eisenhower
Era, 1952–1961* is the first major summary and interpretation of
the whole complex Eisenhower period to appear. Even though
Dwight David Eisenhower and most of his major advisers have
died or passed from the American scene, the literature about the
years of his administration has remained largely episodic or has
taken the form of memoirs. This book's theme and title partially
explain that curious omission. In spite of much evidence to the
contrary (which Alexander brings out), the Eisenhower years in
America have the reputation of being dull and uneventful. Most
historians, beguiled by the dynamic image of a John Kennedy,
the ebullience of a Lyndon Johnson, or the combativeness of a
Harry Truman, have simply slid by the Eisenhower era, often
treating it as an unimportant transitional stage between Truman's
Fair Deal and Kennedy's New Frontier. The result has been an
unfortunate distortion of the postwar period.

History is an unbroken skein, and the Eisenhower administration initiated or changed policies which later administrations had
to live with. One could argue with ease, for example, that the
Eisenhower policy regarding the 1954 Geneva Accords was far
more decisive than any other single factor in the course of events
leading to all-out American involvement in the Vietnam war. Certainly a distinctive yet typically American cultural pattern developed in the fifties, one mockingly characterized by the garish
tail-fins on automobiles but better understood as expressing a
remarkably homogeneous, middle-class optimism. Socially, the
seeds of change sown by the rhetoric of the Roosevelt administration and the promises of the Truman years began to bear some
fruit as black Americans openly challenged established racial
discrimination. Although their efforts usually continued along
traditional lines, particularly via the courts, civil disobedience
with its often-denied but unmistakable implied threat of violence
began on a bus in Montgomery, Alabama, and slowly spread

into a national movement. Clearly, the Eisenhower years possess a uniqueness as well as a continuity which warrants our attention.

Alexander's study will evoke both pleasant and painful memories among those who lived through the fifties, and it vividly recreates for today's readers the atmosphere and history of the eight important years of Eisenhower's Presidency. To many Americans, the Eisenhower decade is increasingly thought of as "the good old days"; economic problems were less pressing, the cold war seemed a simple and understandable battle between good and evil, a unified American society was supposed to be righting by peaceful and orderly means those few wrongs which existed, and people felt secure and confident—even if there was a certain smugness about that feeling. What those Americans tend to forget is that, by 1961, everything had taken on a new aura of urgency, confusion, and change. The way America handled those new attitudes is another story, but Charles Alexander has offered a persuasive, witty, and revealing explanation of how and why they came about.

WARREN F. KIMBALL

RUTGERS UNIVERSITY
NEWARK COLLEGE

Preface

Although Dwight D. Eisenhower was not flamboyant, not an inspirational or charismatic leader, not one who stirred great popular passions, in his own way he dominated American life during the years 1952–1961 as much as more vigorous and colorful Presidents like Andrew Jackson, Theodore Roosevelt, and Franklin D. Roosevelt had dominated earlier periods. This book is an effort to survey and interpret those years, a span of time that can justifiably be termed the Eisenhower era. While the period after 1952 has received relatively little concentrated attention from professional historians, there does exist—in the writings of many journalists and memoirists, in most analyses by political scientists, and in general treatments of recent United States history—something of an orthodox or traditional view of Eisenhower and his administration. According to this view, the only Republican President between 1933 and 1969 was a genial, well-meaning, but indecisive and basically out-of-touch chief executive, whose performance fell far short of that of Franklin Roosevelt and Harry Truman, his Democratic predecessors, or John F. Kennedy and Lyndon Johnson, his Democratic successors. The Eisenhower administration—characteristically depicted as standpattist in domestic affairs, unimaginative in its foreign policy, and neglectful of the nation's defenses—supposedly constitutes a stifling interlude in the three and a half decades of high drama which began with Franklin Roosevelt's New Deal and ended in the debris of Lyndon Johnson's Great Society. A study of the Eisenhower administration, one of my friends has suggested, might well be entitled "The Mild Bunch."

I did not set out consciously to overturn this common in-

terpretation of the Eisenhower period. In many respects I am in
agreement with it. Yet without trying to be a "revisionist," I
have come to share the inclination—evident in such recent books
as Garry Wills's *Nixon Agonistes* (1970) and Herbert Parmet's
Eisenhower and the American Crusades (1972)—to look more
favorably at the thirty-fourth President, his policies, and some of
the men around him. This change in attitude has involved rejecting or at least softening a number of opinions I formed during
the 1950s and held for a long time thereafter. Coming to maturity
while Eisenhower was President, I cast my first ballot in a presidential election in 1956—not for the incumbent Eisenhower but
for Adlai Stevenson. In 1960 I ardently supported John F. Kennedy, who seemed to have all the qualities—a sophisticated, dynamic conception of the Presidency, a grasp of global realities, a
strong commitment to social justice—which Eisenhower had
seemed to lack. Of course for me, as for many other people, the
experiences of the past decade—particularly the disastrous
American intervention in the Indochina war—have made for a
greatly altered perspective. Yet I have had no difficulty resisting
the current fashionable tendency to wax nostalgic about the
fifties. Anyone who remembers the temper of American public
life during that decade of grim cold war confrontation should
have little reason for nostalgia.

Insofar as this book has a single unifying theme or thesis,
it is that the Eisenhower era was a time for holding the line in
American government and society. The administration in power
was generally content to hold the line against—and not really
try to reverse—the movement toward the welfare state under
way since the 1930s. Despite their early pledges to "liberate"
areas under Communist domination, the makers of American
foreign policy ended up accepting the objective of "containing"
the Soviet Union and the People's Republic of China which had
guided the Truman administration. Eisenhower and his three
Secretaries of Defense also labored diligently but with mixed
results to hold the line against unremitting cold war pressures to
expand the size and cost of the military establishment; and
Eisenhower became the only President in the post–World War II

period to address himself forthrightly to the rapidly growing power and influence of what he labeled the "military-industrial complex." At the same time, the collective disposition of the American people was to continue to accept uncritically the cold war consensus formed before Eisenhower became President, and to hold the line against efforts to raise fundamental questions about their political, economic, and social institutions.

Except for chapter four, which looks cross-sectionally at aspects of American economic, social, intellectual, and cultural experience in the 1950s, my treatment of the Eisenhower years is roughly chronological. Chapter three focuses on the workings of foreign policy in 1954–1955; otherwise I have combined discussions of national and international developments within chapters. Separate handling of events at home and abroad might have made for more orderly presentation. One of my objectives, however, was to show something of the interrelationship between foreign affairs and domestic politics and policies. I also wanted to avoid compartmentalization as much as possible in the interest of conveying some sense of the enormously complex, disorderly character of the period.

Andrew H. Wilkins served well as my research assistant during the early stages of the book, and Anthony L. Newberry's help was invaluable toward the end. Deborah Eckels, Mary Alice Samuels, and Sue Milhoan shared the typing chores while attending to numerous other duties. Alonzo L. Hamby and John L. Gaddis, my colleagues in the Ohio University History Department; Stephen B. Oates and Robert Griffith of the University of Massachusetts; David D. Van Tassel of Case Western University; and Warren F. Kimball of Rutgers University, Newark, cheerfully read all or parts of my manuscript. These friends and fellow historians brought their particular knowledge and expertise to bear in making the manuscript much better in every way than it would otherwise have been. Kimball, moreover, was kind enough to ask me to contribute to the Indiana University Press series America since World War II, of which he is general editor. He proved a skillful and understanding overseer. A different kind of understanding was furnished by my wife, JoAnn, and my daughter, Rachel, who stayed out of the way when they should have, got in the way when they were needed, and generally made my life happy.

Charles C. Alexander

Athens, Ohio
March 1974

Holding the Line

I

Korea, Communism,
Corruption

EVEN though the first Sunday in July 1952 was hotter than usual in the District of Columbia area, Baizie Miller Tankersley was able to attract some 4,000 people to a Republican fund-raising carnival held at her Maryland estate. Mrs. Tankersley, niece of Robert R. McCormick, the ultraconservative publisher of the *Chicago Tribune,* collected a helpful $5,000 for her choice for the Republican presidential nomination that year, Senator Robert A. Taft of Ohio. Taft himself was on hand, stiffly submitting to the ceremony of having his political fortune told inside a closed tent. Among other Republican luminaries present was Taft's Senate colleague Joseph R. McCarthy, taking a break from his noisy pursuit of Communists in nearby Washington. Perhaps the most popular sideshow at Mrs. Tankersley's carnival featured impersonations of the "political monstrosities" of the Democratic party, including "Acheson the Dean of Hisses," "Perle the Gem of the Notion," "Lattimore the Friend of China," and "Caudle the Mink Cuddle."

These objects of Republican ridicule not only largely summed up the animosities of Taft and the conservative wing of the Grand Old Party but also symbolized what agitated vast numbers of American voters about the incumbent Democratic administration. Dean Acheson, the mustachioed, urbane Secretary of State, was the man Taft and his followers held most responsible for what they saw as a succession of disasters in American foreign policy, especially the "loss" of China to the Maoist Communists and the agonizing military stalemate in Korea. Acheson seemed the archetype of the "striped-pants diplomats" from upper-class, Ivy League origins who had run the State Department for twenty years. Those in charge of American foreign policy, so Republican mythology insisted, had "betrayed" the countries of eastern Europe as well as China at the Yalta Conference in 1945, contrived the "defeatist" doctrine of containing instead of rolling back Soviet power, and "coddled" domestic Communists and Communist sympathizers. Most notable of them was Alger Hiss, accused of espionage for the Soviet Union and convicted of perjury before the House Committee on Un-American Activities (HUAC). Senator McCarthy, in the course of making the Communism-in-government issue almost his personal property since 1950, had smeared the reputation of many people, including Professor Owen Lattimore of The Johns Hopkins University, an Asian specialist and State Department consultant. Lattimore, McCarthy had wildly charged, was "the top Russian espionage agent" in the country and "the principal architect of our far-eastern policy."

The other two "political monstrosities" on exhibit had less sinister but almost as infamous associations for victory-hungry Republicans in 1952. Perle Mesta, a good friend of President Harry Truman, who billed herself as "the hostess with the mostest," had been the impresaria of social life in the nation's capital before her appointment as ambassador to Luxembourg. T. Lamar Caudle symbolized various instances of conflict of interest and corruption within the Truman administration which had come to light during the past year. In the Bureau of Internal Revenue alone, Truman had fired nearly 250 employees. Also fired was Assistant Attorney General Caudle, head of the Tax Division of the Justice Department, who had accepted bribes for not prosecuting tax evaders.[1]

Korea, Communism, corruption (the $K_1 C_2$ formula, Senator Karl Mundt called it) would be the basis for the Republican onslaught against the Democrats in the fall. Taft, of course, wanted to lead the onslaught. When he arrived in Chicago for the Republican convention not long after appearing at the Tankersley

---

1. In 1957 T. Lamar Caudle received a two-year sentence in federal prison.

carnival, Taft and his managers were still outwardly confident. But the presidential nomination, which Taft had sought twice without success, was already slipping away once again. Taft was the overwhelming choice among congressional Republicans, and he was probably the favorite of a majority of GOP party workers west of the Hudson River. Since the end of the Second World War Taft had emerged as the foremost spokesman for conservative Republicanism. While favoring federal aid to education and federal financing for public housing, in other respects Taft staunchly upheld private enterprise and opposed the expansion of the functions and power of the national government.

For their position on foreign policy, Taft and his supporters were denounced by both the Truman administration and eastern Republicans as "isolationist." Originating before Pearl Harbor in the debates over Franklin Roosevelt's policy of aiding Great Britain and France as they struggled against Nazi Germany, the term "isolationist" had continued to be a useful epithet in the cold war since 1945. By so branding their critics, as *Life* magazine observed, Truman and Acheson had reserved for the Democrats "a near-monopoly of respectable opinion about foreign policy." "Isolationism" scarcely described any important segment of American opinion, certainly not the views of the Taftites. Taft's personal beliefs were complex. Troubled by the rise of a huge military establishment and the threat it posed to personal liberty and national solvency, Taft was also obsessed with fighting Communism both abroad and at home. The United States, he thought, had global economic and strategic interests which must be backed up by the nation's vast military power. In wielding its power, however, America should go it alone. Taft's approach to foreign policy, part of a tradition reaching back to the beginnings of the Republic, is thus best described as "unilateralist."

Unilateralism featured three fundamental and closely related propositions. First, the United States should enter no "entangling alliances" such as the North Atlantic Treaty Organization (NATO), which the Truman administration had fostered in 1949 to counter a purported Soviet military threat to western Europe and, more importantly, to further political stability and cohesiveness among non-Communist Europeans. Traditionally distrusting the European countries and convinced that the United States should pursue an independent course, Taft and his followers were skeptical about the United Nations organization; some Republicans (though not Taft himself) regarded the UN with outright disdain.

Second, Taft—and midwestern and western Republicans generally—favored a foreign policy that stressed the Pacific region and Asia over Europe; it was in those regions, they insisted, that America's vital interests and moral obligations were and would continue to be. This "Asia First" orientation explains the implacable bitterness with which Taft and most other Republicans reacted to the victory of Mao Tse-tung's armies in the Chinese civil war and the withdrawal, at the end of 1949, of the remnants of Chiang Kai-shek's Nationalist armies to Formosa and other offshore islands. It also explains the passionate attraction of the Republican right wing to General Douglas MacArthur. Much of the popular hysteria triggered when Truman removed MacArthur from his command of United Nations forces in Korea the previous year had dissipated by mid-1952. MacArthur nevertheless remained the foremost symbol and the foremost political casualty of the Truman-Acheson "no-win" policy in the war on that ravaged peninsula.

The MacArthur controversy points up the third major proposition on which unilateralists operated: As MacArthur had admonished, America should never get bogged down in a land war on the Asian continent. In Korea the United States, furnishing almost all the international forces involved in the UN's "police action," was obviously very much bogged down. In the fall of 1950 the military and political adventurism of MacArthur, with Truman's blessing, had carried American and South Korean armies to the Yalu River in an effort to unify the peninsula and destroy the Communist North Korean regime. But then the intervention of vast numbers of Chinese troops had forced the UN forces to retreat to the prewar partition line at the 38th parallel. After that the fighting had settled down to a grueling, indecisive succession of mostly localized struggles, accompanied by prolonged, inconclusive, and frustrating truce negotiations.

For Taft, congressional Republicans, and Americans in general, Korea had become an intolerable situation. Taft's position on the war had vacillated considerably since its outbreak in the summer of 1950, but by 1952 he had come to insist that the United States either go all out for military victory, as MacArthur urged, or withdraw from the peninsula entirely. And Taft seemed to care little for how the UN as a whole or America's European allies might react if the United States brought to bear its full military power in Korea, including perhaps the use of atomic bombs.

Taft thus found himself the leader of militant American unilateralism—that huge body of opinion which continued to believe passionately in what the British historian D. W. Brogan in 1952 called the "illusion of American omnipotence." Taft spoke for those who assumed that "any situation which distresses or endangers the United States can only exist because some Americans have been fools or knaves," as Brogan put it. The taciturn Taft usually did not join in the anti-Communist hyperbole of McCarthy and other Republican senators like Richard Nixon and William Jenner, or the Democrat Pat McCarran. Yet Taft also saw fools and knaves behind America's troubles. The State Department's policies were pro-Communist, he declared early in 1952; McCarthy's insistence on a complete investigation of subversives at State was "fully justified." Taft was never McCarthy's friend and seems to have had some reservations about his tactics. Even so, he both agreed with McCarthy's assumptions about the internal "Red menace" and drew substantial support from those who shared the perfervid anti-Communism of the junior senator from Wisconsin.

More than anything else, Taft's stance on foreign policy frightened the "moderate," "internationalist" element of the GOP. Such Republicans, strongest on the east coast, had thwarted Taft's bids for the GOP presidential nomination in 1940 and 1948. While eastern Republicans had become increasingly strident in their criticism of the Truman administration, they continued to believe that foreign policy should be Atlantic- and European-oriented, that it should be founded on "collective security" arrangements recognizing the interrelationship between American interests and those of other nations, and that it should be backed by a broad, bipartisan consensus. In the last three campaigns

Republican presidential candidates Wendell Willkie and Thomas E. Dewey had personified these views. During late 1951 and early 1952, as Taft took the inside track in the drive for the GOP nomination, Dewey and like-minded Republicans sought a man with enough popular appeal to counter Taft's strength among congressional Republicans and party workers.

By late March 1952 they had their man, the only one they had ever really sought. General of the Army Dwight D. Eisenhower, commander of NATO since early the previous year and the triumphant leader of Allied forces in Europe during World War II, let it be known from NATO's Paris headquarters that within two months he would resign from the Army and return to the United States to announce his candidacy for the Republican presidential nomination.

In 1952 the sixty-one-year-old Eisenhower was very much of a political novice. Four years earlier his popularity had been so great—and his political identification so indistinct—that he could easily have had the presidential nomination of either major party. In 1948, in fact, the liberal Americans for Democratic Action (ADA) had pushed Eisenhower for the Democratic nomination over President Truman until the general put an end to such efforts. Before 1952 Eisenhower's most overtly political acts had been to vote for (but not openly support) Thomas E. Dewey for President in 1948 and John Foster Dulles, the unsuccessful Republican candidate in a special New York senatorial election, the next year. Upon assuming the presidency of Columbia University in 1948, Eisenhower had said that "nothing in the international or domestic situation especially qualifies for the most important office in the world a man whose adult years have been spent in the military services. At least, this is true in my case."[2]

Four years later, however, the genuinely reluctant general finally gave in to the entreaties of Dewey, Senator Henry Cabot Lodge of Massachusetts, Eisenhower's good friend Roy A. Roberts, publisher of the *Kansas City Star*, and other leading Repub-

---

2. Eisenhower served as president of Columbia until late 1950, when President Truman named him NATO commander. He then received a leave of absence from the Columbia trustees, continuing as the University's nominal president.

licans. Early in February 1952 Eisenhower's supporters held an improbable midnight rally in New York's Madison Square Garden after the Friday night boxing matches. Some 18,000 people nearly filled the Garden to thunder "We like Ike." After the rally the noted aviatrix Jacqueline Cochran piloted her aircraft to Paris, where she gave Eisenhower a film of the demonstration. In the New Hampshire Republican primary in March, Eisenhower polled 50 percent of the vote to Taft's 38 percent; he also ran a powerful second to native-son Harold Stassen in the Minnesota primary, despite the fact that, because his name did not appear on the ballot, his supporters had to write in a great variety of spellings of Eisenhower. Later that month President Truman—still getting little more than 25 percent in the Gallup poll's approval ratings and recently embarrassed by a poor showing in the New Hampshire Democratic primary—announced that he would not seek reelection.

Eisenhower's enormous popularity was borne out not only by the New Hampshire and Minnesota primaries but also by the public opinion polls, which showed him to be the favorite among all the potential candidates in both parties. An especially significant poll taken by the Gallup organization early in May made him the choice of 52 percent of the independent voters, as compared to only 14 percent for Taft. Here was graphic evidence that Taft, despite his image as "Mr. Republican," was woefully weak with people whose votes the outregistered Republicans had to have to win.

In the face of such evidence, Eisenhower doubtless was attracted by the prospect of power, as most men would be. In Eisenhower's case, however, the political drive seems to have been relatively weak; certainly he had little taste for the rough and tumble of politics. Two factors were critical in bringing about his decision to seek the Presidency. One was the general's uncommonly strong commitment to duty, a commitment born of nearly four decades of sacrificing home life and often personal comfort in Army service. Eisenhower, as the political scientist James David Barber has described him, was "a sucker for duty." The other factor was Eisenhower's genuine fear of what a Taft Presidency would do to American foreign policy. Just before he

left for Europe to assume his NATO command, Eisenhower had
met secretly at the Pentagon with Taft to seek the Senate minority
leader's bipartisan support for the European alliance. When Taft
spent most of the time talking about limiting the number of
American divisions in NATO, Eisenhower became worried that
"isolationism was stronger in the Congress than I had previously
suspected."

Eisenhower was not fundamentally unhappy with the course
of the country's foreign and military policies since 1945. As NATO
leader he had been a willing instrument of those policies, probably the most effective such instrument the Truman administration had. The general had become as confirmed a cold warrior
as anyone; like Taft, McCarthy, Truman, Acheson, and the vast
majority of the American people, Eisenhower believed in a
monolithic conspiracy directed from the Kremlin which aimed
at nothing short of Communist global domination through intimidation, subversion, and, unless the United States maintained
powerful defenses, military aggression. Even so, Eisenhower did
not share the Republican right wing's obsession with the specter
of Communist espionage and subversion at home. For Eisenhower
the principal menace was abroad and was best countered by
American leadership in the formation of strong military alliances
accompanied by programs of overseas military and economic
assistance. In short, Eisenhower and the Republican "internationalists" who rallied around him essentially accepted the Truman
administration's policy of containing Communist power until, so
the presumption went, patience and firmness brought a loosen-
ing of the Kremlin's grip on the Russian and eastern European
peoples, perhaps even internal convulsions leading to the overthrow of Communist tyranny. As for Asia, Eisenhower shared the
general dismay over the Communist victory in China and the
standoff in Korea. But while he and his party would be able to
use the war issue with great effect in the 1952 campaign, Eisenhower had no clear-cut proposals for ending the conflict.

On June 4, 1952, Eisenhower formally began his bid for the
Republican nomination in a nationally televised but rain-marred
speech at a park named after him in his hometown, Abilene,
Kansas. The speech was a rather vapid effort. Eisenhower spoke

broadly of the need for strong national defense, for unwavering vigilance against international Communism, for holding down the cost and size of government, and for more attention to "those simple virtues—integrity, courage, self-confidence, an unshakeable belief in [the] Bible . . . ." The next day, to the consternation of some of his managers, Eisenhower endorsed the GOP's 1950 Declaration of Principles, which had defined the difference between Republicans and Democrats as "liberty versus socialism." Eisenhower thus revealed that many of his views were, as Herbert Parmet has commented, "considerably to the right of the men who had promoted his candidacy." Yet as Parmet has also pointed out, Eisenhower's nomination "would give the GOP a candidate much less representative of Republican thinking than was Senator Taft."

The Republican convention opened on Monday, July 7, in Chicago's International Amphitheatre. It was the first presidential nominating convention to be nationally televised, although by 1952 coaxial-cable transmission had not yet reached all parts of the southeastern and Rocky Mountain states. Carried by all four television networks (which then included the small Dumont system), the proceedings reached an estimated 50 million voters watching in public places and on some 18 million home sets. More than one-half the American people supposedly saw at least part of the convention.

"Mr. Republican" had a clear lead in delegates, but he was still considerably short of the 604-vote majority needed for the nomination. After the delegates finished cheering the keynote speech by General MacArthur, himself hopeful for the nomination if Eisenhower and Taft deadlocked, what turned out to be the decisive battle shaped up over the seating of contested delegations from several southern states. In those states the Taft-dominated regular party oganizations—which, because of historic Democratic party dominance, were little more than patronage dispensers—had met spirited resistance from Eisenhower backers, who were mostly former Democrats. After the state party conventions, controlled by the regular Republicans, refused to accommodate the Eisenhower forces, both factions sent delegations to Chicago. Just before the convention the Republican National Committee and the Committee on Rules, again with pro-Taft sentiment pre-ponderant, voted to seat Taft delegates in most cases. Behind the scenes Taft offered a few of his contested delegates to Eisenhower, but the general's managers, realizing that they had everything to gain by dramatizing their grievances, determined to carry their fight before the convention.

The Eisenhower challenge took the form of the shrewdly named Fair Play Amendment, which proposed to change the party rules so as to prohibit contested state delegations from voting on the status of other delegations in dispute. The critical vote came when Taft's backers tried to emasculate the amendment. After this effort failed by a vote of 658 to 548, the Fair Play Amendment carried by acclamation. Here was dramatic proof that, for all their strength in the GOP hierarchy, Taft's supporters could not control the convention. The next night, after bitter debate, the convention voted to give Eisenhower a majority of the disputed delegates from Georgia, Florida, Louisiana, and Texas. By this time the convention was clearly moving toward an Eisenhower nomination.

On Thursday night the delegates adopted the report of the Platform Committee without opposition. The platform endorsed Senator McCarthy's claim that the Democrats had "shielded trai-tors to the Nation in high places." The principal author of the foreign policy section was John Foster Dulles, a Republican who had worked in various capacities for the State Department under Truman and who now castigated the containment policy of the administration he had served as "negative, futile and immoral." In an all-out bid for the votes of Americans of eastern European ancestry, the GOP promised that a Republican administration would "repudiate all commitments contained in secret understand-ings such as those of Yalta which aid Communist enslavement." Strongly endorsing collective security in Europe, the platform also disclaimed any intention of withdrawing from Asia and denounced the Democrats for not doing enough to help Chiang Kai-shek's Nationalist Chinese regime. Designed by Dulles to satisfy both European-oriented Republicans and Asia Firsters, the platform pleased Eisenhower; despite what he later described as its "purple, 'prosecuting attorney' style," it had repudiated "isolationism."

On Friday afternoon the GOP convention proceeded with relative dispatch to make Eisenhower its nominee. On the first ballot the general received 595 votes to 500 for Taft; the remainder were scattered among Governor Earl Warren of California, Harold Stassen, and other favorite sons. Before the clerk could announce the first-ballot totals, the Minnesota delegation switched its nineteen votes from Stassen to Eisenhower. Other states clamored to do the same; when the switching stopped Eisenhower had 841 votes, Taft fewer than 300.

In choosing his vice-presidential running mate, Eisenhower depended mainly on the advice of Dewey, Lodge, Governor Dan Thornton of Colorado, and Herbert Brownell, a New York corporation lawyer soon to become his campaign manager. Richard M. Nixon, the thirty-nine-year-old junior senator from California, was the man he picked. Although Eisenhower knew little about Nixon before his name was brought up, the general soon saw that Nixon would give an almost perfect balance to the ticket. First gaining notoriety during HUAC's inquiry into left-wing influences in the motion picture industry, Nixon had then led the committee in its dogged pursuit of Alger Hiss. In his 1950 senatorial campaign and then as a senator, Nixon had continued to use the issues of Communist subversion at home and Democratic betrayal abroad to great advantage for himself and his party. At the same time, he had supported the European alliance and the United Nations, and had maintained good relations with eastern Republicans. Reserved, introspective, yet intensely combative, Nixon had impressed friends with his toughness and determination. Among his growing number of enemies, he stood for ruthlessness and duplicity.

Eisenhower's acceptance speech on Friday night was a lofty address. He told the delegates, "you have summoned me on behalf of millions of your fellow Americans to lead a great crusade—for freedom in America and freedom in the world." His aim, he proclaimed, was "to sweep from office an Administration which has fastened on every one of us the wastefulness, the arrogance and corruption in high places, the heavy burdens and anxieties of a party too long in power." Closing with a call for party unity, Eisenhower implicitly acknowledged what must be his major task in the weeks ahead. Denied the nomination a third time by the "Eastern Establishment," Taft and many of his supporters had left the convention bitter and disheartened.

Ten days later the Democrats came together in the same building in Chicago for their twenty-ninth quadrennial national convention. If anything, the Democratic party was more deeply divided than the GOP. The Democrats had suffered deep wounds in 1948, when delegates from the Deep South had walked out of the convention to protest the adoption of a strong civil rights platform and had gone home to organize their own party. The "Dixiecrat" candidate, Senator J. Strom Thurmond of South Carolina, had taken four states away from President Truman that year, although Truman had managed a narrow reelection. The party presumably would have to moderate its stand on civil rights, especially its earlier pledge to secure voting rights for massively disenfranchised black southerners, or there might very well be another schism.

On the Democratic left, however, the spectrum of opinion had narrowed considerably since the 1948 debacle of Henry A. Wallace's Progressive party, formed by liberals and radicals who thought Truman's uncompromising policy toward the Soviet Union was destroying chances for world peace. The fact that the Progressive leadership included a considerable number of American Communists, together with the steady worsening of American-Soviet relations, had effectively discredited the Wallace candidacy. Wallace had received little more than a million votes, fewer even than Thurmond. The Progressive party represented the last real challenge to the increasingly pervasive cold war consensus in American political life. After 1948 Democratic party liberals, keyed by the fervently anti-Communist Americans for Democratic Action, became full converts to the Truman administration's hard-line cold warriorism. Foreign policy pronouncements from the Democratic left and the Republican right came to seem almost equally militant.

Despite their commitment to fighting Communism around the globe, the Democrats still had to defend an administration that was not only plagued by scandal and charges of Communist infiltration at home but also was unable to promise either peace or more aggressive actions to vanquish the nation's enemies abroad. Confronting Eisenhower's towering prestige and magnetic appeal, experienced politicians might have been expected to wait for a more promising opportunity. Yet with President Truman formally out of the running, a cluster of men actively sought the Democratic nomination: United States Senators Estes Kefauver of Tennessee, Richard Russell of Georgia, and Robert S. Kerr of Oklahoma; Vice President Alben W. Barkley; and Mutual Security Administrator W. Averell Harriman of New York. Kefauver was a strong southern liberal, who had first gained national exposure by vigorously leading a Senate committee in its televised investigation of national organized crime. Campaigning for more than a year, Kefauver had beaten President Truman in the New Hampshire primary and led in pledged delegates as the convention opened.

The emerging Democratic favorite, however, was Governor Adlai E. Stevenson of Illinois. Stevenson had proved even more reluctant to seek the presidential nomination than Eisenhower. Backed by Truman, by the powerful Chicago-Cook County political organization, by an energetic Draft Stevenson organization made up of Chicago-area academicians and students, by ADA's national leadership, and by a swelling number of Democratic leaders convinced that only he could win, Stevenson had nevertheless denied repeatedly that he wanted the nomination. All he did want, he claimed, was to run for reelection in Illinois that year. Fifty-two years old, the grandson of one of Grover Cleveland's Vice Presidents, Stevenson had won the governorship in 1948 by a record majority after serving in various appointive posts under the Roosevelt and Truman administrations, most importantly as acting ambassador to the UN. Stevenson's governorship had been generally progressive and successful. Basically shy, inclined to be philosophical, something of an intellectual yet also an astute politician, Stevenson seemed the man most likely to bring together the many diverse elements within the Democratic party.

Stevenson never said flatly that he would not accept the nomination, and his noncandidacy gained momentum when he spoke to the convention on the first day as host governor and prompted an impressive demonstration. Meanwhile septuagenarian Barkley's slim chances evaporated when the heads of several labor unions in the Congress of Industrial Organizations formally turned down his plea for support. Nor could Kefauver, Harriman, or the other declared contenders pick up many additional delegates.

The Democratic platform predictably took credit for the rapid advances in personal income under the Truman administration (without mentioning big advances in living costs), for record employment, and for government efforts to maintain profitable farm income levels. The Democrats called for basic changes in the Taft-Hartley Act, denounced as crippling by labor unions since its passage in 1947, and for expanded federal activity in public power and resource conservation. Their foreign policy statement pointed to the party's enlightened internationalism and lauded the Truman administration for stopping the spread of Communist power. The Democratic position on civil rights was somewhat weaker than in 1948. A group of northern liberals—led by Franklin D. Roosevelt, Jr., Senator Hubert Humphrey of Minnesota, and Senator Blair Moody and Governor G. Mennen Williams of Michigan —did get the convention to approve a loyalty pledge whereby southern Democrats promised to try by "all honorable means" to keep the party's national nominees on their state ballots in November. All delegates would have to sign such a pledge. After the loyalty pledge carried by voice vote, the delegations from South Carolina, Virginia, and Louisiana refused to sign it and thus lost their voting rights at the convention. The next day, however, the convention voted to restore the ballot to the dissident Southerners.

The balloting for the presidential nomination began on Friday afternoon, July 25, amid fruitless efforts to form a stop-Stevenson coalition.[3] For the last time for at least a generation, the choice of a presidential nominee would take more than one ballot. Although Kefauver led on the first two tallies, he was still far short

3. The delegates began the balloting in the relieved knowledge that the previous day a settlement had been reached in a 53-day-old steel strike which had kept some 600,000 workers off the job. The strike had followed a U.S. Supreme Court decision holding unconstitutional President Truman's emergency seizure of the steel mills to maintain steel output for national defense.

of the 616-vote majority. During the second ballot late in the afternoon, President Truman flew into Chicago. At his hotel he had dinner with a group of party officials, including Paul Fitzpatrick, the New York state chairman. When the balloting resumed that night, Fitzpatrick read a statement from Averell Harriman announcing his withdrawal and calling on his supporters, mainly the big New York delegation, to shift their votes to Stevenson. After the third ballot Stevenson lacked only two votes for a majority. At this juncture Kefauver stepped to the rostrum to capitulate and to release his delegates. Shortly after midnight, in about as close to a genuine draft as is possible, the Democratic convention made Stevenson its nominee.

In the early morning hours, after most radio listeners and television viewers had themselves capitulated and gone to bed, Truman presented Stevenson to the tired but noisy delegates. Appearing to be awed, even a little stunned by the day's developments, Stevenson began by quoting Scripture: "So if this cup may not pass away from Me, except I drink it, Thy will be done." Then he went on to give the kind of eloquent, forthright, frequently witty address that became the hallmark of his campaign that year. "Let's face it," he admonished his listeners. "Let's talk sense to the American people. Let's tell them the truth." Ahead were not "easy decisions," but "a long, costly, patient struggle against the great enemies of men—war and poverty and tyranny."

But Stevenson's rhetoric of sacrifice, patience, and endurance was hardly what most Americans wanted to hear after nearly a generation of depression and inflation, and wars hot and cold. Over the past twenty years the Democrats had simply accumulated too many political liabilities. Stevenson, campaign manager Wilson Wyatt, and Stephen A. Mitchell, chairman of the Democratic National Committee, tried as best they could to dissociate their efforts from the Truman administration and what Republican orators never tired of terming "the mess in Washington." Democratic campaign headquarters, set up at Springfield, the Illinois capital, not Washington or New York, were staffed mainly by people not closely connected with the administration. In an awkward meeting at the White House in August, Stevenson tried as gently as possible to tell Truman that he should stay out of the campaign. Such tactics riled the pugnacious President, who later wrote that the Stevenson forces had "needlessly sacrificed basic political backing. . . ."

Added to Stevenson's troubles was the fact that, while the southern delegations had not bolted the convention this year, most Democratic politicians in the South found Stevenson hardly more palatable than they did Truman or the ADA. Trying to appease the southerners, Stevenson made Senator John Sparkman of Alabama, who had supported Truman's Fair Deal program short of civil rights measures, his vice presidential running mate. Nevertheless, many Democrats went home from the convention to form Democrats for Eisenhower organizations and to join Republicans in trying to carry the South for the general. Such leaders as Senator Harry F. Byrd of Virginia and Governors James F. Byrnes of South Carolina, Robert Kennon of Louisiana, and Allan Shivers of Texas openly supported Eisenhower.

Of particular concern in Louisiana and Texas, as well as California, was the complex question of federal-versus-state title to offshore oil deposits in the so-called tidelands. In 1945 Truman had issued an executive order affirming exclusive federal ownership of all mineral deposits in the continental shelf regions down to 600 feet. The Supreme Court upheld the administration's position in suits brought by California and Texas, and in the spring of 1952 Truman vetoed legislation to transfer title to the states. The Republican platform came out unequivocally for "returning" the tidelands to the states, while the Democratic platform and Stevenson endorsed federal ownership. The states with tidelands claims had lost substantial revenues for educational purposes because they could no longer charge oil companies for offshore drilling leases. By 1952 this abstruse constitutional question had become a highly emotional political issue, one that involved a clear conflict between a group of states and Washington. For conservatives the federal hold on the tidelands was another instance of the arrogant expansion of federal power.

Eisenhower also had serious differences with the Taft wing of the GOP, but he was able to bring his party together, at least for the purpose of winning the election. Herbert Brownell arranged for him to meet with Taft on September 12 at the general's official residence in Manhattan, which Eisenhower continued to occupy as president of Columbia University. The general was noncommittal about the results of their breakfast conference, but Taft announced that he and Eisenhower were in basic agreement on domestic policy, especially on the need to hold federal spending at $70 billion for fiscal year 1954 and roll it back to $60 billion for fiscal 1955. Their differences on foreign policy, said Taft, were only of "degree."

Although the Stevenson forces got some political mileage out of Eisenhower's "great surrender" to Taft, the general and his strategists had effectively created the appearance of party unity. In fact the views of the two Republicans when it came to the economy and the nature and functions of government were strikingly similar. Formally opening his campaign at Boise, Idaho, Eisenhower declared that "The great problem is to take the straight road down the middle," between extremes of radicalism and reaction. Yet he went on to say, "We have had for a long time a government that applies the philosophy of the left—a government that does everything but wash dishes for the housewife." Though somewhat less passionate than the Republican rightists in condemning the New Deal–Fair Deal direction of government over the past twenty years, Eisenhower believed as much as Taft that a sound budget was the key to a sound dollar, and that a sound dollar was the key to a sound and prosperous economy which maximized opportunity for private investment and profit.

On foreign policy there were major areas of disagreement. Eisenhower believed fervently in the European alliance, which Taft continued to see as a wasteful and potentially dangerous entanglement with countries that had proved to be ingrates in the past and would do so again. Taft's win-or-get-out position on Korea was too much for Eisenhower, who saw the war as a necessary part of the global strategy to contain Communism. Eisenhower was also less exercised than the Republican right over the Communist threat at home.

The fact remained that in 1952 many Americans really believed the charges made by McCarthy and others that their government, because of Democratic laxity or connivance, had become systematically infiltrated and subverted by the Communist party. The Republicans exploited such feelings to maximum effect. McCarthy, who quickly became a featured speaker in Eisenhower's "crusade," announced that "There is only one issue for the farmer, the laborer, the businessman—the issue of Communism in government." On occasion Eisenhower himself could sound like the most ardent Red-baiter, as when, in an October 5 speech at Billings, Montana, he promised to "find the pinks; we will find the Communists; we will find the disloyal."

Two nights earlier Eisenhower, by *not* saying something, had created one of three great sensations in the 1952 presidential race. Eisenhower had become deeply disturbed by the attacks McCarthy and his allies had leveled at his old military superior and comrade-in-arms, General of the Army George C. Marshall. As Eisenhower's foremost sponsor in the Army, Marshall had been chiefly responsible for his appointment as Supreme Allied Commander in Europe during World War II. Shortly after the war Marshall had gone to China as President Truman's special emissary in a futile effort to mediate between warring Chinese Nationalists and Communists. Then, as Truman's Secretary of State, Marshall had helped formulate the plan named after him for massive economic assistance to western Europe. He had also served a stint as Secretary of Defense.

Outraged by the fall of the Nationalist government in China, Republican Senator William Jenner in 1950 had called Marshall "a front man for traitors," who was "either an unsuspecting stooge or an actual co-conspirator with the most treasonable array of political cutthroats ever turned loose in the Executive Branch of Government." The next year McCarthy had accused Marshall of having an "affinity for Chinese Reds," of conniving in the "sellout of Asia," and of being part of "a conspiracy of infamy so black that, when it is finally exposed, its principals shall forever be deserving of the maledictions of all honest men."

Eisenhower told his campaign speech writers that he wanted to put a passage praising Marshall into an address he was to give in Milwaukee the night of October 3. When McCarthy visited him in Peoria, Illinois, the day before, Eisenhower is supposed to have angrily refused to omit the statement on Marshall. On the train north, however, Eisenhower let himself be persuaded by Governor

Walter Kohler of Wisconsin and by Sherman Adams, the former governor of New Hampshire who had become campaign "chief of staff," that to go out of his way to laud Marshall would be unnecessarily provocative and might damage his chances in Wisconsin. At Appleton, his home base, McCarthy introduced Eisenhower; at Green Bay the presidential candidate said that he and McCarthy differed only on the methods of exorcising disloyal elements from government. And in his Milwaukee speech Eisenhower made no mention of the much-maligned Marshall. Unfortunately for Eisenhower, copies of the speech containing the Marshall passage had already gone out to the press. The incident brought wit and sarcasm from Stevenson and consternation from such Eisenhower backers as the *New York Times,* but the general's drive kept its momentum. Several times later in the campaign, Eisenhower did offer praise for Marshall.

By the time he submitted to the McCarthyites on the Marshall issue, Eisenhower had already surmounted—even gained from— a potentially much more damaging controversy precipitated by the disclosure of questionable behavior on the part of his running mate. On September 18 the *New York Post,* one of the few pro-Stevenson daily newspapers, reported that for some time Richard Nixon had been the beneficiary of a "secret fund" of more than $18,000 raised by a group of wealthy Californians, and that Nixon had regularly drawn on the fund for personal expenses since coming to the Senate. Actually the fund was not secret; Nixon had mentioned it to several people and had even replied to newsmen's questions about its existence. It was, moreover, fairly common for congressmen to take what amounted to maintenance money from individuals and organizations. But in a campaign which was supposed to be a crusade to bring morality and decency back to Washington, Nixon's conduct seemed at least an impropriety, perhaps a serious breach of public ethics.

Eisenhower's public reaction was a combination of righteousness and sagacity. Everyone in his crusade must be "as clean as a hound's tooth," he indicated to reporters. Then he simply waited. As the days passed the fund became more and more of a cause célèbre. There was much arguing among Eisenhower's advisers and telephoning back and forth between the Eisenhower retinue

in the East and Nixon on the West Coast. Dewey, Stassen, and the
powerful pro-Eisenhower *New York Herald-Tribune* urged Nixon's withdrawal, which Eisenhower recognized could be politically disastrous. Instead, he had Sherman Adams arrange an audit
of Nixon's finances by a battery of lawyers and by the famous
accountancy firm of Price, Waterhouse and Company; and he also
let Nixon know that he favored a nationwide radio-television talk
in which the vice presidential candidate would candidly make his
defense. This strategy proved sound. The audit showed that there
was nothing clandestine about the fund, that the money had been
used mostly to supplement campaign expenses, and that Nixon
had remained clearly within the letter of the law. The release of
the audit coincided with the disclosure that Governor Stevenson
had also used an unofficial fund—in this case to·beef up the salaries of his staff in Springfield.

With Eisenhower still reserving his verdict, the Republican
National Committee paid $75,000 for thirty minutes of prime net-
work television and radio time so that Nixon could speak to the
country. On the evening of September 23, to a television audience
estimated at nearly half of the available viewers and to many
millions more listening over radio, Nixon presented his case. Perhaps appropriately, he spoke from the El Capitan Theater in
Hollywood. The vice presidential candidate was alternately de-
fensive, aggressive, and beseeching. His wife, he said, had received no mink coat (which, with the deep freeze, had become a
symbol of influence-peddling and bribery in Truman's Washington). No, Pat wore only a "respectable Republican cloth coat."
The sole gift his family had got from anyone was a little dog
named Checkers, which the children loved, and "we're gonna
keep it." Nixon claimed to be innocent of any wrongdoing, but it
would be a good idea, he added, for the Democratic candidates to
make public their own financial records. Whatever happened, he
would continue his fight against "the crooks and the Communists
and those that defend them. . . ." Above all, he would fight on to
insure Eisenhower's election.

The "Checkers speech," as it was quickly dubbed, was a
masterful performance, destined to become part of American political folklore. Eisenhower still withheld his judgment when he

spoke in Cleveland that night. But by the next morning, with stacks of telegrams praising Nixon accumulating in Cleveland, in Los Angeles, at Republican headquarters in New York, and elsewhere, Eisenhower realized that what had once seemed a dread campaign liability had become a considerable campaign plus. In perhaps the first truly effective use of television by a national political figure, Nixon had made himself virtually indispensable to Eisenhower.

The general ordered his running mate to fly across the continent and join him at Wheeling, West Virginia. There Nixon, still not knowing his fate, stepped from his aircraft and met an ebullient Eisenhower, who slapped him on the back and assured him, "You're my boy!" A little later, speaking at a local football stadium, Eisenhower announced Nixon's full vindication. From then on Nixon drew campaign crowds almost as big as Eisenhower's.

Eisenhower traveled mostly by train and made numerous brief whistle-stop appearances in towns and small cities, whereas Stevenson usually flew to the sites of his addresses. The Democratic candidate's polished efforts often sounded more like political science lectures than campaign speeches. He won the admiration of many columnists and intellectuals, but his campaign lacked the boisterousness and impact of the Republican assault. Then Truman, angry about a lot of things but especially the Marshall episode, came into the fray against the better judgment of Stevenson and his advisers. Trying to reenact his amazing come-from-behind performance of 1948, Truman undertook the most energetic and extensive speaking tour ever made by an outgoing President. Over a thirteen-day period in October Truman gave more than a hundred speeches as he whistle-stopped across the country. His themes were the same ones he had used four years earlier: The Republicans would dismantle the social welfare programs established under the New Deal and Fair Deal, destroy the prosperity won under Democratic rule, oppress organized labor, and, in foreign policy, revert to suicidal "isolationism."

Stevenson seemed to take inspiration from Truman's noisy intervention. Stepping up his own rhetoric, he began to draw great crowds wherever he went. Leaving no doubt that he was

firmly within the cold war consensus, Stevenson approved the
dismissal of Communist teachers in schools and colleges, endorsed
the Truman administration's prosecution of Communist leaders
under the Smith Act, and defended Truman's loyalty program,
which had led to the resignation or removal of thousands of
federal employees, often on dubious constitutional grounds.
Americans lived in "a world half slave and half free," Stevenson
declared, "a world besieged from the East for the first time since
the Turks were turned back from the gates of Vienna. . . ." For
Stevenson, "The challenge of our faith and time is the 'insensate
worship of matter' organized in a vast international conspiracy."

The K_1, C_2 formula, though, was too potent a mixture for the
Democrats to counteract. The 1952 campaign, the bitterest in
memory, featured even more than the usual number of distortions,
smears, and appeals to blind prejudice. Yet behind the cascade of
calumny and vilification turned loose by the Republicans, there
remained several very good reasons for electing Eisenhower.

The man who presented the best case for an Eisenhower Presidency was Walter Lippmann, columnist for the *New York Herald-
Tribune*, whose essays and books published over the previous
thirty years had earned him a reputation as America's wisest
commentator on public affairs. Lippmann believed that the Democrats, by succumbing to corruption and leading the country into
a seemingly endless war, had forfeited their claims to leadership.
No Democratic President could end the Korean conflict, because
any settlement short of total victory, which was plainly unattainable, would look like surrender to the Republicans and could
prove fatal to the Democratic party. Because of his prestige as a
military figure and his personal popularity, Eisenhower would be
able to reach a realistic settlement which his party would have to
accept. Eisenhower's talents were as a mediator, conciliator, and
healer. Thus he could also quiet the rabid anti-Communists on
the Republican right, undercut McCarthy's popular base, and
close the nation's wounds. On the other hand, another Republican
defeat following Dewey's startling upset in 1948 might send the
GOP into a paroxysm; loyal opposition would give way to irrecon-
cilability. For Lippmann, in short, the timeworn slogan "It's time
for a change" had taken on a new and desperate urgency in 1952.

The public opinion polls indicated that most voters favored Eisenhower. Yet after their embarrassing experience of predicting a Dewey victory four years earlier, the polling organizations were reluctant to speculate on how big the GOP's margin might be. What insured an Eisenhower landslide—and provided the third great sensation of the campaign—was the general's announcement at Detroit on October 24, eleven days before the election, that securing "an early and honorable" peace in Korea "requires a personal trip to Korea. I shall make that trip. . . . I shall go to Korea."

This declaration was about as close to a specific proposal for ending the war as Eisenhower ever came. Actually neither Eisenhower nor his party had any coherent or consistent views on how the war should be terminated. John Foster Dulles, Dewey, and on one occasion Eisenhower discussed the need to send more Republic of Korea troops into the front lines to replace American units; Dewey predicted that Eisenhower, as President, would have South Korean forces doing nine-tenths of the fighting within a year. Taft was somewhat amenable to this "Koreanization" alternative; basically, though, he still favored either General MacArthur's all-out strategy or complete withdrawal.

So in 1952 presidential candidate Eisenhower, like presidential candidate Nixon sixteen years later, asked the electorate to trust him, to believe that somehow he could bring an honorable end to a bloody, stalemated Asian war. Unlike Nixon in 1968, Eisenhower never claimed to have a secret plan for peace; he promised only to go and see for himself. For most voters, however, this promise from the nation's greatest living hero was enough.

The turnout on election day was by far the heaviest in the country's history—nearly 61,500,000. Eisenhower received almost 34 million votes to more than 27 million for Stevenson. With 55.4 percent of the total, Eisenhower carried 41 states; Stevenson, with 44.4 percent, carried only seven southern states plus West Virginia. Eisenhower's electoral vote was 442, Stevenson's 89. Some 670 nonsouthern counties which had gone to the Democrats since 1932 now went to Eisenhower. Even in the South, Eisenhower showed remarkable strength, polling 48.9 percent of the region's votes, carrying Texas, Virginia, Tennessee, and Oklahoma, and

narrowly losing Louisiana and South Carolina. A majority of
voters in all income groups cast their ballots for the general, who
also elicited substantial defections from Franklin Roosevelt's New
Deal coalition among ethnic and religious minorities. Whereas
Truman had carried all the major cities in 1948, Eisenhower won
majorities in Newark, Buffalo, Louisville, Miami, and every urban
center west of Kansas City.

Yet the Eisenhower landslide portended no major political
realignments. Not only did Stevenson receive the largest popular
vote since Roosevelt's in 1936 but also the Democrats still controlled state governments throughout the South and in much
of the rest of the country. Despite Eisenhower's vote-getting
prowess, the Republicans gained a majority of only eight seats in
the national House of Representatives and a split in the Senate
(which, because of Vice President Nixon's tie-breaking vote as
presiding officer, they would be able to organize when the Eighty-
third Congress convened in January).

The Republicans, looking forward to the first GOP inauguration since 1928, could rejoice that the "drift toward socialism"
had been reversed, that the crooks and Communists would be
driven from Washington, that the crusade had triumphed. On
election night Eisenhower and his wife, Mamie, left the Republican celebration at the Commodore Hotel in New York, walked
out onto Park Avenue to enter their waiting automobile, and
found two complete strangers sitting in the front seat. They were
Secret Service men, already assuming their assignment to guard
the President-elect.

II

The Ordeal of Power

DWIGHT D. Eisenhower was the third professional soldier to go directly from military service into the White House. The other two were Zachary Taylor and Ulysses S. Grant. Neither they nor any of Eisenhower's other predecessors except George Washington had enjoyed such universal acclaim and admiration before coming to the Presidency. Though mainly a consequence of his military achievements, Eisenhower's overwhelming popular esteem also had much to do with the President-elect's origins, background, and personality, which seemingly made it possible for ordinary Americans to identify closely with him.

Eisenhower's father was working as a railroad laborer in Denison, Texas, when David Dwight, the third of seven sons (of whom six survived childhood), was born on August 14, 1890. Not long after that the Eisenhower family moved to Abilene, Kansas, where the father worked at a local creamery. Despite his mother's membership in a pacifist Protestant sect and his father's lack of money or influence, Eisenhower managed to get an appointment to the United States Military Academy. He enrolled at West Point as Dwight David, the name he used thereafter. Determined to excel in athletics, Eisenhower suffered a nearly crippling leg injury and became a desultory student, finishing far down in the class of 1915, behind several men he would later outrank.

A year after his graduation, Second Lieutenant Eisenhower married into the prosperous Doud family of Denver, Colorado. After spending the First World War stateside as a tank instructor, he began to work his way up the ranks in the postwar years. Following a stint in the War Department during the Hoover administration, Eisenhower served on General MacArthur's staff in Washington and in the Philippines, with an intervening assignment in the Canal Zone. Major Eisenhower was on the scene in 1932 when Army Chief of Staff MacArthur commanded the troops that drove the rag-tag Bonus Army of unemployed veterans from Washington.

After the attack on Pearl Harbor, General George C. Marshall brought Brigadier General Eisenhower to Washington as his chief of operations. The next year Eisenhower became a major general and assumed command of all United States forces in the European theater. His dramatic rise climaxed in 1944, when he took charge of the buildup for the invasion of western Europe as Supreme Commander of all Allied forces. His achievement in leading the victorious American, British, and Free French armies against Germany made him the nation's preeminent military figure, approached in stature only by MacArthur, hero of the Pacific war against Japan.

Even though Eisenhower often expressed his strong dislike for the maneuver, cajolery, and accommodation basic to the American political process, his success as a military leader involved the exercise of essentially those same qualities. Possessing neither the haughty charisma of MacArthur nor the flamboyance and the zest for warfare of General George C. Patton, his tank operations expert, Eisenhower was long on patience, persuasiveness, tact, and the art of compromise. A master military politician, he adroitly managed to unite and utilize the collection of headstrong leaders from different nations and services under his command. Eisenhower became the archetype of the successful modern military man, one skilled in administering complex operations within a vast bureaucracy, cultivating good relations with civilian authorities and the press, and building a favorable public image.

That public image—which Eisenhower nurtured carefully and used so well as politician and President—was of an amiable, unpretentious average American who got the job done, a man interested in facts and cases, not abstractions and theories. One can scarcely imagine MacArthur's being called "Mac," but Eisenhower was naturally "Ike" to both his intimates and to the millions of people who saw him only in newsreels or on television. The image had much truth to it. Eisenhower was no intellectual, he was ignorant on many subjects, and his personal tastes were hardly those of the sophisticate. Stumbling over words in his prepared speeches and mutilating syntax in his press conferences, he often seemed unable to command either information or language. Also something of a moralist, Eisenhower meant it when he talked glowingly of the old-fashioned values—honesty, perseverance, duty, thrift.

All these personal traits may have endeared him to the masses, but for critics like George Kennan, a valuable career Foreign Service officer who found himself unwelcome in the new administration, Eisenhower lacked the insight, intellectual vigor, and toughness to be a successful President. "He incorporated, in personality, manner, and appearance, all that Americans liked to picture as the national virtues," Kennan has written. "He was the nation's number one Boy Scout." The liberal journalist Richard Rovere, moreover, saw Eisenhower as deficient in "the kind of knowledge of the American condition he might have gained if his background had been in politics rather than in the military. He went through most of the fifties and on into the sixties with an image of the country formed in Kansas *circa* 1910."

Yet if Eisenhower was not a brilliant man, he did possess a shrewd and disciplined intelligence. Behind his amiability and his famous grin was an intolerance of sloppy administrative work and poorly thought-out proposals. To his subordinates, both military and civilian, his angry outbursts were as legendary as his smiling countenance became familiar to the rest of the American people. As President, Eisenhower achieved only a portion of what he sought. His failures and frustrations were attributable mainly to the limitations of his—and the country's—understanding of the realities of the 1950s, especially the realities of international politics. Like his immediate predecessor and the vast majority of his countrymen, Eisenhower saw the flow of world events through a prism of cold war conflict, of incessant struggle against a multi-faceted, nearly omnipresent Communist enemy.

The fact remains that when Eisenhower entered the White

House, the nation was being torn apart by the Korean war and the controversy over domestic Communism. As Walter Lippmann had predicted, Eisenhower's Presidency had the effect of healing wounds and moderating passions. After getting the United States out of one shooting war, he kept it out of others and thus became the only real peacetime President since 1945. More than any other postwar chief executive, he held down the seemingly insatiable appetite of the military establishment for money and hardware. Dwight Eisenhower obviously was what America wanted in the 1950s; within the context of the times, he generally answered its needs.

I

While vacationing after the 1952 election, Eisenhower received word from the White House that the United States had just set off the first thermonuclear explosion at the island of Elugelab in the Pacific Ocean. The successful test was the outcome of work authorized by President Truman in 1950 to develop a weapon based on the hydrogen fusion principle, which would be far more powerful than the atomic bombs the United States and the Soviet Union then possessed. The November 1952 blast completely obliterated the test island and yielded an unexpectedly high level of three megatons, the equivalent of three million tons of TNT. It was 150 times as big as the atomic blasts which had destroyed the Japanese cities of Hiroshima and Nagasaki in 1945. While what was detonated at Elugelab was a cumbersome "device" and not a deliverable bomb, obviously the destructive capability commanded by the President of the United States was about to take an exponential leap. For Eisenhower the "ordeal of power," to use the phrase of his speech writer Emmet John Hughes, had already begun.

Late in November the President-elect kept his campaign promise to go to Korea. Taking along a party that included General Omar N. Bradley, chairman of the Joint Chiefs of Staff, Attorney General–designate Herbert Brownell, and Charles E. Wilson, his choice for Secretary of Defense, Eisenhower slipped away from New York and began the long air journey across the continent and the Pacific. Clandestine rendezvous, elaborate cover stories issued from Eisenhower's Commodore Hotel head-quarters, and ostentatious comings and goings effectively con-cealed the trip from the press. In Korea Eisenhower got the views of General Mark Clark, United Nations commander, and Admiral Arthur W. Radford, commander of the Pacific Fleet, and talked with South Korean President Syngman Rhee. He also visited the front lines and shared meals with soldiers. While Eisenhower may have learned little that he could not have gotten from Pentagon briefings at home, at least he fulfilled his promise.

By December 5, when news of the trip was finally released in the United States, Eisenhower had returned to the island of Guam. From there his party proceeded aboard the cruiser *Helena* to Wake Island, where Eisenhower made connections with other members of his incoming administration, most notably Secretary of State–designate John Foster Dulles, George Humphrey, slated to become Secretary of the Treasury, and Joseph Dodge, who would head the Bureau of the Budget. Aboard ship Eisenhower had his first chance to talk seriously with the men who would staff the major offices in his administration.

Their main topic was government spending as it related to military power. Dodge reported that President Truman's budget of about $80 billion for fiscal year 1954 could be cut only by jeopardizing national defense. This news pleased no one, least of all Humphrey, who argued that at least the wartime price con-trols instituted by the Truman administration should be ended. It was vital, they all agreed, to recognize that "The relationship between military and economic strength is intimate and indivisi-ble," as Eisenhower phrased it. The United States could spend itself into bankruptcy through wasteful outlays for military and other purposes. The basis for a sound economy was a sound budget. Thus the new administration should plan not for some short-run crisis period, when Soviet power might exceed that of the United States in some categories, but rather for the "long haul," balancing essential military power with a healthy economy. This wedding of military policy to overall economic considera-tions formed what Eisenhower administration spokesmen came to call the "Great Equation."

The two men who dominated the *Helena* conferences were

Dulles and Humphrey. Together with Secretary of Defense Wilson (who was not aboard the *Helena*), they would be Eisenhower's most visible cabinet officers. Dulles seemed the natural choice to head the Department of State. As Eisenhower once said to him, "After all, you've been training yourself to be Secretary of State ever since you were nine years old." Aged sixty-four when he accepted Eisenhower's appointment, Dulles was the nephew of Robert Lansing, who had been Secretary of State under Woodrow Wilson; Dulles's grandfather had held the same post under Benjamin Harrison in the 1890s. Able to boast of a career in the diplomatic service stretching back to the Hague Conference of 1907, Dulles would doubtless have been Thomas E. Dewey's choice for Secretary of State had Dewey not fumbled away the presidential election in 1948. A partner in the old and prestigious New York legal firm of Sullivan and Cromwell, Dulles was one of that species of wealthy men—mostly lawyers and mostly from the Northeast—who had gone into public service, often within the State Department. In the Truman administration Dulles had held a multiplicity of assignments. Besides performing various duties in connection with the United Nations, he had been chief negotiator of the Japanese peace treaty in 1951 and also military pacts with Japan, the Philippines, and Australia and New Zealand.

Articulate, bright, and tremendously energetic, Dulles was the author of a number of books and articles on international affairs. As the Republican party's leading spokesman on foreign policy during the 1952 campaign, he had hammered away at the necessity for rejecting the Truman-Acheson strategy of containment in favor of more dynamic and innovative efforts to "liberate" the "captive peoples" under Communist control. A leading Presbyterian layman, Dulles was a stern moralist, and his absolutist preachments went far beyond Eisenhower's. Epithets like "immoral," "enslavement," and "banditry" frequently enlivened his public rhetoric; his approach to the Soviet Union and the People's Republic of China was consistently doctrinaire and uncompromising. Arthur Larson, who held various posts in the Eisenhower administration, has written of Dulles: "His face . . . was permanently lined with an expression of unhappiness mingled with faint distaste—the kind of face that, on those rare occasions when it was drawn into a smile, looked as though it ached in every muscle to get back into its normal shape."

Dulles became the most traveled diplomat up to that time. During his seventy-five months in office he journeyed 559,988 miles, making nineteen visits to France, eleven to Great Britain, six to West Germany, and four to Italy. Enjoying an extremely close relationship with Eisenhower, and also strengthened by the presence of his younger brother, Allen, as Director of the Central Intelligence Agency, Dulles became one of the four or five most powerful Secretaries of State in the nation's history. Under the Dulles brothers the foreign policy and national intelligence bureaucracies worked intimately, often surreptitiously, to further what they understood to be American interests around the world. Even so, John Foster Dulles was able to guide policy only to the extent that he kept the confidence of the President, and on important occasions Eisenhower would override his judgment. Contrary to the view that became common in the mid-fifties, Dulles did not dictate American foreign policy.

In fact, Eisenhower more regularly followed the counsel of Secretary of the Treasury Humphrey than that of Dulles. An archconservative from Cleveland who had run a business empire as president of the M. A. Hanna Company, Humphrey had supported Robert A. Taft until the Republican convention nominated Eisenhower. The new President and the new Treasury Secretary agreed fully that it was imperative to cut expenditures and taxes, to balance the budget and insure a stable dollar, to remove controls on prices and wages, and generally to cut down government intervention in the economy. Expansion, they both believed, must come through private investment and profit-taking, not more and more government spending. Big and expensive government would ultimately erode American initiative and self-reliance, which for Humphrey and Eisenhower were the foundation of American liberty.

Secretary of Defense Wilson, who had been president of the General Motors Corporation, was basically in accord with this outlook. To Wilson went the baffling task of trying to hold down the most demanding and profligate sector of the federal budget, military spending. In his efforts to economize in the Pentagon,

Wilson would struggle manfully against his own cold warriorism and that of the administration for four and a half years, before finally turning over his department to an equally baffled successor.

The oft-heard characterization of the Eisenhower administration as a "businessman's government" should be qualified. Even in the 1930s a considerable number of corporate executives had held government posts, especially in the early New Deal. As the Roosevelt administration's military buildup got under way in 1940, businessmen flocked into Washington to man agencies involved in war production and finance. By 1945 the "dollar-a-year man" had become an even more familiar figure in the capital than the ardent young New Deal lawyer. After the war the Truman administration had continued to draw heavily on businessmen from both political parties to staff the upper echelons of government.

All the same, there were important contrasts between the background and orientation of the people who had held the top offices in the Truman administration and those who filled the same positions under Eisenhower. Under Truman, foreign-military policy and domestic policy had operated in separate realms, and had been handled by different kinds of people. Dominating the State and Defense departments had been investment bankers, corporate attorneys, or career Foreign Service officers; whereas those who dealt in domestic policy had been mostly Democratic politicians and liberal lawyers. By contrast, the Eisenhower administration tried to establish an essential unity, or "equation," between foreign, military, and domestic concerns. Eisenhower recruited people who had been mainly executives and attorneys from manufacturing and merchandising companies. With a few exceptions, most notably the Dulles brothers, people who had dealt in production, profits, and payrolls held the major positions throughout government. Moreover, the Eisenhower appointees were nearly all faithful Republicans, as opposed to the bipartisan composition of the Truman administration, particularly in the State and Defense departments.

After 1952 the administration in power, more than any time since the 1920s, tended to assume that the well-being of the nation depended on the well-being of corporate enterprise. Charles

E. Wilson spoke bluntly but typically when he said during his Senate confirmation hearings, "I thought what was good for our country was good for General Motors, and vice versa."[1] Douglas McKay, an Oregon automobile dealer who became Secretary of the Interior, put it even more bluntly: "We're here in the saddle as an Administration representing business and industry."

As Democrats quipped, Eisenhower's cabinet consisted of "eight millionaires and a plumber." The plumber was Martin Durkin, head of the plumbers and steamfitters union within the American Federation of Labor, whom Eisenhower, for reasons not wholly clear, appointed Secretary of Labor. A Stevenson supporter in 1952, Durkin came into the administration believing that Eisenhower would seek major changes in the Taft-Hartley Act. It soon became obvious that that was not the case, and before the year was out Durkin angrily left the government, to be succeeded by James Mitchell, a personnel manager. The cabinet became a collection of eight millionaires and a millionairess in the spring of 1953, when Congress, at Eisenhower's urging, upgraded the Federal Security Administration (FSA) to cabinet level as the Department of Health, Education, and Welfare. FSA Administrator Oveta Culp Hobby, commander of the Women's Army Corps during the Second World War and wife of the wealthy publisher of the *Houston Post,* became the second woman to hold cabinet rank.

Like every President from Franklin Roosevelt to Richard Nixon, Eisenhower brought to the office an expansive, forceful conception of his role as maker and executor of foreign policy. Unlike other recent Presidents, however, he had a rather narrow constitutionalist view of his role in domestic matters. His legislative responsibility, he thought, was to propose needed measures on the advice of his cabinet and other high-level officials, but not to lead, persuade, and pressure congressmen into voting as he wished. For the first two years he left congressional leadership to Senate Majority Leaders Taft and William Knowland and Speaker of the House Joseph Martin; after the 1954 elections,

---

1. Wilson's statement was usually misquoted as "What is good for General Motors is good for the country."

which restored Democratic majorities in Congress, he had to rely
heavily on Lyndon B. Johnson, the new majority leader in the
Senate, and Sam Rayburn, who resumed the speakership of the
House. Eisenhower also was never really comfortable as head of
his party, and he found discussions of patronage distribution almost physically painful. The President, the journalist Marquis
Childs wrote as late as 1958, had "a civics-textbook concept of
the co-ordinate powers of the three branches of the federal
government."

Though somewhat of an exaggeration, Childs's comment does
suggest a central fact: Eisenhower's view of functions and divisions of power in government was essentially formalistic. Franklin
Roosevelt and Truman had both relied on amorphous, largely
extraconstitutional and extrastatutory groups for advice and
execution. Subsequently John F. Kennedy, Lyndon Johnson, and
Richard Nixon would operate in much the same fashion. Eisenhower, however, nearly always worked within formal lines of
authority. He restored the cabinet, whose collective role had
declined under Roosevelt and Truman, to its traditional function
as the highest consultative body in the executive branch. Besides
meeting almost weekly with his cabinet and seeking the opinion
of each department head on each issue, Eisenhower enlarged
the cabinet meetings to include UN Ambassador Henry Cabot
Lodge[2] and the Directors of the Bureau of the Budget, the International (later United States) Information Agency, and the
Central Intelligence Agency. Eisenhower also relied heavily on
the National Security Council, with which he met an average
of once a week during his first two years in office.

Alongside these executive bodies was Eisenhower's elaborate
and much-criticized staff system, headed by Sherman Adams, with
the title Assistant to the President. Adams's organization closely
resembled a military command structure, and Eisenhower doubtless had just such an operational model in mind when he instructed Adams to set up the White House staff. Drawing also
on the findings of the Hoover Commission's study of the executive

2. In 1952 Lodge had lost his Senate seat from Massachusetts to
young U.S. Representative John F. Kennedy.

branch in the immediate postwar years and of other study groups on government operations, Adams set up a line of authority running from himself directly to the components of the presidential staff. Thus the various secretaries, counsels, administrative assistants, and special assistants all were responsible to Adams. At the same time, nearly all documents generated in the executive branch and intended for the President had first to go through Adams's office.

Brusque, tireless, and efficient, Adams ran an extraordinarily tight ship. Frequently frustrating efforts of people to gain personal access to the President, Adams was generally able to determine who and what got to see Eisenhower and when. He also exercised considerable influence through the daily information summaries he and his staff provided Eisenhower. All the same, Adams's importance has probably been exaggerated. No power behind the throne, he remained most typically an administrator of the mundane rather than a high-level policy maker.

II

After his return from Korea and the *Helena* talks, the President-elect had a much-publicized conference in New York with General MacArthur, who had written Eisenhower that he had a plan for ending the Korean war. While President Truman fumed that any such plan should come straight to him, MacArthur told Eisenhower that the only way to end the war was to give the Chinese and North Korean governments an explicit warning that the United States would use atomic bombs unless a peace settlement were quickly reached. Although Eisenhower did not publicly disclose what MacArthur had said until he published his memoirs a decade later, a similar warning, given indirectly and less bluntly, actually figured in the administration's moves to conclude the war later that year.

The meeting with MacArthur, a New York session with his full cabinet, and other matters kept Eisenhower busy in the remaining weeks before his inauguration. Contacts with the outgoing administration, however, made no great demands on his time. Aside from one short, chilly, and mutually unrewarding meeting be-

tween Eisenhower and Truman and Lodge's fifty-minute briefing
from the State Department Policy and Planning Board, the new
and old regimes rather studiously ignored each other.

On January 20, 1953, Eisenhower took the oath of office administered by Chief Justice Fred M. Vinson. After that the mass
of joyous, long-suffering Republicans, together with the grim-
faced Truman and a few other Democrats, heard his inaugural
address. Although it was not one of America's great state documents, the speech was important because, virtually ignoring
domestic matters, it unequivocally committed the new administration to maintaining the American conception of international
order through collective security efforts, founded on "the basic
law of interdependence." If any further denial of Republican
unilateralism was necessary, this statement should have sufficed.

While Eisenhower worked with aides on his State of the Union
message, Senate confirmation hearings on his cabinet and other
appointees went forward. Questions of possible conflict of interest
held up the ratification of several choices. Running into the most
trouble was Secretary of Defense–designate Wilson. Besides offering his aphorism about the mutual well-being of General Motors
and the nation, Wilson proved most reluctant to dispose of several
million dollars worth of stock in GM, a corporation with almost $5
billion in military contracts. After he finally agreed to sell the
stock, Wilson won confirmation with only six dissenting votes.
Formal separation from corporate offices and stock holdings did
not, of course, remove the basic problem, which resulted from
the fact that so many of Eisenhower's appointees—as had also
been the case under Roosevelt and Truman—came from companies doing much of their business with the government. Shortly
after his confirmation Wilson forbade Defense Department officials to take part in contract negotiations involving firms they
had been connected with, but that helped little. In 1953 Eisenhower apparently failed to recognize that such a problem existed.
Irritated by holdups in Senate action on Wilson and others, he
confided to his occasional journal that "sooner or later [Presidents]
will be unable to get anybody to take jobs in Washington except
business failures, political hacks, and New Deal lawyers."

Eisenhower's State of the Union message announced two striking breaks with existing policy. The more sensational announcement was that no longer would the Seventh Fleet—which Truman had ordered into the Formosa Strait right after fighting broke out in Korea—"shield" mainland China from attack by the Nationalist Chinese forces on Formosa. Though both hailed and criticized as a move to "unleash Chiang Kai-shek," the new policy actually had little practical significance. Chiang was in no position then or at any time thereafter to launch a full-scale invasion of the mainland, and in fact the shield had operated mainly to deter Communist Chinese attacks on the offshore islands. The Asia Firsters in Congress, however, took heart from what looked like a bold military initiative.

The other major announcement, more prosaic but more consequential, was that the administration would shortly eliminate all the controls on prices and wages the Truman administration had established in an effort to curb runaway inflation bred by the Korean war buildup. This policy was in keeping with conventional Republican doctrine. Articulated especially by George Humphrey, such doctrine held that controls led to economic stagnation and that their removal would promote an expansionary surge, a boom more than sufficient to absorb wage increases, while prices would begin to decline.

Eisenhower and Humphrey—together with Budget Director Dodge and Arthur Burns, the new chairman of the Council of Economic Advisers—also wished ardently to achieve big reductions in the size and costs of government, to cut taxes, and to balance the federal budget. On this score, however, the administration ran into a complex of realities which blunted its efforts in 1953 and led to a succession of disappointments thereafter. Between 1932 and 1953 the federal budget had grown from less than $4 billion to nearly $85½ billion, while the number of federal employees had climbed from about 630,000 to more than 2½ million. The administration quickly found out that much of what the government spent consisted of built-in costs like veterans' and Social Security benefits and interest payments on the national debt, which had soared to more than $273 billion. Early in 1953, moreover, Eisenhower refused to countenance major reductions in military expenditures because of the war and other national security needs. The $80-billion budget Truman proposed for fiscal year 1954 projected a deficit of $9.9 billion, which the administration was able to pare by only $4.4 billion. That meant that Eisenhower had to oppose any effort to cut taxes in 1953.

At the end of April Eisenhower, Humphrey, and Dodge broke the news on budget and taxes to the Republican congressional leaders. Senate Majority Leader Taft reacted by pounding on the table and shouting, "With a program like this, we'll never elect a Republican Congress in 1954. You're taking us down the same road Truman traveled. It's a repudiation of everything we promised in the campaign."

Taft's emotional outburst expressed his own deepest convictions and those of Republicans in general. He was partly right when he accused the Eisenhower administration of following the path of its predecessor. Taft, like George Humphrey and most Republicans in Congress, wanted at least to stop—if possible to reverse—the trend of the last twenty years toward bigger, more expensive, and more interventionist government. Other Republicans, like the President's brother Milton Eisenhower, Sherman Adams, and Arthur Larson, accepted the basic premises of welfare-state collectivism as enthroned under Roosevelt's New Deal and consolidated under Truman's Fair Deal. Somewhere in between was Eisenhower, who shared Taft's repugnance for big government yet also believed that Washington had obligations to insure some degree of economic opportunity and security. Eisenhower's centrism meant that the administration would become a battleground between so-called Old Guard and so-called moderate or liberal Republicans. The outcome would be a stalling of collectivism in some areas, advance in others, and overall a continuing expansion of the functions and power of the federal government.

Republican conservatives had their way on tax policy and the tidelands issue. The tax reduction Humphrey formulated and Eisenhower endorsed in 1954 was quite in the spirit of the tax programs put over in the 1920s by Secretary of the Treasury Andrew Mellon, whose portrait hung in Humphrey's office. Despite the efforts of most Democrats to get across-the-board tax cuts, most Republicans combined with conservative Democrats to lower levies on transportation and luxuries like jewelry, perfume, and furs, to exempt a portion of stock-divided income, and to give earlier depreciation allowances to businessmen. The Submerged Lands Act of 1953 redeemed the Republican pledge to "return" the oil-rich tidelands to the states, which now would own mineral rights extending three leagues (10.3 miles) into the sea, provided the states had claimed such boundaries when they entered the Union. Much litigation ensued from this ambiguous law; it was 1960 before the Supreme Court upheld the claims of Texas and Florida but limited the offshore oil titles of the other Gulf states to three miles.

The Republicans also tried to overturn New Deal–Fair Deal agricultural policies. By 1953 huge stores of grain, cotton, tobacco, and other commodities had accumulated in federally owned or leased facilities under an increasingly expensive government program of buying up production which could not be sold profitably on the open market. By this system of supports the Department of Agriculture maintained artificial price levels in an effort to insure producers parity in purchasing power with other groups in the economy. Actually, except during the Second World War, the government had never guaranteed more than a certain percentage of parity. Price supports stood at 90 percent of parity by the end of the Truman administration; under the intense pressure of farm lobbies, they remained there for Eisenhower's first year. But Secretary of Agriculture Ezra Taft Benson, a high official in the Mormon Church in Utah and a devout adherent to the concept of the free marketplace, was determined to change things. Backed strongly by Eisenhower, Benson proposed a sliding scale for price supports which, by moving agriculture toward the open market, should greatly reduce surpluses valued at $2.5 billion.

Two 1954 laws largely implemented Benson's thinking. Flexible price supports, providing for as little as 70 percent of parity, would go into effect for grains, cotton, peanuts, and dairy products; tobacco would continue at 90 percent. Surplus commodities could be sold abroad at lower prices or used, as Eisenhower preferred, in school lunch programs, in disaster relief, or as part of American assistance to foreign countries.

In most other ways, however, the Eisenhower administration

accepted and perpetuated the basic reality of the welfare state.
Also in 1954, in the biggest single expansion of Social Security
coverage to that time, Congress brought self-employed people
under the system. Two years later Eisenhower sought and received from Congress, again under Democratic control after
the 1954 elections, an increase in the national minimum wage
from 75¢ to $1.00 an hour. Eisenhower also favored limited ex-
pansion of federal activity in housing, medical care, and education. In 1955 he signed a new housing law to finance the
construction of 45,000 units over the next four years. The administration's plan to subsidize private health insurance programs
died in Congress under attacks from both the American Medical
Association, fearful that the plan portended socialized medicine,
and Democratic liberals who rejected it as wholly inadequate.
The United States thus remained the only major Western nation
without a national health insurance system. Eisenhower's call for
federal grants to the states for school construction similarly
foundered, this time primarily because of southern Democratic
opposition after Adam Clayton Powell, Jr., Harlem's black representative, put a rider on the education bill denying money to
racially segregated school districts. The nation's burgeoning
school-age population continued to use facilities that were largely
old and overcrowded.

The administration was more successful in promoting waterway and highway transportation. For more than three decades
Republican and Democratic Presidents had failed to overcome
regional selfishness, which had blocked a joint United States–
Canadian project to convert the St. Lawrence River into an inland
waterway connecting the Great Lakes with the Atlantic Ocean.
By the time Eisenhower entered the White House, the proposal
had become more urgent because the supply of iron ore in the
Great Lakes region was running out. With midwestern steel
manufacturers beginning to look to Labrador for new ore deposits and with the Canadian government ready to proceed alone,
Eisenhower administration officials, led by George Humphrey,
pushed hard for the project. Finally, in the spring of 1954, Congress established a new government agency, the St. Lawrence
Seaway Development Corporation, to build the deepwater navi-

gation channel with Canada. The St. Lawrence Seaway would reach completion in 1959.

The Administration's approval for the state of New York to develop power sites on the United States side of the seaway was one manifestation of Eisenhower's belief that Washington should do everything it could to decentralize government functions. In providing needed public services, federal officials should work in "partnership" with state and local authorities and private enterprise. Another example was the President's plan for federal school construction grants. But the most far-reaching and costly application of the partnership concept came in the administration's highway program.

By the 1950s it was fairly obvious that the nation's system of overland transportation was reaching crisis conditions. Since World War II the railroads, privately owned and chronically in financial straits, had steadily cut passenger service and abandoned trackage. The existing network of highways, mostly built and maintained by state and local governments, had become less and less adequate for the needs of a people enjoying record prosperity and wedded to automobile transportation. Three factors explain the direction the Eisenhower administration took: the historic American obsession with the automobile, the influence of auto manufacturers and road materials and contractor interests, and the arguments of highway safety and civil defense advocates, who were convinced that building more highways would reduce traffic deaths, while the nation also would get an effective way to evacuate populated areas in case of nuclear attack. Unwilling even to consider outright nationalization of the railroads, the administration and Congress also gave little attention to the alternative of subsidizing private ownership to stabilize, restore, and improve rail service. The administration's decision—as formulated in 1955 by a study group appointed by Eisenhower and headed by General Lucius Clay—was to build a monumentally extensive and expensive national highway system in cooperation with the states, but mainly with federal money.

After much debate and delay over what prerogatives the states would have and how the system would be paid for, Congress finally passed the Federal Highway Aid Act of 1956. The statute authorized what quickly came to be called the "interstate system"—some 42,000 miles of controlled-access, four-to-eight-lane roads linking major cities. The system was to be completed by 1970 at an anticipated cost of $27.5 billion, with Washington paying 90 percent of the bill. The 1956 law also made possible the improvement of existing federal, state, and county highways on a matching-cost basis. To pay for the national highway program, Congress increased and earmarked federal taxes on fuels, tires, and commercial vehicles. By the time Eisenhower left office, more than 7,500 miles of the interstate system were open to traffic. Yet both time and cost estimates proved wildly optimistic. Two decades after its inception the system was still unfinished; its expense had far outrun the original price tag.

The building of the interstate system provided massive indirect subsidies for auto manufacturers, trucking firms, and the construction industry. It thereby pointed up the fact, discussed little in the 1950s, that the traditional dichotomy which had identified big government with liberalism and limited government with conservatism was fast becoming obsolete in practice. Despite Republican rhetoric, increasingly the real issue was not whether government was big or small, but whose interests it served. Even as the Eisenhower administration haltingly furthered the welfare state, the functional meaning of that state was changing.

III

Eisenhower's main attentions were rarely on farm prices, aid to education, housing, or highways. His overriding concern was foreign and military policy, and here he often had trouble bringing his own party around to his way of thinking. For example, Congress showed little interest in a 1953 administration bill to reorganize the Defense Department in the interest of greater administrative centralization. Even more disappointing to the President was the way Congress handled his foreign aid program. By 1953—with the Marshall Plan winding down in Europe and with the United States still contributing fairly small amounts of economic and technical help under Truman's Point Four program for "underdeveloped areas"—foreign aid mostly meant direct gifts of military matériel, plus "defense support" money to relieve other costs so nations could put more into their armed forces. Eisenhower was a firm believer in the concept of foreign aid, or "mutual assistance," as he preferred to call it. For the President it was a cheap way to buy global military capabilities. As he often noted, the yearly cost of maintaining a Greek or Pakistani soldier was but a fraction of the cost of an American soldier.

Republican unilateralists, on the other hand, saw the whole course of American overseas spending in the postwar period as misdirected and wasteful; and they were generally unwilling to support the administration on any grounds in its efforts to continue assistance to foreign countries. Eisenhower's first foreign aid bill, providing $5.1 billion for fiscal 1954, was cut by $700 million in the House Appropriations Committee. The Senate restored only $100 million, leaving Eisenhower with $600 million less than he had asked for.

The divisions within the GOP on foreign policy were nowhere more apparent than in the confused controversy over the issues of "liberation" for the Russian-dominated countries of eastern Europe and "repudiation" of the much-misunderstood and much-despised agreements between the United States, Great Britain, and the USSR at the Yalta Conference early in 1945. Most GOP Congressmen took quite literally John Foster Dulles's vociferous calls for liberation in the 1952 campaign and the Dulles-authored Republican platform pledge to repudiate commitments "such as those of Yalta. . . ." According to the conventional wisdom of the early cold war period, Yalta was at best a tragic blunder, at worst a sellout, a betrayal, and a milestone along what Senator Joe McCarthy called "twenty years of treason." Franklin Roosevelt, either willingly or because of illness and befuddlement, had succumbed to the wiles of Soviet dictator Josef Stalin, had surrendered eastern Europe to Communist imperialism, and had also undermined Chiang Kai-shek's position in China. Or so the story went. While not in a position to disavow the Yalta agreements, the Truman administration, by its tough talk and global military buildup, had indirectly lent credence to the legend of Yalta.

John Foster Dulles kept up a drumfire of liberation rhetoric after becoming Secretary of State. "To all those suffering under

Communist slavery," he declaimed in a filmed television speech early in 1953, "let us say: you can count on us." Dulles was usually careful to qualify his calls for liberation with phrases like "by all peaceful means," and on various occasions he publicly rejected the strategy of inciting armed revolt in eastern Europe. To those who took his rhetoric seriously, however, it seemed that a logical first step in any move away from containment and toward liberation was to repudiate the agreements that had supposedly made possible the "enslavement" in the first place.

Once in power, Dulles and Eisenhower quickly began to have sober second thoughts. By the end of January five different Yalta repudiation resolutions had appeared in Congress. Eisenhower's 1953 State of the Union message did promise to seek a congressional resolution declaring that the United States recognized "no kind of commitment contained in secret understandings of the past with foreign governments which permits this kind of enslavement." Yet the President did not specifically mention Yalta or directly call for repudiation. Both the White House and the State Department had come to feel that outright repudiation might give the Soviets an excuse for, among other things, denying Western access rights to West Berlin, which had been affirmed at Yalta. Eisenhower, moreover, was not keen about repudiating agreements he had himself implemented in 1945 as Allied Supreme Commander.

Consequently the Captive Peoples resolution the administration at last sent to Congress basically reiterated what the Democrats had said about Yalta all along. The resolution mentioned no particular wartime agreements, deplored Soviet "totalitarian imperialism" in eastern Europe, called for national self-determination in the area, and rejected any interpretations or applications of the Yalta provisions "which have been perverted to bring about the subjugation of free peoples." In other words, the essence of Yalta was not betrayal by Roosevelt and his associates but Soviet perversion of what had been agreed to.

Republican congressional reaction to the Captive Peoples resolution ranged from disappointment to dismay. The Democrats were generally willing, at the behest of Minority Leaders Johnson and Rayburn, to give the administration their quiet support. Democratic votes were crucial in getting the administration's resolution through the House. In the Senate Foreign Relations Committee, however, Republicans led by Taft balked at what they considered a weak measure which said nothing about the original legality or illegality of the Yalta agreements. Taft attached an amendment stipulating that as far as Congress was concerned the resolution did not "constitute any determination" of whether the agreements were valid. Early in March, when the Foreign Relations Committee reported out the resolution as amended, Johnson had to inform the perplexed President that the Democrats could no longer support the measure in its present form. At this juncture, conveniently for the administration, the Soviet government announced the death of Stalin, Russian ruler for almost thirty years. Dulles persuaded the Republican leadership that further action on the resolution would be "inopportune" in view of the uncertain situation in the Kremlin. Sent back to the Senate Foreign Relations Committee, the resolution died unobtrusively.

References to Yalta continued to spice Republican rhetoric over the next two years, until in 1955 the State Department released the official papers of the conference. Published in major daily newspapers and eventually in the official documentary series *Foreign Relations of the United States,* the Yalta papers unlocked no sinister secrets and in fact revealed little that was not already known. Their publication largely—though by no means completely—laid to rest the Yalta legend.

The Yalta repudiation imbroglio—so much a matter of semantics and symbolism—suggested how limited the administration's liberation crusade might be. Hard proof of the hollowness of the easy talk about "rolling back" the "iron curtain" over eastern Europe came in June 1953, when workers in East Berlin and other parts of Soviet-occupied East Germany rioted to protest factory speedups and food shortages. While Russian tanks put down the uprising, the American government could do nothing but "deplore" its suppression and praise the heroism of the rioters. Despite the obvious helplessness of the United States, the calls for liberation continued from Dulles, from militant congressmen, from the State Department's Voice of America broadcast network, and from Radio Free Europe, run by eastern European exiles officially with private contributions but in fact mostly with CIA money. The final exposure of the myth of liberation would not come for more than two years.

The summer of 1953 was not generally a happy one for Eisenhower, what with the anguish of the East German revolt, the death from cancer of the strong-willed but loyal Taft in July, and the stalling of major portions of the administration's legislative program. Even so, the President could take satisfaction in the redemption of his foremost campaign promise—to end the Korean war. Like Truman, Eisenhower disregarded the goal of total military victory, which could not be won without the risk of world war. United Nations Commander Clark recalled that on Eisenhower's Korean visit in December 1952, "The question of how much it would take to win the war was never raised." Like Truman, Eisenhower was willing to settle for restoring the prewar partition of North and South Korea at approximately the 38th parallel—in short, for containment. What continued to deadlock the truce negotiations at Panmunjon was not a dispute over territory, but the issue of prisoner exchange. The Peoples Republic of Korea (North Korea) and the People's Republic of China were willing to permit full repatriation of South Korean and United Nations (overwhelmingly American) prisoners of war. The Truman administration, however, had insisted on the right of the much larger numbers of North Korean and Chinese POWs to choose whether they wished to be repatriated or to remain in the south.

To break the deadlock at Panmunjon, the new administration made its only departure from Truman's policy. Eisenhower decided to threaten nuclear warfare for the limited objective of a peace agreement based on the principle of nonforcible repatriation. Soon after the truce talks resumed on April 23, Dulles and Eisenhower became impatient with what they viewed as footdragging by the Chinese. The UN command stepped up its bombing compaign in North Korea; on May 13 American bombers struck a previously undamaged North Korean dam network and inundated a valley area twenty-seven miles long. Then, on May 22, Dulles conveyed through Indian Prime Minister Nehru and the Indian ambassador in Peking a secret and carefully worded warning that unless progress became evident in the truce talks, all previous limits on targets and weapons would be lifted. Implicitly, the United States might use atomic bombs against North Korea and even China's Manchurian provinces.

Whether this warning was the decisive factor in breaking the deadlock is still unclear. At any rate, on June 8 a complicated arrangement for the exchange of prisoners was finally agreed to. South Korean President Syngman Rhee—a figure second only to Chiang Kai-shek in the Republican pantheon of Asian leaders—denounced the agreement and promised to carry on the war without the United States. The Chinese then launched an offensive against a sector in the battle line held by South Korean troops and drove them back seven miles, presumably to demonstrate the weakness of Rhee's army. After that Rhee ostensibly consented to the prisoner exchange provisions, and the negotiations proceeded toward a full armistice.

The cantankerous Rhee had hardly given up. On the night of June 18 he ordered the release of some 27,000 prisoners who had refused repatriation. The prisoners quickly disappeared into the population; fewer than 700 were ever recovered. As the Chinese and North Korean governments stormed and broke off the negotiations once again, Republicans like Senators Knowland and McCarthy applauded Rhee's action. The Eisenhower administration could only privately fume and publicly reassure Rhee of renewed American military intervention if the proposed armistice broke down. Meanwhile a new Chinese offensive, again directed only at South Korean sectors, pushed the battle line still further south. At last Clark and Walter Robertson, Assistant Secretary of State for Far Eastern Affairs, succeeded in convincing Rhee to put aside, at least for the time being, his hopes of conquering the North. Although he accepted the armistice, Rhee still refused to sign the peace document. Clark had to sign both for him and for the United Nations.

On the evening of July 26 Eisenhower went on national radio and television to announce the armistice. The UN "police action," the legal designation for the Korean war, had ended on terms Truman had originally set forth but for which only Eisenhower could win bipartisan assent. Besides costing the United States about $18 billion and devastating most of the Korean peninsula, the war had caused the deaths of some 23,000 Americans and at least a million Koreans and Chinese. And the conflict had ended not with a peace settlement but with a fragile armistice. Sporadic clashes along the truce line continued for the next twenty years, long after a military coup in Seoul had overthrown Rhee. Over that period the United States spent close to $10 billion in the Republic of Korea to rebuild its economy and to make its army one of the biggest and best equipped in the world. The Soviet Union also beefed up and maintained North Korea's forces, although neither the Russians nor the Chinese stationed significant numbers of military personnel north of the 38th parallel. By contrast, the United States kept some 50,000 men in the South. Korea remained one of the deadliest frontiers of the cold war.

IV

The Korean conflict was the most confused and frustrating the nation had fought since the War of 1812. The 1953 armistice removed a deeply divisive element in American life. In the long run the passing of Korea as a political issue contributed to the waning of the Communist phobia which had seized the country in the years since 1945. Yet even though the "no-win" war had done much to feed America's great fear of Communism, the end of the fighting by no means marked the end of the distrust, harassment, and political repression that had come to pervade American society. Many citizens were still haunted by notions of spy plots and Communist subversion in the nation's governmental, educational, and even religious institutions. Continuously playing on their anxieties was Joe McCarthy, an extraordinarily ruthless and effective purveyor of suspicion and hatred. While McCarthy had many allies and even some rivals in Congress and other high places, he, more than anyone else, personified the massive assault on civil liberties and civil sanity which went forward under the banner of anti-Communism. "McCarthyism" had already become, to McCarthy's followers, a synonym for the preservation of American freedoms, while to McCarthy's foes the term was synonymous with efforts to destroy those freedoms. In short,

McCarthyism connoted tendencies and forces which antedated, exceeded, and long outlived the meteoric career of the bombastic junior senator from Wisconsin.

In the 1950s students of American society offered various hypotheses to explain the phenomenon of McCarthyism. The sociologists Seymour M. Lipset, Talcott Parsons, Edward Shils, and Nathan Glazer and the historians Richard Hofstadter and Oscar Handlin saw the anti-Communist hysteria as manifesting basic flaws in American society. The theories they advanced had to do with status anxieties, class jealousies, the compulsive super-patriotism of ethnic minorities and Roman Catholics, and the persistence in mid-century of the putatively conspiratorial, proto-fascist mentality of earlier midwestern agrarian radicalism. There were major elements of truth in all these theories. McCarthy, a Roman Catholic himself, did enjoy a remarkable degree of approval among his coreligionists; Francis Cardinal Spellman of New York City and other Church leaders lavishly praised him for leading the crusade against "Godless Communism." McCarthy also had a heavy following among lower-middle-class Americans, a segment of society that largely overlapped the Roman Catholic population, which in turn included most Americans of eastern and southern European ancestry. Moreover, much of McCarthy's strength lay in the midwestern states. Finally, McCarthy drew many supporters and substantial monetary backing from newly rich businessmen and financiers, who supposedly felt less secure in their money and power than persons of established wealth.

Yet explanations like these—besides revealing a basic disillusionment with popular democracy and a preference for a "pluralistic" political culture of interacting elites—tended to ignore or obfuscate the two most obvious aspects of anti-Communist extremism: That, whatever other collective tensions or neuroses it might suggest, such extremism was preoccupied with the alleged threat of Communism, and that it also had strongly partisan political motivations. As the scholars Michael Rogin, Robert Griffith, and Earl Latham have shown, the kind of sentiment McCarthy exploited in the early fifties had its roots in the frustrations of a party long out of power and in a loathing of radical political ideologies which reached far back into the American past.

Effectively discrediting the theory that McCarthyism was a degraded version of native midwestern radicalism, Rogin has demonstrated that by the late thirties the states of the upper Middle West were already strongly anti–New Deal; on foreign policy the region had intensified its traditional unilateralist aversion to collective security. Thus McCarthy's strength there was consistent with sentiment already firmly entrenched in the years before Pearl Harbor. Rogin has also pointed out that McCarthy's national following reflected established political cleavages. Early in 1954 the public opinion polls gave McCarthy a peak approval rating of 50 percent. More significant, according to Rogin, is the fact that twice as many Democrats as Republicans expressed *disapproval* of McCarthy. A survey of opinion polls throughout McCarthy's years of greatest popularity indicates that party identification determined public attitudes toward the senator much more than religious affiliation, class status, educational level, or any other factor.

Griffith and Latham have shown that McCarthy's rise to power was only one manifestation—albeit the most spectacular—of a longstanding controversy over Communist influence in American government and society. After flaring up in the late thirties, anti-Communism had died down somewhat during World War II when Russia was America's ally. Reemerging with renewed virulence after 1945 with the onset of Soviet-American conflict, anti-Communism gathered momentum from the Communist victory in China, the war in Korea, and the Republican party's inability to regain the Presidency. What Griffith has called "the anti-Communist persuasion"—"a fear of radicalism which sometimes bordered on the pathological"—took in far more than McCarthy's activities. The Wisconsin Republican gave the persuasion new focus, boldness, and viciousness. Yet while McCarthy disrupted the normal routine of American politics, he was also very much a product of that routine. McCarthyism, Rogin has concluded, mirrored "the specific traumas of conservative Republican activists—internal Communist subversion, the New Deal, centralized government, left-wing intellectuals, and the corrupting influences of a cosmopolitan society. The resentments of these Republicans and the Senator's own talents were the driving forces behind the McCarthy movement."

Various hopeful observers thought that Eisenhower in the White House would mean the muzzling or at least muffling of McCarthy. The President's practice of watchful waiting—on the assumption that with enough rope the senator would hang himself—might eventually have contributed something to McCarthy's downfall. During the administration's first year, however, McCarthy became more audacious and ferocious than ever, largely because Eisenhower and most of the people he brought into his administration were themselves much affected by the anti-Communist persuasion.

The administration shared the belief of the militant anti-Communists in Congress that Soviet espionage had severely jeopardized the nation's security, and that such espionage had enabled the Russians to build their atomic capability years ahead of Western predictions. Like the great majority of his fellow citizens, Eisenhower thought not in terms of a broad body of international scientific knowledge which the Soviets could utilize as readily as anyone else, but in terms of scientific secrets which America should be able to monopolize. Thus the President had no doubts about the guilt of Julius and Ethel Rosenberg, who had received death sentences in 1951 for helping transmit data on the atomic bomb to Soviet agents six years earlier. Convinced that the Rosenbergs' actions "may have condemned to death tens of millions of innocent people" and that they had received "the fullest measure of justice and due process of law," Eisenhower followed the example of President Truman in denying the Rosenbergs a stay of execution. On June 13, 1953, while demonstrators pleaded for mercy in front of the White House and at other places in the United States and abroad, the Rosenbergs died in the electric chair at Sing Sing Prison in New York.

Truman's unyielding attitude in the Rosenberg case had done little to counter the charge that his administration and his party were "soft on Communism." Right after World War I some members of the American Communist party, a larger number of "fellow travelers," and a still larger number of past party members or people with current Communist acquaintances had held jobs in various parts of the executive branch. Two other facts, however, are equally certain: First, there was absolutely no concrete evidence of Communist influence on Truman administration policy at any time. Second, as early as March 1947 Truman ordered a thorough check of all federal employees by the Federal Bureau of Investigation and the Civil Service Commission. The check was exceedingly rigorous and, if anything, generally unmindful of the constitutional protections of those under investigation. By the spring of 1951 FBI Director J. Edgar Hoover could report that more than 3,225,000 federal employees had been examined. Nearly 3,000 had resigned while under investigation; another 304 had been formally discharged.

Republican militants still suspected Truman's loyalty program because it distinguished between "loyalty" and "security" and concerned itself with "security risks" only in such "sensitive" areas as the State and Defense departments. These limitations, they claimed, made it possible, even likely, that persons who appeared loyal, but who had Communist associations or personal traits like homosexuality or alcoholism, might be blackmailed into undermining the nation's defenses.

Agreeing that the Truman administration had been slow and unsystematic in removing actual or potential subversives, Eisenhower in April 1953 issued Executive Order 10450, which made federal employment contingent on whether retention was "clearly consistent with the interests of the national security." Under this new directive the administration found not a single Communist, but it did summarily fire people because of questionable associations or personal habits. At Vice President Nixon's urging, the Civil Service Commission disclosed three weeks before the 1954 congressional elections that 6,926 persons had been dismissed since Eisenhower took office. Campaigning across the country, Nixon could brag that "We're kicking the Communists and fellow-travelers and security risks out of the government not by the hundreds but by the thousands." Nixon neglected to mention that the present administration had first hired about 40 percent of the nearly seven thousand reportedly fired since early 1953.

Even though little remained in the way of cleansing the federal bureaucracy of subversives by the time Eisenhower took office, his supposedly tougher policy did much to demoralize the State Department. To mollify McCarthy, Styles Bridges, William Knowland, William Jenner, and other anti-Communist militants in the Senate, Secretary of State Dulles appointed Scott McLeod, an ex-FBI agent who had been on Bridges's staff, State Department security chief. Among those dropped because of McLeod's investigations or at Dulles's initiative were such capable Foreign Service officers as the Asian specialist John Carter Vincent, John Paton Davies (fired after nine security inquiries had cleared him), and George Kennan, who was credited with being the theoretician behind Truman's containment policy. Within eighteen months after Dulles took office, few who had held important positions under Dean Acheson were still at State. One of the holdovers was Robert Murphy, who came back from Japan, where he had served as ambassador, to become Assistant Secretary of State for United Nations Affairs. The extent of popular suspicion plaguing State is evident in a question one of Murphy's friends raised: "Bob, how can you bring yourself to work in that nest of Commies and homosexuals in the State Department?"

When Eisenhower nominated Charles E. Bohlen, a career Foreign Service officer and Roosevelt's interpreter at the Yalta Conference, to become ambassador to the Soviet Union, Senate militants were indignant. Here was the administration trying to appoint to a vital diplomatic post a man who had been associated with the Yalta "betrayal" and subsequently with Truman's disastrous policies. The militants' indignation turned to outrage when Bohlen defended the Yalta agreements before the Senate Foreign Relations Committee. Nevertheless, the committee unanimously recommended Bohlen's confirmation at the urging of Taft, who disliked the whole business but was willing to go along with the administration. Final Senate approval, though, came only after Taft and Senator John Sparkman examined the FBI's file on Bohlen and reported back to the Senate that they had found nothing to reflect on Bohlen's loyalty. In the end thirteen senators, led by McCarthy and Bridges, voted against Bohlen.

In 1953 the spearheads of the congressional anti-Communist crusade included the peripatetic Senate Internal Security sub-

committee, where William Jenner took over the chairmanship
from the florid Democratic Red-baiter Pat McCarran, and the
equally well-traveled House Un-American Activities Committee,
now chaired by ex-FBI agent Harold Velde. Jenner's subcommittee
continued the probe McCarran had begun of American Communists allegedly employed at UN headquarters in New York.[3]
Meanwhile HUAC busied itself with rumors of Reds in New York
City's schools and, for the third time since 1947, in the motion
picture industry.

Yet Joe McCarthy got the biggest and most frequent headlines as chairman of the Permanent Investigation Subcommittee
of the Senate Committee on Government Operations. Far from
muzzling McCarthy, the Republican return to power sent him on
a veritable rampage. Running his subcommittee with an appropriation twice as big as the previous year's, McCarthy first set his
sights on the International Information Agency (IIA) and the
State Department's Voice of America. Fed a steady stream of
half-truths and gossip by his "loyal underground" of disgruntled
minor bureaucrats, McCarthy charged incompetence if not sinister motives in the location of Voice of America transmitters. In
Cambridge, Massachusetts, a Voice engineer whose name had
come up before McCarthy's subcommittee threw himself in front
of a truck after writing in a suicide note, "once the dogs are set on
you, everything you have done since the beginning of time is
suspect." McCarthy also sent his two youthful aides, Roy M. Cohn,
son of a Democratic judge in New York City, and G. David
Schine, heir to a hotel chain, to inspect IIA libraries in Europe for
pro-Communist books. As a result of their whirlwind tour—which
took Cohn and Schine to 12 cities in 6 countries over 17 days—
intimidated IIA officials actually burned a few books and removed
hundreds of others from their library shelves.

In the meantime McCarthy announced that he had personally
negotiated an agreement whereby Greek shipowners would stop
trading with mainland China. Mutual Security Administrator
Harold Stassen denounced McCarthy for interfering in foreign

3. The previous fall the subcommittee's "indiscriminate smears,"
as UN Secretary General Trygve Lie described its tactics, had apparently caused the suicide of Abraham Feller, head of the UN legal staff.

policy, but Secretary of State Dulles, after lunching with the senator, allowed that he had acted "in the national interest." McCarthy backtracked a little, saying that he had only participated in achieving an "informal understanding."

This was one of the few times McCarthy backtracked on anything. His standard tactic was to make some exaggerated or wholly false charge, then to ignore factual rebuttals and move on to other accusations, all the while waving fictitious documents (sometimes just blank paper), citing erroneous statistics, and pretending that only he really had the facts.

Eisenhower had a genuine revulsion for McCarthy and his allies. When embraced by Senator Jenner before a speech in Indiana during the 1952 campaign, Eisenhower had confided to his aides, "I felt dirty from the touch of the man." The President's basic response to McCarthy, however, was to try to hold his lofty perch above political strife, on the grounds that it would do little good to "get down into the gutter with that guy." Urged by a supporter to repudiate McCarthy, the President replied: "It is a sorry mess; at times one feels almost like hanging his head in shame when he reads some of the unreasoned, vicious outburts of demagoguery that appear in our public prints. But whether a Presidential 'crack down' would be better, or would actually worsen, the situation, is a moot question."

In 1953 the administration made two overt moves against McCarthy. One was Eisenhower's pointed criticism of book burners in a speech at Dartmouth College in June. (Three days later the President disabused reporters of any illusions that he favored totally free expression by sanctioning the possible destruction of material that advocated violent revolution.) The second move had to do with an article published in the July issue of the right-wing magazine *American Mercury* by J. B. Matthews. Staff director for McCarthy's subcommittee and a professional ex-Communist who had found a home in postwar Washington, Matthews accused the nation's Protestant clergy of being heavily infiltrated by Communists. Even McCarthy could recognize the absurdity of this charge, and he quickly tried to get out a press release announcing the firing of Matthews. While Vice President Nixon stalled McCarthy on his way to reporters, the White House released Eisenhower's reply to a telegram from the National Conference of Christians and Jews protesting Matthews's article. An hour before McCarthy finally got out his story, the President's letter castigating such "generalized and irresponsible attacks" as that of Matthews was on the wire services. Emmet John Hughes, who helped prepare the Eisenhower letter, has recalled that this affair was "the only notable reverse suffered by McCarthy in a period of more than a year."

On the other hand, the administration sometimes matched the worst excesses of McCarthy and his fellow Communist-stalkers in Congress. In November Attorney General Brownell charged that early in 1946 President Truman had received two FBI reports that Assistant Secretary of the Treasury Harry Dexter White was a Soviet spy. Truman, according to Brownell, had ignored the reports so he could make White the American representative on the International Monetary Fund. In the course of denying Brownell's claims over national television and radio, Truman denounced McCarthy, who in turn demanded and got equal time to attack the Democrats. Chairman Velde of HUAC then tried to bring Truman and former Secretary of State James F. Byrnes, who seemed to back up Brownell's story, before his committee, but both Truman and Byrnes refused HUAC's subpoenas on constitutional grounds. When Eisenhower defended Truman's loyalty, Brownell quickly followed with the assurance that he had questioned only Truman's "laxity," not his loyalty. Although Jenner's Senate subcommittee later took testimony from Brownell and J. Edgar Hoover about the White episode, the controversy generated by this rather futile exercise in flogging dead horses soon subsided.

Of much greater import was the Oppenheimer case. Among the many people victimized by the doctrine of guilt by association used so effectively by anti-Communist crusaders, the most famous was J. Robert Oppenheimer. A professor of physics at Princeton University, Oppenheimer had directed the Los Alamos atomic laboratory during World War II and since then had been a valuable consultant to the Atomic Energy Commission (AEC). Although no evidence of disloyalty on Oppenheimer's part ever turned up, he was considered a security risk because he had opposed the decision to develop the "super" or hydrogen bomb in 1949–1950, and because he had maintained close associations with past or present Communists, including his wife. Late in 1953 Eisenhower personally ordered Oppenheimer cut off from all classified nuclear information. Oppenheimer demanded and got a hearing before the AEC security board, which voted 2-1 to withhold his security clearance and to dismiss him as an AEC consultant. The commission itself then voted 4-1 to uphold the board's decision on the grounds that Oppenheimer had shown "fundamental defects in his character."

The dismissal of Oppenheimer, perhaps the country's most respected native-born scientist, provoked an intense and long-running debate in the press and within the American scientific establishment, where confidence in the Eisenhower administration diminished substantially. The Oppenheimer case was a major testament to the strength and pervasiveness of the anti-Communist persuasion in the early fifties. While that case was reaching its climax, however, other events were in motion which would at last fatally undermine the foremost exploiter of the anti-Communist persuasion, Joe McCarthy. On April 22, 1954, the Army-McCarthy hearings began.

The hearings were the outgrowth of a long succession of allegations and counterallegations between McCarthy and Roy Cohn, on one hand, and Secretary of the Army Robert T. Stevens and various high Army officials, on the other. However absurd it might seem to a later generation of Americans, McCarthy had actually convinced himself that the United States Army was soft on Communism. During his subcommittee's inquiry into alleged espionage at the Signal Corps laboratory at Fort Monmouth, New Jersey, McCarthy discovered that the Army had promoted a dentist named Irving Peress to the rank of major, and then had given him an honorable discharge upon learning that Peress had once taken the Fifth Amendment when questioned about Communist connections. After Secretary Stevens refused to turn over Peress's file to McCarthy's staff, the senator brought General Ralph Zwicker, who had overseen Peress's discharge, before his subcommittee and gave him a severe tongue lashing. At this point the Army mounted a counterattack in the form of twenty-nine charges against McCarthy, subcommittee counsel Cohn, and the subcommittee's staff director. The most spectacular charge was that McCarthy and Cohn had tried to blackmail the Army into giving a commission and special treatment to draftee G. David Schine. McCarthy retorted that the Army was using Schine as a "hostage" to keep the subcommittee from getting at the truth.

McCarthy's subcommittee voted to hold hearings on the whole tangled sequence of events and accusations, with Senator Karl Mundt temporarily assuming the chairmanship. Telecast daily and covered by some 180 newsmen, the hearings dragged on until June 17. Under Mundt's generally inept chairmanship, they consisted mostly of dreary haggling over picayune matters, interrupted frequently by McCarthy's calling "Point of order, Mr. Chairman." Even the closest follower could make little sense of the confused proceedings. The subcommittee's four reports were equally confused and inconclusive. The Army-McCarthy hearings did, however, reveal McCarthy at his boorish and ruthless worst, while they also made Army counsel Joseph Welch a national personality. At one point Welch left McCarthy speechless by asking, "Have you left no sense of decency?" Together with Edward R. Murrow's careful critique of McCarthy's methods earlier that spring on CBS television's "See It Now," the hearings probably did change some people's minds about the junior senator from Wisconsin. At any rate, for the first time since 1950 it seemed that McCarthy had lost his momentum.

What finally brought McCarthy down, though, was not public outrage over his studied disregard of constitutional liberties and his sustained abuse of power. Nor was it vigorous action on the part of the administration to discredit McCarthy, unless one assumes that the administration's strategy was to try to appear even more zealous in its pursuit of Communists. In June Eisenhower announced that forty-one second-echelon Communist party officials had been convicted in federal court for violating the Smith Act of 1940, which made it a federal crime to advocate the overthrow or to belong to an organization advocating the overthrow of the United States government.[4] Eisenhower also reported

4. The Truman administration had earlier prosecuted the eleven top Communist leaders.

that 84 "alien subversives" had been deported and that 62 new groups had been added to the Attorney General's list of subversive organizations.

Nor did McCarthy fall because Congress had lost its enthusiasm for the Communist issue. During its second session in 1954, the Eighty-third Congress enacted eight different laws placing further curbs on subversive activities. By far the most significant was the Communist Control Act, passed unanimously by the Senate and with only two negative votes in the House of Representatives. Besides adding "Communist-infiltrated" organizations to the "Communist-action" and "Communist-front" organizations already required to register with the Attorney General under the 1950 McCarran Act, the Communist Control Act in effect made membership in the Communist party illegal. The statute designated the party an "agency of a hostile foreign power" and denied it the "rights, privileges and immunities" other political organizations had.

In this instance, as had been the case with the McCarran Act four years earlier, liberal Senate Democrats subordinated their regard for civil liberties to their determination to prove that they were as passionately anti-Communist as the Republican rightists. In 1950 Democratic Senators Paul Douglas and Harley Kilgore had proposed, as a substitute to the McCarran bill, legislation authorizing the President to intern all suspected subversives after he declared an "internal security emergency." This intended substitute had eventually become part of the McCarran bill, which President Truman vetoed but Congress repassed. In 1954 Senator Hubert Humphrey, another favorite of the Americans for Democratic Action, was mainly responsible for the section of the Communist Control Act that stripped Communists of their political rights. Senator Wayne Morse, an independent liberal from Oregon, attested to the strength of the militance behind the deluge of anti-Communist legislation in 1954: "In the Senate there is no division of opinion among liberals, conservatives and those in between when it comes to our utter detestation of the Communist conspiracy and our united insistence that as a Senate we will fight the growth of the Communist conspiracy."

McCarthy thus found himself in trouble not because the anti-Communist persuasion had weakened appreciably. He had, though, by vilifying the Army and Secretary Stevens, become an embarrassment to the administration and the GOP. By his rashness, his irresponsibility, and his general disregard for the canons of procedure and decorum fixed in the Senate, he had also alienated senators who had no real quarrel with him otherwise. Thus a substantial bipartisan bloc had come to oppose McCarthy, mainly for the wrong reasons. What offended most senators was not McCarthy's beliefs but rather his methods and his unruly behavior.

Early in August 1954 the Senate voted overwhelmingly to establish a select committee to study a set of censure charges brought against McCarthy by a fellow Republican, Ralph Flanders of Vermont. Chairing the select committee of four Republicans and three Democrats was Arthur V. Watkins, a Utah conservative, who carried out the investigation with a remarkable absence of the rancor and disruption usually associated with McCarthy. Even McCarthy behaved himself fairly well when he appeared before the committee. On September 27 the Watkins committee unanimously recommended McCarthy's censure for contempt of the Senate (because he had refused to appear before a Senate committee probing election irregularities in 1952) and for his abuse of General Zwicker.

The Senate put off considering the committee's report until after the congressional elections. Finally beginning on November 29, the Senate debate was long, tedious, often acrimonious. McCarthy regained form and blasted away at the Watkins committee, prompting Minority Leader Johnson to snap that McCarthy's statements "do not belong in the pages of the *Congressional Record*. They would be more fittingly inscribed on the walls of a men's room." First-termer Sam J. Ervin of North Carolina, one of the Democrats Johnson had put on the Watkins committee, added that the Senate should not just censure McCarthy, it should expel him. Technically, the Senate did not even censure McCarthy, although practically speaking it did. On December 2 it voted 67-22 to "condemn" McCarthy for contempt of the Senate in 1952 and for contempt and abuse of the Senate and its select committee in 1954.[5] Every Democrat present, independent Wayne Morse, and 22 Republicans, mostly from the Northeast, voted for condemnation. Led by Majority Leader Knowland, 24 Republicans, nearly all former supporters of Taft from the Middle West and West, backed McCarthy.

Although the Senate was never willing to confront the fundamental questions raised by McCarthy's antics, its formal condemnation proved a mortal blow. With the Senate under Democratic control after 1954, McCarthy lost his locus of power as chairman of the Permanent Investigation Subcommittee. He also became more and more of a liability to the Republicans. McCarthy still had some of the old fight left in him. Hearing about Eisenhower's felicitations to the Watkins committee, he apologized to the American people for asking them to vote for Eisenhower. But McCarthy's attacks no longer scared anyone. Six months after the censure vote, Eisenhower—with undue smugness in view of the paltry contribution the administration had made to the push against McCarthy—asked his cabinet if they had heard the story making the rounds that McCarthyism had become "McCarthywasm." McCarthy did not live out the second six-year term Wisconsin's voters had given him in 1952. Obscure and almost friendless in the Senate, he died in May 1957 of a liver ailment presumably aggravated by heavy drinking. He was only forty-seven.

The anti-Communist persuasion, a basic feature of American political life, would far outlive McCarthy. Yet with the Korean war over and with the passage of time, the Communist issue eventually lost much of its power to inflame public emotions. Hounded by federal and state authorities and wracked by internal disputes which, as Joseph Starobin has pointed out, produced a mirror image of McCarthyite paranoia, the American Communist party had been declining steadily since the late forties. Then, in 1956–1957, the party was literally torn to pieces as a result of quarrels over Soviet party head Nikita Khrushchev's long recapitulation of the "crimes of Stalin" and Khrushchev's

5. The count charging McCarthy with abusing General Zwicker had previously been dropped.

brutal suppression of the Hungarian revolt. From an FBI estimate of 20,000 in 1956, party membership shrank to around 5,000 by 1960. Yet state officials, organizations like the American Legion and the Christian Anti-Communist Crusade, and especially HUAC carried on the hunt for Reds. As late as 1957 Francis E. Walter, HUAC's Democratic chairman, could still seriously claim—FBI figures to the contrary notwithstanding—that there were 200,000 American Communists, "the equivalent of twenty combat divisions of enemy troops. . . ."

The 1954 congressional elections gave the Republicans their last opportunity to do much with the issue of Communist influence in American government and society. When Vice President Nixon and other Republicans proudly quoted figures on the total number of federal employees discharged since January 1953, the Democrats retorted that they had fired even more real security risks under Truman. This avid numbers game prompted Richard Rovere to observe that "visitors from another civilization would have been forced to conclude that in the United States the measure of political virtue was the number of unworthy civil servants a government managed to dismiss."

Though losing their slim congressional majorities, the Republicans fared considerably better than parties in power usually do in midterm elections. Yet the 1954 elections, Robert Griffith has commented, "did seem to signal the end of the political dynamic which had supported McCarthy and the Communist issue." Likewise Richard Rovere, one of the earliest and most perceptive students of McCarthy, has written that "surely the fevers of McCarthyism subsided in 1954, and most of us knew it and felt it." The nation thereafter seemed a lot less wrought up over spies and subversives at home.

Yet there was no discernible accompanying shift in public thinking on international affairs. Despite the death of the tyrant Stalin, the Soviet Union continued to appear as a worldwide menace, to be met by the worldwide military, economic, and political might of the United States. Communist China, moreover, seemed bent on dominating all Asia. The basic framework of the cold war thus remained intact, as did the cold war consensus on American foreign policy.

III

Rhetoric and Reality
in Foreign Policy

AMERICANS of the mid-1970s, hearing from almost every quarter that the United States had entered a period of detente with both the Soviet Union and the People's Republic of China, might wonder at the intensity of American hostility toward the "Communist bloc" in the 1950s. In those years the overwhelming majority of the American people—whether Republicans or Democrats, conservatives or liberals, businessmen, industrial workers, or members of the professions—had few doubts that their country faced a worldwide conspiracy whose center was Moscow and whose ultimate objective was nothing less than universal Communist conquest. This premise formed the crux of the cold war consensus, a consensus that had functioned without significant critical challenge since the late 1940s, and that determined the way Americans reacted to events both within and beyond their continental borders. Foreign policy debates in the fifties focused not on whether America was actually in peril but on the way this supposed peril should be dealt with. On ends there was fairly general agreement: The United States must strive continuously to frustrate the Communist conspiracy, thereby either forcing Moscow to moderate its policies, as George Kennan anticipated, or creating conditions under which the hundreds of millions living in Communist tyranny could rise up and smash their masters, as John Foster Dulles passionately envisioned.

I

Dulles's militant rhetoric to the contrary notwithstanding, American policy really functioned in terms of a global balance of power. That meant that the United States and its allies must block Communist expansion at every turn. Thus while the Eisenhower administration talked about "rolling back the Communist tide" and "liberating the captive peoples," in practice it found itself having to settle for the basic strategy of containment inherited from the Truman administration. Dulles's spread-eagle pronouncements proved useful in appeasing anti-Communist militants in Congress and creating the appearance of a sharp break with previous Democratic policy. Yet as Kennan has commented, from the outset Dulles "knew very well that whatever he might say publicly, he was going to have to pursue in reality . . . pretty much the policy [of containment] toward the Soviet Union with which my name had been often connected." Kennan is scarcely an unbiased commentator, and he makes Dulles appear more hypocritical and less idealistic than he doubtless was. Nevertheless, even Dulles and certainly Eisenhower recognized how limited the areas of cold war maneuver actually were, and thus how limited were the gains they could expect without bringing on hot war.

Within the framework of the inherited and sustained strategy of containment, there were still several points of contrast between the Eisenhower-Dulles policies and those of Truman and Acheson. After 1952 American foreign policy did become more dogmatic, more absolutist, often less flexible. To Dulles it was absolutely "immoral" for India and other newly founded nations in Asia and Africa to remain neutral under mounting cold war pressures. Even though Eisenhower was somewhat more tolerant of neutralism than Dulles, the President shared his Secretary of State's conviction that the clash between the Western and Communist countries was a confrontation of fundamental good versus fundamental evil, and that whatever happened in the world had to be considered first within this Manichean bipolarity. The administration simply could not understand how various states in what was collectively termed the "underdeveloped areas" (later called the "Third World") could take American economic and even military assistance and still refuse to align themselves with the United States. American policy remained basically out of touch with the realities of a world of rapidly multiplying nations with a diversity of interests and a common fear of being sucked into the cold war power struggle.

Dulles and Eisenhower were not always of one mind, even though their differences were usually matters of emphasis. No less convinced than Dulles that the United States must resist Soviet designs at every point where they became manifest, the President did believe there were some issues on which the two superpowers might be able to agree. Though tied to a set of assumptions that made significant accommodation with the Russians unlikely, Eisenhower did genuinely want to reduce existing armament levels and lessen cold war tensions. The President's hopeful attitude on the question of East-West negotiations seemed more plausible after Stalin's death early in 1953. Within a few months the new Soviet "collective leadership" had offered a more conciliatory line.

Dulles was highly skeptical when not outright alarmed by the prospect of negotiating with America's mortal enemies. In Dulles's thinking the USSR, under the burden of the arms race, must eventually reach a condition of economic exhaustion which would be conducive to internal strife, convulsion, and the ultimate collapse of the Communist regime. Meanwhile the crises and tensions of the cold war cemented the elaborate and far-flung alliance system Dulles was forming on foundations laid by the Truman administration. Cold war crisis also insured the continued willingness of Congress to appropriate money for America's global defenses. Peace overtures, such as Eisenhower's April 1953 speech before the National Press Club calling for a relaxation of tensions, seemed useful to Dulles not as steps toward accommodation with the Soviets, but as weapons in the incessant psychological warfare America must wage. Like Acheson, his predecessor at State, Dulles was frankly convinced that the United States and the USSR, locked as they were in "an irreconcilable conflict," really had nothing to negotiate about. For Dulles diplomacy was almost exclusively a matter of forming and shoring up alliance systems, of maintaining Western unity and stiffening the resolve of the "free world" to resist Communist advance. While Dulles was Secretary of State, from 1953 until terminal cancer forced his resignation in the spring of 1959, every one of the Eisenhower administration's peace initiatives originated in the presidential staff system. Not one came from the State Department.

For all his cold war militance and disdain for negotiation, Dulles still staunchly backed Eisenhower's protracted campaign to reduce and hold down the size and cost of the American military establishment. Eisenhower, Dulles, Secretary of Defense Wilson, and Admiral Arthur Radford, Eisenhower's choice to head the Joint Chiefs of Staff, all were realists enough to see that in the nuclear age omnipotence was a wasteful and dangerous illusion. The United States simply could not afford the capability to fight any kind of war, anywhere, at any time. The chief lesson Eisenhower and his associates drew from Korea was that limited wars, fought with conventional weaponry on the periphery of the Communist world, only drained the nation's resources and weakened its allies' resolve. Yet the Communist threat was always and everywhere present. The administration's synthesis of the seemingly antithetical objectives of military economy and global defense was the doctrine of strategic deterrence, which Dulles, in one of his most troublesome coinages, called "massive retaliation." Relying mainly on the intercontinental striking power of the Strategic Air Command's hundreds of nuclear-armed bombers, strategic deterrence looked like a dramatic yet rational alternative to the Truman administration's practice of scattering funds among the three military services in a futile effort to surpass or at least match the Soviets in every arms category. Strategic deterrence formed the essence of what Admiral Radford, in a speech late in 1953, called the "New Look" in American military policy.

The New Look rejected the major premise of the Truman administration: That ahead, presumably in the year 1954, lay a period of "maximum danger," when Soviet and maybe Chinese aggressiveness might bring on full-scale war. The United States should therefore build up both conventional and nuclear forces to be ready for any contingency. As for costs, Truman's economic advisers had presupposed that a healthy, expanding economy could easily absorb and maybe even benefit from increased military outlays. In turn, a healthy economy would effectuate speedy mobilization and conversion to wartime production.

The contrasting premises under which the Eisenhower administration formed its military policies were: (1) That the United States faced a protracted period of danger in its relations with the Communist powers, whose military capabilities would not change a great deal for some years; (2) that militarily the United States should plan for the long haul, thereby avoiding the economic uncertainties and contractions which had resulted from maximum-danger planning; (3) that arms costs must be cut as part of an overall reduction in federal expenditures to achieve a balanced budget and a sound credit and currency system, which in turn would enable the country to afford its military establishment; (4) that any future armed conflict between the major powers would quickly move to a nuclear exchange; and (5) that the United States should therefore concentrate on developing its nuclear arsenal and delivery capability at the expense of conventional ground and naval forces.

As early as May 1952, in an article in *Life* magazine, Dulles had sketched the basic approach to military policy the Eisenhower administration later adopted. Dulles had even used the phrase "retaliatory striking power" in an early draft of the 1952 Republican platform, although at the insistence of Eisenhower, who thought it too strong, the phrase did not appear in the final version. The administration could do little with the fiscal year 1954 military budget because the Korean war was still on. But by the fall of 1953—with the war over and the administration supposedly no longer constrained by the mistakes of the Truman years—Eisenhower and his strategists could move to implement the new departure in military policy for fiscal 1955.

A National Security Council policy paper (NSC–16212), which the President approved on October 5, 1953, set forth the essentials of the New Look. To counter localized Communist aggression the United States, instead of reacting with its own conventional forces, would rely for a first line of defense on American-equipped and trained indigenous troops. Backing up these native forces would be American tactical air and sea power, presumably furnished with "tactical" nuclear weapons—atomic bombs and shells about the size of the bombs used against Hiroshima and Nagasaki in 1945. Here, articulated for the first time in a formal policy statement, was the notion that the development of the hydrogen bomb had made 1945-style atomic weapons part of the regular equipment of tactical warfare. Dulles remarked that atomic weapons were "becoming more and more conventional." And in the spring of 1955 Eisenhower added: "Where these things are used on strictly military targets and for strictly military purposes, I see no reason why they shouldn't be used just exactly as you would use a bullet or anything else."

The same policy paper also envisioned a 25 percent reduction by 1957 in the number of Americans under arms, to be achieved mainly by cutbacks in Army and Navy manpower. Meanwhile, the Air Force—which could deliver "more bang for a buck," as Secretary of Defense Wilson put it with customary pungency—would receive substantially more money and manpower authorizations. Total military expenditures should drop from about $50 billion in fiscal year 1954 to less than $35 billion by fiscal 1957.

The New Look expressed commonly held views within the Eisenhower administration. Secretary of the Treasury Humphrey, for example, insisted that "The United States has no business getting into little wars. If a situation comes up where our interests justify intervention, let's intervene decisively with all we have got—or stay out." Yet it was Secretary of State Dulles, with his penchant for extravagant phrase-making, who became identified more than anyone else with what looked like an all-or-nothing military policy. On January 12, 1954, in a speech before the Council on Foreign Relations, Dulles acknowledged that there was no "local defense" which would "contain the mighty land power of the Communist world."[1] In the face of the Communist bloc's superiority in ground forces, America must support its allies and protect its worldwide interests with "the further deterrent of massive retaliatory power." The Eisenhower administration, Dulles said, had made the hard decision "to depend primarily

1. The Council on Foreign Relations, a prestigious private organization, for more than thirty years had given strong support to an activist foreign policy based on collective security.

upon a great capacity to retaliate, instantly, by means and at places of our own choosing." Five days later, in his second State of the Union message, Eisenhower added that the United States possessed and would preserve "a massive capability to strike back."

The scariest word in Dulles's analysis, echoed by Eisenhower, was "massive." The administration evidently was saying that any Communist advance in any part of the world would prompt the dispatch of SAC's armada of bombers to drop their nuclear payloads. Actually the kind of unlimited reaction implied by the concept of massive retaliation had a clear inner logic. If in fact the United States and its allies confronted an omnipresent conspiracy masterminded from the Kremlin—if virtually any disturbance of the global status quo resulted from a flexing of the tentacles of the Communist octopus—then surely the appropriate response was an all-out blow at the head of the beast.

While Dulles's critics did not quarrel with the premise of a global Communist conspiracy, they did shudder at the prospect of a nuclear war precipitated by another situation such as the North Koreans' crossing of the 38th parallel in 1950. Moreover, how did massive retaliation relate to the kind of guerilla warfare leftist elements had earlier fought against the government of the Philippines, and the similar fighting still going on against British rule in Malaya and French rule in Indochina? Adlai Stevenson summed up the chorus of criticism greeting Dulles's speech when he accused the administration of "putting all its eggs in one basket."

Despite repeated efforts in the administration to qualify and minimize the significance of what Dulles had said, the concept of strategic retaliation remained central to its military thinking. Eisenhower's budget for fiscal year 1955, submitted to Congress early in 1954, stipulated an Army manpower level of one million, a cut of one-third, and reduced Navy manpower from one million to about 870,000. Conversely, the Air Force would be slightly enlarged, from 950,000 to 970,000. The administration slashed the Army's budget by more than $4 billion, while the Navy was to receive $1½ billion less than in fiscal 1954. Only the Air Force, already with the biggest budget, would get more money. With an added $800 million, the Air Force's total outlay would be $16.4 billion.

The Army leadership was understandably indignant and more than a little frightened. General Matthew B. Ridgway, Army Chief of Staff, heatedly denied that the Joint Chiefs had agreed unanimously on the fiscal 1955 military budget; instead, according to Ridgway, the administration and Chairman Radford had pressured the Chiefs into submitting a "directed verdict." Ridgway resigned his post, retired from the Army, and in 1956, at the nadir of the Army's size and influence, published an angry memoir which compared Ridgway's experiences in the Eisenhower administration to being shot at from ambush or bombed by one's own aircraft. Although some Navy traditionalists were equally unhappy with the New Look, other Navy leaders, typified by Radford, applauded the increasing emphasis on carrier-based air power. Carriers would insure a key Navy role in strategic planning.

It was ironic that the Air Force should be the main beneficiary of an economy drive by a President who was himself a career Army man. Eisenhower, though, continued to be sold on the strategic deterrence synthesis embodied in the New Look, which was the only way, he thought, to restrain the military services' hunger for money and projects at the same time that the nation bolstered its global might. To get the New Look budget through Congress, Eisenhower skillfully played on the popular feeling that "If Ike doesn't know what the military needs, then who does?" In private, moreover, Eisenhower revealed that he had as much confidence as the public in his judgment. Writing to a boyhood friend, he prophesied that "some day there is going to be a man sitting in my present chair who has not been raised in the military services and who will have little understanding of where slashes in their estimates can be made with little or no damage. If that should happen while we still have the state of tension that now exists in the world, I shudder to think of what could happen in this country."

In his drive for military economy Eisenhower received general support from congressional Republicans, many of whom still were more agitated about domestic Communism than about Communist military power. The Democrats, with congressional majorities after 1954, tried often and with eventual success to make political capital of alleged shortcomings in the nation's defenses—as in their criticism of the weakening of the Army's capability to fight conventional wars and their warnings of a "bomber gap" in 1955 and a "missile gap" beginning in 1957. All the same, Eisenhower usually had Democratic support for an activist, presidentially dominated foreign policy. Many of his fellow Republicans, however, had a lingering fear from the Roosevelt-Truman years of the chief executive's preeminence in international affairs. Such Republicans—basically the midwestern and western, formerly Taftite, element in the GOP—furnished most of the support for the effort to limit presidential power in foreign policy. That effort took the form of the Bricker Amendment.

As early as 1951 Republican Senator John Bricker of Ohio had introduced a constitutional amendment which, though taking several different forms over the next three years, retained three main provisions: (1) The executive branch could enter into no treaty that conflicted with the Constitution. (2) Any treaty, to become effective as internal law in the Unied States, must have supporting legislation "which would be valid in the absence of a treaty." (3) In addition to the constitutional requirement that two-thirds of the Senate must approve a treaty, Congress would gain the power to reject or regulate all executive agreements with foreign countries just as if they were formal treaties. Although Bricker had originally offered his amendment out of opposition to Democratic foreign policy, especially the Yalta agreements, he revived the measure early in the Eisenhower administration with the backing of a majority of Republican senators. The amendment also had endorsements from the American Bar Association, the American Legion, the American Medical Association, and other powerful organizations.

The first part of the Bricker Amendment was essentially a superfluous truism. The third provision—viewed in the context of two undeclared wars (Korea in the fifties and Indochina in the sixties and seventies), plus numerous executive agreements committing the country to other potential conflicts—might have been a sensible way to curb executive circumvention of the Senate's role in treaty-making. It was the second article—a strange, bewildering evocation of the doctrine of states' rights—that generated the greatest controversy, rallied the opposition in both parties, and eventually caused the amendment's demise. The administration could charge that the "which" clause, by forcing the State Department to square every treaty with existing laws in every state, would reduce foreign policy to its feeble condition under the Articles of Confederation.

Contenting himself with platitudes and suggestions for compromise, Eisenhower shrewdly left the major attack on the Bricker Amendment in the hands of the State Department. Privately, after listening to various proposals for appeasing Bricker and his associates, Eisenhower exploded, "I'm so sick of this I could scream. The whole damn thing is senseless and plain damaging to the prestige of the United States. We talk about the French not being able to govern themselves—and *we* sit here wrestling with a *Bricker Amendment.*"

As the debate over the amendment dragged through 1953 into the next year, the administration finally succeeded in organizing the "internationalist" opposition inside and outside Congress. In the end the administration narrowly won its case. In February 1954 Walter F. George of Georgia, ranking Democrat on the Senate Foreign Relations Committee, offered a modified version which would simply have required all international agreements to have Senate ratification. Still opposed by the administration, the George proposal fell one vote short of the two-thirds majority needed to pass constitutional amendments. Thirty-two of the 60 favorable votes came from Republicans, including Majority Leader William Knowland, 28 from Democrats. Seventeen Democrats and only 14 Republicans voted with the administration. Subsequent versions presented by other senators mustered substantially less support.

II

The failure of the Bricker Amendment left the Eisenhower administration with a relatively free hand in foreign policy. Building on the inherited frameworks of the North Atlantic

Treaty Organization, the Organization of American States (OAS), the ANZUS treaty with Australia and New Zealand, and various bilateral pacts, Secretary Dulles brought into being an elaborate global system of alliances. Supplemented by more bilateral treaties, the expanded American alliance system encircled and pointed SAC's nuclear power at the hearts of the Soviet Union and mainland China. Moreover, while they paid more heed to congressional opinion than would their successors, the President and Secretary of State were usually able to commit American armed forces whenever and wherever they perceived a threat to the global status quo. Finally, the Central Intelligence Agency, with Eisenhower's full approval and indeed enthusiastic support, vastly broadened its role and functions. Under Director Allen Dulles the CIA went beyond its original statutory responsibility for gathering data on conditions in foreign countries (i.e., espionage) and became a powerful instrument for implementing American policy and objectives. On a number of occasions the CIA intervened clandestinely in the internal politics of other nations, sometimes to shore up shaky regimes favored by the United States, at other times to help subvert and overthrow objectionable governments.

The first occasion was in Iran within six months after Eisenhower entered the White House. An abundantly oil-rich but impoverished Middle Eastern kingdom, Iran had been the subject of one of the earliest cold war confrontations, precipitated by Russian occupation of the northern part of the country early in 1946. The Soviets had shortly withdrawn under intense pressure from the United States and Great Britain, opening the way for the British-owned Anglo-Iranian Oil Company to consolidate its monopoly. In 1951 Mohammed Mossadeq, the frail but fiery ultranationalist premier of Iran, had secured the nationalization of the company against the wishes of the pro-Western shah, Mohammed Riza Pahlevi. At first the Truman administration had continued modest military and economic assistance to the Iranian government despite British desires to get rid of Mossadeq. By the beginning of the Eisenhower Presidency, however, key portions of the American national security bureaucracy had come not only to share the British view that overthrowing Mossadeq was necessary to insure Western access to Iranian oil, but to believe that

Mossadeq was sympathetic to his country's Marxist Tudeh party and was moving into the Soviet orbit. Eisenhower and Dulles quickly agreed with this assessment, despite the fact that Mossadeq had outlawed the Tudeh and had repeatedly rebuffed its overtures for a political coalition.

After Mossadeq refused to give in to the new administration's threats to withdraw its aid, the CIA began working under cover to bring him down. Kermit Roosevelt, grandson of Theodore Roosevelt and the CIA's top covert agent in the Middle East, operated closely with the American Military Assistance Mission in Tehran, the Iranian capital. In the summer of 1953, when the shah dismissed Mossadeq, rioting in Tehran forced the monarch to flee the country. With a coup d'état imminent, Roosevelt and his team of operatives speedily organized a countercoup, sending paid anti-Mossadeq rioters into the streets at the same time that they gave money and equipment to the Iranian army to insure its loyalty to the shah. These efforts were brilliantly successful. Late in August the Mossadeq government capitulated, the shah made a triumphant return, and an army general friendly to the Western powers was installed as premier.

The new government agreed to the formation of an international oil consortium which broke the British monopoly and gave American companies a 40 percent interest in Iranian oil operations. In return, during 1954 the United States gave $85 million to Iran, the beginning of a flow of money which would continue unabated over the next two decades. The Iranian people remained overwhelmingly poor and illiterate, but the shah's army became one of the largest and best equipped in the Middle East. Later on in the fifties Iran became the United States' formal ally.

The Iranian affair might be viewed as something of a warmup for the better-known American intervention in Guatemala, where the CIA and the State Department operated within more complex circumstances but with equal success. In Guatemala, as in Iran, economic considerations neatly meshed with the administration's determined anti-Communism. In 1954 the Guatemalan republic was governed by a moderately leftist regime, made up mostly of past or present military officers who had overthrown the harsh dictatorship of Jorge Ubico ten years earlier. Marxists were sprinkled throughout the government bureaucracy, while other Marxists held key positions in the Guatemalan labor unions. The country's economy was almost totally dominated by foreign investors, the largest of which was the American-owned United Fruit Company.

United Fruit enjoyed an extraordinary degree of influence within the Eisenhower administration. In the 1930s John Foster Dulles's legal firm, Sullivan and Cromwell, had drafted the basic agreements between the Ubico dictatorship and United Fruit. At one time Allen Dulles had served on United Fruit's board of directors. John Moors Cabot, Assistant Secretary of State for Latin American Affairs, was a major stockholder in the company, which also retained as corporate counsel Spruille Braden, who had held Cabot's post in the Truman administration. Finally, Eisenhower's personal secretary was the wife of United Fruit's vice president for public relations.

In 1953 President Jacobo Arbenz Guzmán, who had been popularly elected two years earlier, initiated a program of land reform. In Guatemala about 2 percent of the population held title to 70 percent of the land. The Arbenz government expropriated 234,000 acres of uncultivated United Fruit Company land, to be paid for in government bonds equaling the value of the property reported for tax purposes. The company insisted on compensation at more than twenty-five times what the government offered, and its position had the full support of the State Department. The expropriation reinforced the growing feeling within the administration that Arbenz either already had or soon would come under the control of Communists.

In March 1954, at the Tenth Conference of the Organization of American States held at Caracas, Venezuela, John Foster Dulles got the Latin American delegations to agree that they would take "measures necessary to eradicate and prevent subversive activities" and consult on collective action in case of a Communist takeover in one country. Mexico and Argentina abstained; only Guatemala voted against Dulles's resolution. Meanwhile the CIA picked Colonel Carlos Castillo Armas of the

Guatemalan army to lead an insurrection against Arbenz, and
began training a band of Guatemalan mercenaries in Honduras
and on an island off the Nicaraguan coast.

In May a Swedish freighter delivered to Guatemala two tons of
rifles and machine guns, which Arbenz had had to buy from
Czechoslovakia after vainly seeking arms from the United States
and other Western countries. This arms purchase from the Communist bloc seemed final and convincing proof of Arbenz's pro-
Communism. Secretary Dulles, allowing his imagination to range
freely, speculated that the arms might be used against the Panama
Canal (a thousand miles from Guatemala). In the meantime
Senate Minority Leader Lyndon Johnson introduced a resolution,
quickly passed by a vote of 69-1, reaffirming the Monroe Doctrine
and labeling the Guatemalan situation an instance of "Soviet
interference" and "external aggression." The Pentagon stepped up
its arms shipments to Nicaragua, while the CIA began secret drops
of arms and supplies inside Guatemala near United Fruit headquarters.

On June 18 Castillo, at the head of about 150 troops, crossed
into Guatemala from Honduras and began a desultory march on
Guatemala City, which was bombed and strafed by American
aircraft of World War II vintage, flown by CIA pilots. Abandoned
by the army and even by the supposedly Communist-dominated
labor unions, Arbenz could only appeal to the United Nations. In
the Security Council the Russian delegate staunchly supported
UN intervention in Guatemala, while Ambassador Henry Cabot
Lodge of the United States, besides denying any involvement by
his government in the fighting, argued with considerable emotion
that the OAS had primary jurisdiction in the situation. On June 25
the Security Council voted four to five—with the USSR, New
Zealand, Lebanon, and Denmark voting affirmatively and the
United States and four of its client states (Turkey, Nationalist
China, Colombia, and Brazil) opposed—not to place the Guate-
malan appeal on its agenda.

That same day rebel forces, supplied with more arms and aircraft at Eisenhower's personal direction, forced Arbenz to flee to
eastern Europe. Castillo arrived in Guatemala City in the United
States embassy's plane and, under the aegis of Ambassador John

Peurifoy, agreed to form a military junta to rule the country. Later Castillo took complete power, outlawed opposition parties, disfranchised all illiterates (about 70 percent of the people), and jailed thousands of suspected political enemies. American aid, which had totaled $600,000 in the ten years before the 1954 coup, now poured in at a rate of $45 million a year. In exchange for such American beneficence, Castillo restored all expropriated lands to United Fruit and did away with taxes on foreign investors' dividends. Although Castillo was assassinated in 1957, the Guatemalan government remained in friendly hands. In Eisenhower's last year in office it willingly made available sites for training Cuban exiles, whom the CIA was preparing for an operation against another leftist regime unacceptable to the United States.

III

During the time that the administration was planning and pulling off its coup in Guatemala, the President and Secretary Dulles were much more closely occupied with what was happening at Geneva, Switzerland, and halfway around the world in Indochina. In those places events were unfolding that posed the severest challenge so far to the administration's stand against alterations of the global status quo by the forces of radical revolution. Out of the complex circumstances in the spring and summer of 1954 came the fateful American decision to take over from France as the principal agent of counterrevolution in Southeast Asia.

Years before Eisenhower took office, the United States had become the foremost supplier for the French armed forces fighting to quell the revolutionary movement in the eastern part of Indochina. After World War II the French had reoccupied and reorganized their colonial possessions in Indochina as the Associated States of Vietnam, Laos, and Cambodia. Supposedly giving autonomy to the three areas, the arrangement in fact preserved French economic and political control. Since the early postwar years a Vietnamese insurgent movement known as the Vietminh—led by the confirmed Marxist-Leninist Ho Chi Minh and controlled by the Vietnamese version of the Communist party

—had struggled to overthrow French rule. For both sides the war
was long and bloody, but it also severely strained the rebuilding
French economic system and proved a major source of chronic
political instability at home.

Under Franklin Roosevelt, American policy in Indochina had
started out hostile toward the French colonialists. Indecisive and
neutral in the early Truman period, the American government had
begun to give moderate assistance to the French by 1949. After
the Communist victory in China and the onset of the Korean war,
the Truman administration had committed increasing quantities
of money and matériel to bolster what now looked like a parallel
struggle by the French against "Communist aggression" in Asia.
American aid accelerated under the Eisenhower administration,
which in its first year sent nearly $800 million worth of arms and
equipment into Indochina along with several hundred mechanics,
technicians, and military advisers. Eisenhower and his associates
retained something of the traditional American dislike of colonialism, at least as practiced by other countries, and insisted that a
French promise of complete independence for Vietnam was
indispensable to an effective military effort. Yet the administration
also was convinced that, as the United States ambassador to the
Associated States proclaimed in a *Life* article, "France is fighting
the good fight in Indochina, the fight of the free world against
Communism, just as the U.N. fought to check Communist aggression in Korea." By the beginning of 1954 the United States was
bearing nearly three-fourths of the cost of the war against the
Vietminh. While the Vietminh received some help from mainland
China and Soviet Russia, the amount of outside assistance going
to the insurgent forces was a tiny fraction of what the United
States gave the French.

The French and French-led native Vietnamese forces were
generally ineffective against the Vietminh campaign of localized
but devastating guerilla operations. Seeking to draw a large contingent of Vietminh into open battle, the French committed one
of the supreme follies of recent military history when they
established an isolated fortress position in the midst of Vietminh
territory at Dien Bien Phu, in northwestern Vietnam near the
Laotian border. There, in the early months of 1954, the French

garrison of 11,000 found itself surrounded by a superior Vietminh force, which began systematically to reduce the fortress perimeter.

On March 20, 1954, with the predicament of the Dien Bien Phu garrison becoming daily more critical, French Chief of Staff General Paul Ely flew to Washington to seek direct American military intervention, a request that provoked a protracted debate within the government and between the United States and its Western allies. Somewhat to Ely's surprise, Admiral Radford suggested an American air strike against the Vietminh positions at Dien Bien Phu, to be executed by sixty B-29s from the Philippines accompanied by 150 fighter escorts operating from carriers off the Indochina coast in the Gulf of Tonkin. Three "tactical" atomic bombs would be dropped. The French high command quickly agreed to the plan, code-named Operation Vulture, and formally requested the air strike. Air Force Chief of Staff General Nathan Twining, an enthusiastic supporter for such action, later reminisced that "You could take all day to drop a bomb, make sure you put it in the right place. . . . And clean those Commies out of there and the band could play the Marseillaise and the French would come marching out of Dien Bien Phu in fine shape."

Eisenhower and John Foster Dulles agreed on the need for an air strike, although they demurred on the use of A-bombs. In a press conference on April 7 the President gave his own rationale for "saving" Indochina from Communism. Besides pointing out that the region contained valuable reserves of tin, tungsten, and rubber, and that the loss of the Indochina market would force Japan to seek new markets on the Chinese mainland, Eisenhower set forth what came to be called the "domino theory": "You have a row of dominoes set up, and you knock over the first one, and what would happen to the last one was the certainty that it would go over quickly. So you have a beginning of a disintegration that would have the most profound influences." Ultimately, Eisenhower implied, all of Southeast Asia could fall under Communist control.

While they both favored some kind of military action to relieve Dien Bien Phu, Eisenhower and Dulles also agreed that any American intervention must be preconditioned by a French promise to give the Associated States their independence, by the willingness of the British and other allies to act jointly with the United States, and by congressional approval for military operations. None of these preconditions could be met. The French were willing to be part of the global holy war against Communism, but they refused to make their part of the war even holier by granting full independence to the peoples of Indochina. British Prime Minister Winston Churchill and Foreign Minister Anthony Eden, steadily dismantling their own colonial empire, thought the French cause hopeless and looked to the upcoming international conference on the Far East in Geneva at the end of April as a chance for a face-saving negotiated settlement. Thus the British leaders politely but firmly rebuffed Dulles's overtures. Without British participation, the Republican and Democratic congressional leadership flatly refused prior approval for an administration-prepared resolution sanctioning intervention.

Meanwhile Army Chief of Staff Ridgway argued not only against the proposed air strike but also against a plan to land American ground forces at the northern Vietnamese port of Haiphong. The French opposed such an expedition anyway because they wished to minimize the United States' physical presence in Indochina. Sometime earlier Eisenhower had let the French know that if American troops went in, the United States would expect to assume direction of the war.

Frustrated in their dealings with their allies, with congressional leaders, and even with portions of the American military leadership, Eisenhower and Dulles had no choice but to go along with the Geneva Conference.[2] Dulles attended only the initial sessions at Geneva, refusing even to look in the direction of the delegates from the People's Republic of China, which the United States had refused to recognize diplomatically since the Communist victory in 1949, or at the Vietminh. In American thinking the main culprit in Indochina was the Communist regime in Peking, which the administration regarded as the inspiration of the Vietminh and as a threat to overrun all of Southeast Asia.

After Dulles unhappily returned to Washington, Undersecre-

2. The Geneva Conference, which was supposed to take up a range of issues relating to the Far East, had been set up at the Berlin meeting of foreign ministers in January 1954.

tary of State Walter Bedell Smith remained to represent American interests. No progress at all was made on Korea, a matter that was supposed to share equal billing with Indochina on the conference agenda. Nor was there appreciable movement toward an agreement on Indochina, despite the surrender of the remnants of the Dien Bien Phu garrison on May 7. The conference finally began to make headway only after a peace coalition headed by Pierre Mendès-France replaced Joseph Laniel's government in Paris and after the Russian leadership began to pressure the Chinese and Vietminh to reach a settlement.

Meanwhile Dulles, Smith, and Ambassador Douglas Dillon again approached the French on the question of intervention, this time ignoring the British. By now, though, the French were committed to a negotiated settlement, whereas the deterioration of the situation in Indochina had convinced the Joint Chiefs of Staff and Secretary of Defense Wilson that intervention would be militarily useless. Finally, on June 15 Dulles informed the French foreign minister that there was no longer any possibility of American military action.

It still took another month to reach a settlement at Geneva. On July 20–21 the French and the Vietminh signed an armistice agreement, and representatives of France, Great Britain, China, the Soviet Union, and the Vietminh declared their approval of (but did not actually sign) a more general agreement called the Accords. Smith, the American representative, observed the final proceedings, but on instructions from Washington he refused to approve the Accords. He did say, however, that his country would "refrain from the threat or use of force to disturb them." At the same time, Eisenhower announced ominously that the United States "has not itself been party to or bound by the decisions taken by the Conference."

The Geneva settlement established a truce between the Vietminh and the French and temporarily partitioned Vietnam at the 17th parallel, with the French agreeing to withdraw south of the partition line. National elections were to take place within two years to choose a government for all of Vietnam; the elections were to be administered in the South by the French and supervised by an international commission. Neither part of Vietnam was to join a military alliance or allow the establishment of foreign military bases. National elections were also to be held in Laos and Cambodia, with the Communist-led Pathet Lao forces remaining intact.

Certainly the Geneva agreements were not popular in Washington, where there was a general feeling that partition meant the irretrievable loss of the northern part of Vietnam to Communist "enslavement." Yet Eisenhower and Dulles also apparently shared Smith's view that the agreements were "the best which we could have possibly obtained under the circumstances"—those circumstances being mainly the determination of the French and British to gain peace. As Smith observed to a group of congressmen when he got back from Geneva, "diplomacy has rarely been able to gain at the conference table what cannot be gained or held on the battlefield." After all, Ho Chi Minh, by accepting the 17th parallel truce line, had given up a sizable area already under Vietminh control. Moreover, with the fighting halted and the French exhausted and dispirited, prospects were bright for the establishment of a much more powerful American presence in southern Vietnam and perhaps in other parts of Indochina. The United States could transform Vietnam south of the 17th parallel into a bastion of anti-Communism, a vital outpost on the cold war frontier.

To bring about this transformation, the Eisenhower administration took three major steps in the immediate post-Geneva period. First, it endorsed Ngo Dinh Diem as the leader of the temporary government of South Vietnam. At American urging and over the opposition of the pro-French Emperor Bao Dai, the French had made Diem premier of Vietnam during the Geneva deliberations. At the time Diem was living in exile at a Roman Catholic seminary in New Jersey. Besides being a devout Catholic, Diem was a fervent Vietnamese nationalist, both anti-French and anti-Communist and thus, from the American standpoint, seemingly the perfect choice. Diem became closely associated with the American Military Assistance Advisory Group in Saigon and especially with Colonel Edward G. Lansdale, an Air Force officer working for the CIA. Lansdale had a reputation as a guerrilla warfare expert. Perhaps imagining himself as a sort of "Lawrence of Southeast Asia" (with Diem as his King Faisal), Lansdale transmitted glowing reports on Diem to Washington and thus became a major factor in the administration's eventual decision to back Diem.

The second move was spelled out in a National Security Council policy paper which Eisenhower approved on August 30, 1954. The United States would henceforth bypass French officials and give military and economic assistance directly to Diem's government in South Vietnam. American military representatives were to cooperate with the French as little as possible, while as much as possible "The French were to be dissociated from the levers of command." The United States would work with Diem but would encourage him to create a popular, democratic basis for his government. "The Government of the United States," Eisenhower wrote Diem in October, "expects that this aid will be met by performance on the part of the Government of Vietnam in undertaking needed reforms."

Third, Secretary Dulles acted quickly in the months after Geneva to create an Asian alliance system which would counter the putatively aggressive designs of "Red China." At Manila on September 6, 1954, Dulles met with representatives of Great Britain, France, Australia, New Zealand, Thailand, Pakistan, and the Philippines to form the Southeast Asia Treaty Organization (SEATO). The Manila Pact bound the signatories to assist each other in case of armed attack and to consult in case of internal subversion. Although the Geneva agreements prohibited Vietnam, as well as Laos and Cambodia, from joining military alliances, the SEATO treaty brought these newly independent areas under its protection. Unlike the North Atlantic Treaty Organization, SEATO did not require its members to supply troops for a common defense force; rather, the new alliance would depend on the strategic deterrent capability of the United States. Ratified by a vote of 81–1 in the Senate, the SEATO treaty was Dulles's major contribution to alliance-making, one of the most important of a succession of agreements by which, at the end of the Eisenhower adminstration, the United States found itself bound to defend forty-three different countries.

One may grant the Eisenhower administration's sincerity in

expressing its hopes that the Diem regime would govern demo-
cratically and with popular support. Within less than a year, however, it faced a cruel choice: Either continue to back Diem's
increasingly authoritarian government, or accept a united Vietnam, probably, in the assessment of Eisenhower himself, with Ho
Chi Minh as its national leader. The American choice, went the
quip around Washington, was to "sink or swim with Ngo Dinh
Diem."

In February 1955 Diem rebuffed North Vietnam's call for
normalized relations between the two zones and interzonal postal
service. That May—at a time when the State Department had
about lost patience with Diem because he had failed to gain the
support of the various political factions and religious sects in the
south—rightist elements tried to overthrow his government. After
Diem's police and civil guard, largely trained by Colonel Lansdale's CIA team, put down the revolt, Secretary Dulles quickly
invalidated a cable he had just sent instructing the American embassy in Saigon to stop supporting Diem. Now on firmer ground,
the Diem government refused even to participate in planning
sessions for the 1956 national elections. In October Diem staged
a tightly controlled "national referendum," proclaimed that more
than 98 percent of the people of the South had opted for a Republic of Vietnam with himself as president, and ousted Bao Dai
and other dissidents in the Saigon government.

The last French troops pulled out in April 1956, three months
before the scheduled national elections they were supposed to
administer. Announcing that the elections would not be held,
Diem killed the last chance for the peaceful unification of Vietnam. Meanwhile American aid flowed into southern Vietnam at
the rate of a half-billion dollars a year, American advisers outfitted
and trained Diem's army and police force, and the Eisenhower
administration worked to create the fiction that the Geneva partition line was now a national boundary, separating the Republic
of Vietnam in the South from the Democratic Republic of Vietnam, with its capital at Hanoi.

For many American observers Diem's government had become
a model of dedicated, efficient anti-Communism. Diem was "the
tough miracle man of Vietnam," as a *Life* writer described him

in the spring of 1957. Having "roused his country and routed the Reds," Diem had set "a pattern of leadership which could provide an alternative to neutralism in southeast Asia . . . ." Weakened by political unrest and dislocation caused by its bloody campaign against private landownership, Ho's government in Hanoi was essentially powerless to prevent Diem's cancellation of the national elections and the rapid consolidation of his hold in the South. Meanwhile the Soviets and Chinese would do no more than protest and offer reassurances of "socialist solidarity" with the Democratic Republic.

In 1957 Diem stepped up his efforts to eliminate opposition among the Buddhist sects, Montagnard mountain tribesmen, middle-class political liberals, and remnants of the southern Vietminh. Resistance to Diem's government, organized or not, was growing fast. Yet even though American intelligence estimates placed the number of "organized Communists" in South Vietnam at fewer than 1,500, Diem's police jailed or executed thousands of dissidents, all indiscriminately labeled "Viet Cong" —Vietnamese Communists. The government's terrorism provoked counterterrorism against local officials and informers by antigovernment forces, often but by no means always led by former Vietminh. A trickle of men and matériel began to move from North Vietnam across the 17th parallel and through Laos to help the southern insurgents, seemingly lending credence to Diem's insistence that South Vietnam faced aggression engineered by Hanoi. By 1958 the second Indochina war—a conflict as yet little noticed by most Americans but one to which the United States had already massively committed itself—was well under way.

IV

Throughout the fifties the United States' stance toward the Communist regime on the Chinese mainland remained implacably hostile. The outbreak of the Korean war—and especially the Chinese intervention after United Nations forces overran North Korea and reached the Yalu River—destroyed whatever possibility there might have been for normalized relations with the revolutionary regime in Peking. Instead, the Truman administration began to picture the Chinese Communists as voracious expansionists who were bent on dominating all East and Southeast Asia and even the western Pacific. Like its predecessor, the Eisenhower administration stubbornly withheld diplomatic recognition from this government of 650 million people and successfully pressured America's allies and client states to block China's admission to the UN. Chiang Kai-shek's Nationalist government, exiled on Formosa and other offshore islands, continued to receive more American money and military equipment than any non-NATO country.

Besides making the essentially rhetorical gesture of removing the Seventh Fleet from the Formosa Strait and "unleashing" Chiang, the Eisenhower administration if anything stiffened American recalcitrance toward mainland China. According to official American policy, the Nationalist regime on Formosa was still the legitimate government for all of China. The Nationalists thus continued to hold China's place as one of the five permanent members on the UN Security Council. There were, though, some limits to how far the administration would go in denouncing the Chinese Communists. In 1953 it successfully beat down William Jenner's Senate resolution declaring that the United States would never recognize the Peking regime, as well as a rider attached to a UN appropriations bill stipulating that American financial support would stop if the UN ever voted to admit the People's Republic.

American policy aimed as much as possible to isolate the Chinese Communists. One feature of this policy was the State Department's ban on travel to mainland China by American citizens. In August 1956 Peking announced that it was willing to admit American newsmen if Washington reciprocated. After initially giving a flat no to the proposal, Secretary Dulles then said that each Chinese reporter would have to be individually approved, and he implied that no Communists would be allowed in. Under such strictures, prospects for an exchange of newsmen collapsed. When William Worthy, a reporter for a leading black newspaper, defied the travel ban and broadcast a shortwave report from Peking carried over CBS radio, the State Department pressured CBS into discontinuing Worthy's other scheduled broadcasts. At the end of the Eisenhower Presidency mainland China remained a forbidden land, a huge and powerful country about whose internal affairs Americans knew next to nothing.

Conversely, the Chinese Communists kept up a steady barrage of bombast and vituperation against the United States and Chiang's Formosa regime. In particular, Mao Tse-tung, Chou En-lai, and their associates in Peking continually threatened to invade the offshore islands, over which they claimed sovereignty as a result of World War II agreements pledging the return of all former Chinese territories held by Japan. Such an invasion never came, nor did Chiang ever try to fulfill his vaunted promise to lead his Nationalist forces back to the mainland. Yet the Formosa Strait remained one of the tensest and most perilous areas of cold war confrontation throughout the Eisenhower years. On two occasions China and the United States came close to war over the Nationalist-held Quemoy and Matsu island groups lying immediately off the central Chinese coast, more than a hundred miles across the strait from the Nationalist bastion on Formosa. The first and closer of the two brushes with war had its inception in the fall of 1954, almost on the heels of the Indochina crisis.

After Eisenhower announced in his first State of the Union message that the Seventh Fleet would no longer shield the mainland from Nationalist attack, Chiang, while not able to mount an invasion (which Eisenhower would have vetoed anyway), did order bombing raids against mainland shipping and ports. The Communists took no action until late summer 1954, when Premier Chou En-lai proclaimed that his government was prepared to "liberate" Formosa. Eisenhower quickly retorted that an invasion of Formosa "would have to run over the Seventh Fleet." The President knew that the People's Republic lacked the capability for such a large-scale amphibious operation; the question was actually whether the United States would commit itself to defending the string of small islands running for some 350 miles along the Chinese coast, which Chiang's forces had occupied and fortified.

Early in September 1954, just before Dulles arrived in Manila to organize the SEATO treaty, Communist shore batteries began heavy shelling of the Quemoy islands at the entrance to Amoy harbor. Subsequently the Matsu and Tachen island groups to the north also came under fire. Dulles returned from the Manila signings by way of Taipei, the Nationalist capital, where he and Chiang agreed on a mutual defense treaty. Signed in Washington early in December, the treaty bound the United States to come to Chiang's aid if the Communists attacked Formosa or the nearby Pescadores Islands. The treaty did not mention other offshore islands, but formal statements supplementary to (not part of) the treaty gave the United States the option to intervene if they were attacked. The supplementary statements also "released" Chiang by stipulating that he could undertake offensive operations only with American consent.

The tension continued to build as the Senate began deliberations on the treaty and as Communist forces seized one of the northernmost islands. On January 23 Eisenhower sent to Capitol Hill a resolution under which Congress would give him full authority for whatever actions he thought necessary to defend Formosa and the Pescadores. Wanting to keep his options as open as possible, the President carefully avoided any mention of the offshore islands. The House gave Eisenhower what he wanted by a vote of 410–3. In the Senate Walter George—leading his Democratic colleagues in the absence of Lyndon Johnson, who was recuperating from a severe heart attack—skillfully steered the measure around the efforts of Hubert Humphrey and Herbert Lehman to limit presidential military authority to Formosa and the Pescadores. Within five days the Senate passed the Formosa Resolution 83–3. It not only empowered the President to defend Formosa and the Pescadores but also authorized "the securing and protecting of such related positions and territories of that area now in friendly hands," as he judged appropriate. Never before in a time of nominal peace had Congress given the chief executive such sweeping power to make war.

Afterward, in a press conference, Eisenhower acknowledged that in a general Asian war the United States would use atomic weapons. He neglected to add that Nationalist forces already had American-made howitzers which could fire atomic shells if the United States provided them. On advice from the Pentagon in February that the Tachens were indefensible, Eisenhower and

Dulles got Chiang to withdraw his troops from these islands, some of which the Communists had already occupied. By this time, however, the President and his Secretary of State had also apparently become convinced—despite the opposition of General Ridgway and the skepticism of the other Chiefs—that holding Quemoy and Matsu was both materially and psychologically vital to the protection of Formosa, which in turn was vital to the defense of the whole western Pacific.

On March 10 Dulles told Eisenhower, "I believe there is at least an even chance that the United States will have to go to war." Two weeks later Admiral Robert B. Carney, Chief of Naval Operations, privately told a group of newsmen that the President was considering a plan of action "to destroy Red China's military potential and thus end its expansionist tendencies." Serious discussions of preventive nuclear war obviously were under way within the administration. Here was the most critical occasion when, as Dulles said a year later, the administration had gone "to the brink" of war.

At this point the Chinese edged back from the brink. In April, at the conference of Asian and African nations held at Bandung, Indonesia, Chou En-lai indicated that China was willing to enter into direct discussions with the United States on the question of the Formosa Strait. When he got back to Peking, Chou added that "The Chinese people are willing to strive for the liberation of Formosa by peaceful means as far as this is possible." Although the United States did not officially recognize the existence of the Peking government, representatives of the two countries began meeting in Geneva in May, at the same time that an informal cease-fire went into effect in the strait. Somewhat later the Chinese released eleven American airmen, who had been captured in Korea and sentenced to prison terms for espionage. While the Geneva talks dragged on inconclusively, the first Formosa Strait crisis died down.

The passing of the crisis of 1954–1955 brought no improvement in American-Chinese relations. In American thinking the Chinese Communists had become an even more fearful menace than the Soviet Union to the "free world," which, largely as a result of the Korean war, now took in all of non-Communist Asia.

The Eisenhower administration continued to beef up its nuclear forces on the perimeter of China in the hope that the Communist regime would steadily weaken and eventually collapse after American power had thwarted what Secretary Dulles termed its "aggressive fanaticism."

One of the signal international developments of the fifties was the steady enlargement of both the American conception of the free world and the Soviet Union's conception of its own area of interest and activity. In the second half of the decade both Americans and Russians bid strongly with money and flattery for the favor of the "uncommitted nations." The historic Bandung Conference in 1955, attended by delegates from 29 mostly new nations of Asia and Africa, served notice directly on the United States and indirectly on the USSR that the countries of the "underdeveloped areas" wanted nothing so much as to avoid major power dominance and stay out of the cold war. To be sure, the Chinese were warmly received as representatives of a revolutionary nation which had thrown off Western dominance, while the Soviets posed with some success as the anticolonialist sponsor of the Afro-Asian states' political and economic development. Except for its Filipino and Pakistani clients, the United States lacked advocates. Yet the most significant outcome of the Bandung gathering—which claimed to speak for 65 percent of the world's population—was the declaration that "colonialism in all its manifestations is an evil which should speedily be brought to an end." While both Russians and Americans would strive over the next decade to influence the proliferating nations of the Southern Hemisphere, most of the time the two superpowers would find that their programs of economic and military assistance did not buy fast friendships, but contributed to an even more determined spirit of independence and neutrality.

V

However worried the Eisenhower administration might have been about political changes in Asia and Africa, the focus of American foreign policy remained in Europe, as it had since the end of World War II. Central Europe, especially divided Germany and the divided city of Berlin, was where the United

States and the Soviet Union confronted each other most directly and most ominously. Eisenhower and Dulles inherited more than the NATO alliance from Truman and Acheson; they also inherited and made central to their European policy the Truman administration's goal of an economically and militarily integrated western Europe, a system that would present a stronger barrier to the USSR.

The few hundred thousand Western troops in Europe, mostly American, were vastly outnumbered by the forces of Russia and its eastern European satellites. While the American troops were there mainly for political and psychological purposes, both the Truman and Eisenhower administrations justified their costly presence in terms of a purported Russian military threat to western Europe. Yet Eisenhower and his military advisers also assumed that NATO's ground forces should be more than a "trip-wire," even though there would never be enough of them to stop the Red army. Because Western forces should be able to hold long enough for SAC to carry through with "massive retaliation," America's European allies needed to build their own military capabilities. Not only would additional European forces bolster NATO's conventional power but they would allow the United States to bring home some of its troops and reduce its overseas spending—goals that were dear to the administration.

American integrationist objectives in Europe involved fulfilling two programs proposed during the Truman period. The more successful one originated in 1950 as the European Coal and Steel Community, which laid the foundations for the economic integration of France, Italy, West Germany, and the Benelux countries (Belgium, the Netherlands, and Luxembourg). But efforts to bring about military integration in a European Defense Community (EDC), under separate European control but linked to NATO, foundered primarily because the French feared such an international force would be German-dominated.

The French assembly was still debating the EDC treaty when Eisenhower took office. Late in 1953, stepping up pressure on the French to ratify the treaty, Dulles threatened an "agonizing reappraisal" of American policy in Europe if EDC failed. Shortly thereafter the Senate unanimously declared that it would vote to end assistance for countries refusing to ratify EDC. According to Sherman Adams, the desire to get France into EDC was as strong a motive behind American support for the French in the Indochina war as the desire to stop the Vietminh. All the administration's efforts, however, were to no avail. Late in the summer of 1954 the French assembly voted down the EDC treaty.

Fearing German rearmament, the French did not really grasp how determined the administration was to rebuild Germany's military power under the leadership of Konrad Adenauer, the militantly anti-Russian chancellor of the Federal Republic. British Foreign Minister Anthony Eden shortly came up with an alternative which involved expanding the Western European Union (WEU)—originally a postwar Anglo-French accord aimed at blocking a resurgent Germany—to include both West Germany and now Great Britain, which France had wanted in EDC all along to counterbalance German power. The Western European Union would be looser and more decentralized than EDC. Supplemented by Dulles's assurances that American troops would stay in Europe and by Adenauer's guarantee that West Germany would not manufacture atomic weapons or try to reunify Germany by force, the new arrangement was finally acceptable to the Mendès-France government. Overcoming stiff opposition in the assembly, Mendès-France won approval for WEU at the end of 1954.

The Eisenhower administration insistently pushed for some form of military integration of western Europe at the same time that the post-Stalin Russian leadership become more conciliatory in its foreign policy pronouncements. After Stalin's death, the Kremlin acknowledged for the first time that both the USSR and the United States would suffer irreparable damage in a nuclear war; Communist society would survive no better than capitalist. Soviet Premier Georgi Malenkov also proclaimed that there were no issues between Russia and the West which "cannot be decided by peaceful means, on the basis of mutual understanding by interested countries." In August 1953, after announcing that the USSR had exploded its own hydrogen bomb, Malenkov again called for the peaceful settlement of international disputes. Eisenhower's response was an admission that the United States was no longer physically secure, coupled with a warning that the

West must now build even greater military power to prevent Communist world domination.

In 1954 the adminstration was not really interested in accommodation with the Soviets. To Secretary of State Dulles the principal significance of the Soviets' gestures of conciliation was that they might undermine American efforts to build a more solid and powerful anti-Communist front in western Europe. By the first months of 1955, however, Eisenhower had come to believe, against the counsel of Dulles, that something might be gained from a meeting of the leaders of the major powers "at the summit," as Winston Churchill had phrased it in calling for such a gathering two years earlier. Developments in the spring both intensified pressure for a major power conference and brightened hopes for improving the cold war atmosphere.

Giving new urgency to efforts toward accommodation were the formal inauguration of the Western European Union and the admission of the Federal Republic of Germany to full membership in NATO on May 9, and the Soviets' counterorganization of the Warsaw Pact alliance five days later. The Moscow air show on May 19 ostensibly demonstrated that the Russians had great numbers of long-range bombers. (By flying the same aircraft repeatedly past the reviewing stands, the Soviet air force managed to create the illusion of many more big bombers than it actually had.) The NATO war games the next month further frightened Europeans when it became known that the scenario of the maneuvers assumed that a full-scale war would bring down 171 atomic bombs on western Europe alone.

There were also hopeful signs that same spring of 1955. On May 15 the Western powers and the Soviet Union ended their ten-year occupation of Austria by agreeing to a peace treaty which established an independent Austria, forbade its reunification with Germany, and guaranteed Austrian neutrality. Although he signed it, John Foster Dulles did not like the treaty because he feared neutralization might come to look like an attractive formula for a German settlement. Later that month Soviet Premier Nikolai Bulganin and Chairman Nikita S. Khrushchev of the Soviet Communist party made a remarkable trip to Yugoslavia, where they offered their humblest apologies to Tito for Stalin's ostracism of the Yugoslav Communist dictator because he had insisted on following a course independent of Moscow.[3]

It was also in May that the Soviets offered a concession which seemed to promise a breakthrough in the long and so far futile wrangling over international disarmament. On the tenth of the month Jacob Malik, head of the Soviet delegation to the UN Subcommittee on Disarmament, which had been meeting at London for several years, startled the assemblage by agreeing for the first time to accept surveillance and inspection posts on Russian territory. Malik's statement came in answer to the previous summer's Anglo-French proposal for a four-phase program of disarmament beginning with conventional arms, then proceeding to nuclear weapons, and finally eliminating nuclear stockpiles. The Anglo-French plan had been an attempt to reconcile heretofore impossibly contradictory American and Soviet disarmament stands. First set forth in the Baruch Plan of 1946 and basically reiterated ever since, the United States' position was that it must keep its nuclear weapons until other countries had disbanded their nuclear arsenals under close international inspection. The Russians had repeatedly insisted on uninspected nuclear disarmament as a first step toward total disarmament. Now, Malik said, the USSR would not only allow inspection sites but was also willing to exchange information on existing military establishments and national budgets. This cooperation would constitute the basic methodology behind a two-year schedule for reducing the parity force levels of the USSR, the United States, and mainland China, for stopping nuclear tests and the production of nuclear weapons, and for liquidating all military bases in foreign countries. Taken aback by the bold Russian initiative, the Western powers used the upcoming summit meeting in Geneva as an excuse for adjourning the disarmament talks.

Meanwhile Senator Joe McCarthy embarrassed the Eisenhower administration one last time by introducing a resolution which demanded that the Russians put the status of the eastern European countries on the summit agenda as a prerequisite to American participation. To compound the administration's chagrin, the

3. By 1955 Georgi Malenkov had been ousted from the Russian premiership.

Democratic majority on the Foreign Relations Committee reported out the resolution, thereby forcing Eisenhower, Dulles, and Minority Leader William Knowland to organize vigorous opposition against their fellow Republican. McCarthy was finally able to get only three other senators to vote for his resolution.

Although Eisenhower was willing to attend the first meeting of Soviet and Western leaders since the Potsdam Conference of 1945, he was almost as skeptical as Dulles about how much could be accomplished. On July 12, just before leaving for Geneva, the President and Secretary of State met with congressional leaders of both parties to assure them that, in Sherman Adams's words, "Geneva was not going to be another Yalta." With the Bricker Amendment still not entirely dead, the President promised to make no agreements with the Russians without congressional approval. Eisenhower also expressed worry over Russian efforts to foster neutralist tendencies among America's European allies. The British and French, he feared, were starting to view the cold war as merely a competition between superpowers, disregarding the fundamental moral differences between East and West. Dulles added that the western Europeans seemed less concerned than the United States about the plight of the Russian satellites.

By mid-July hordes of dignitaries, newsmen, photographers, and sightseers had congregated in Geneva for the most spectacular international event of the postwar era. On the eighteenth Eisenhower, Bulganin, Anthony Eden (who had succeeded Churchill as British prime minister), and Premier Edgar Faure of France met together with their entourages in the Palais des Nations. Posing for photographers after this first session and throughout the conference, Eisenhower disregarded the advice of Dulles, who had suggested that the countenances of the Americans should be as serious as their purposes, and repeatedly displayed his trademark grin alongside Bulganin and the other heads of government. Soon newsmen were writing of a "spirit of Geneva"—a new mood of amicability, maybe even cooperation, in Soviet-American relations.

Behind the glamour and apparent goodwill, however, the American delegation was unhappy, especially over Russian intransigence on the question of German reunification. The United

States wanted Germany reunified through free national elections, which would presumably lead to a capitalist and westward-leaning Germany with, the Eisenhower administration insisted, the option to join NATO. Such a scheme was quite understandably repugnant to the Russians, who were still haunted by the ghastly losses of World War II and terrified by the specter of a Germany reunified, resurgent, and rearmed. At one point, Eisenhower later wrote, the Americans "seriously discussed the wisdom of leaving the meeting abruptly as a protest against obvious Soviet resistance to any logical solution to the [German] problem."

From the American standpoint the crest of the Geneva summit came on July 21, when Eisenhower made his famous Open Skies proposal. Putting down his written statement and removing his glasses to give an appearance of extemporaneity, Eisenhower looked across the table at the Russians and offered to exchange "a complete blueprint of our military establishments from beginning to end, from one end of our countries to the other; lay out the establishments and provide the blueprints to each other." Moreover, the United States was willing, if the Soviets were, to allow complete aerial surveillance and photography in order to minimize the possibility of surprise attack, "thus lessening danger and relaxing tension."

The Open Skies proposal was the product of intense planning sessions by a group which had begun meeting secretly in the spring at the Marine base at Quantico, Virginia, then had transferred to Paris on the eve of the Geneva talks. Chaired by Nelson Rockefeller and including, among others, Deputy Secretary of Defense Robert B. Anderson, Admiral Radford, and Harold Stassen, who had become the President's Special Assistant for Disarmament Studies in March, this Quantico panel worked to formulate a proposal which Eisenhower could use to counteract the propaganda advantage the Russians had gained with their May 10 disarmament overture. Heading an administration that had made much of the need for a psychological-warfare offensive, Eisenhower wanted to have ready some kind of dramatic gesture for the summit. The Quantico group worked without consulting Dulles, who so strongly opposed its plan that the President still had not made up his mind to present it when he arrrived at Geneva. Again overriding his doubting Secretary of State, Eisenhower finally decided to go ahead with the proposal. The anticipated propaganda dividend was fully forthcoming when most of the international press publicized Open Skies as a sound, reasonable new peace proposal.

The Russians were not impressed. During a break following Eisenhower's statement, Nikita Khrushchev, according to Charles Bohlen, told Eisenhower that Open Skies was "a very transparent espionage device, and those advisers of yours who suggested it knew exactly what they were doing. You could hardly expect us to take this seriously." Open Skies was no disarmament plan at all. Actually it was a step backward from the longstanding American position on inspections, because now the United States wanted aerial as well as ground surveillance. For years the Soviets had rejected the idea of aerial surveillance, and there was no reason to expect that they would change their minds in 1955. The USSR's nuclear striking power was clearly inferior to that of the United States, as American intelligence was well aware. What Eisenhower had proposed was that the Soviets lay open their military establishment to Western inspection before any steps had been taken toward disarmament.

The degree of openness in the American military program was greatly exaggerated in the West. The fact remains that Open Skies would have given the Pentagon most of the closely guarded information it needed about Soviet capabilities, while the Russians would have learned relatively little they did not already know. Open Skies also expressed the premise, inherited from the Truman years and still doggedly adhered to, that any effort to slow down the nuclear arms race was contingent on absolutely foolproof safeguards, which were manifestly impossible in the 1950s.

The appearances of amicability lasted to the end of the Geneva talks on July 23. Addressing the nation on his return, Eisenhower said that "a new spirit of conciliation and cooperation" had featured the four-power conference. In his memoirs he wrote that the Geneva summit was a turning point in the movement toward coexistence in Soviet-American relations. The first postwar cultural exchanges between the two countries and the subsequent visits of Deputy Premiers Anastas Mikoyan and Frol

Kozlov to the United States and of Vice President Nixon and Milton Eisenhower to the USSR were all, according to Eisenhower, attributable to the groundwork laid at Geneva. More importantly, Stephen Ambrose has observed, at Geneva "The West had admitted that it could not win the Cold War, that a thermonuclear stalemate had developed, and that the *status quo* in Europe and China . . . had to be substantially accepted."

Yet the spirit of Geneva produced absolutely no concrete progress on the fundamental issues dividing the two superpowers. Although the Soviets extended formal diplomatic recognition to the Federal Republic of Germany in September, they also proclaimed that the Communist Democratic Republic in East Germany now had full control over East Berlin. The following January East Germany entered the Warsaw Pact. The Big Four foreign ministers meeting at Geneva in October 1955 brought another Western call for national elections to reunify Germany, and another vehement Soviet rejection. And when the UN Subcommittee on Disarmament reconvened in London in September, American delegate Stassen, instead of replying directly to the May Soviet proposal, announced that the United States was invalidating "all of its pre-Geneva substantive positions . . . pending the outcome of our study . . . of inspection methods and control arrangements . . . ." In effect, Stassen was saying that within the American government the dominant view was that disarmament, even with ground inspections, was too dangerous because there remained a certain margin for evasion. Thereafter the Eisenhower administration steadily moved away from the problem of disarmament and toward the more limited goal of "arms control."

Though aware that it could benefit both economically and in terms of its national security from curbing the arms race, the USSR also recognized by the mid-fifties that it was making progress toward achieving mutual deterrence vis-à-vis the United States. In the post-Stalin era the Soviets went in for their own "New Look," meaning, as in the United States, reductions in conventional arms and the rapid expansion of strategic forces. Yet unlike the United States, which continued to develop and mass-produce huge numbers of intercontinental bombers, the Russians concentrated on ballistic missiles for their principal deterrent force. Throughout the fifties the Soviets produced comparatively few long-range bombers, despite loud warnings by leading Democrats of a bomber gap in mid-decade. In the United States, on the other hand, missile efforts remained uncoordinated and, it would later appear, underfunded. Not until January 1955 did the Air Force award a contract for the development of America's first intercontinental ballistic missile (ICBM), the Atlas. And not until the following September—perhaps significantly, the same month in which American disarmament negotiators backtracked at London—did Eisenhower order Atlas development placed on a highest-priority, "crash" basis. Within two years the administration and the Republican party would find themselves facing much more politically damaging charges of a missile gap.

VI

In the fall of 1955, though, the peril of nuclear holocaust seemed to have receded a little. The first crisis in the Formosa Strait had passed; Europe was still basking in the glow of Geneva. And Vietnam? Relatively few Americans could even find it on the map, and even in those sections of the American government where Indochina was an acute concern, there was general satisfaction that the situation in South Vietnam seemed to have stabilized. For the first time since 1945 no shooting war was going on anywhere in the world.

On September 24, 1955, at the warmest point in the cold war "thaw" of the mid-fifties, and with the economy fully recovered from the short-lived post–Korean war recession and reaching new peaks of prosperity, Eisenhower suffered a "moderately severe" coronary seizure while vacationing in Colorado. Journalists commented that if the President had scheduled his heart attack, he could not have chosen a more opportune time. For several weeks, while the President's physicians forbade him even to read a newspaper, Vice President Nixon, Secretary Dulles, and the presidential staff in Washington, together with Press Secretary James Hagerty and Sherman Adams in Colorado, took care of most of the affairs of state. But the President's recovery was rapid; by mid-October he was easing back into his work routine. The next

month he returned to Washington for a few days and then set
up operations at his Gettysburg, Pennsylvania, farm. Adlai
Stevenson, already an announced candidate for the 1956 presidential nomination, and other leading Democrats questioned
whether Eisenhower was physically fit even to continue for the
rest of his present term, let alone serve out a second. The President nevertheless regained his strength, became nearly as active
as ever, and contemplated running again in 1956. The pressure
from his party for him to do so was tremendous; with the polls
indicating that Eisenhower's popularity was as high as ever and
that he was far ahead of Stevenson or any other Democrat in
voter preference, National Chairman Leonard Hall and the rest
of the GOP leadership hoped desperately for an affirmative decision.

Exactly when Eisenhower made up his mind is not known. But
the chances that he would run again were better than ever after
Paul Dudley White, a renowned heart specialist who had become
his chief physician, said publicly in mid-February that there was
no reason why the President could not carry on basically as he
had. Then, at his news conference on the morning of February
25, Eisenhower said that he would be willing to accept his party's
renomination. That night on national television and radio he announced that he had decided to seek a second term because "the
work I set out four years ago to do has not yet reached the state
of development and fruition that I then hoped could be accomplished within the period of a single term of office." The sigh of
relief from Republicans across the land was almost deafening.

Eisenhower's decision to run again came at the apex of the
relative peace and general prosperity that distinguished the years
1955–1957. These years might be described as a period of pause,
even to some extent of relaxation—in short, as the time of the
"Eisenhower equilibrium." Such a concept of equilibrium not only
is helpful for understanding the complex political and diplomatic
history of the Eisenhower era, but also offers a good vantage point
from which to survey the even greater complexities of American
economic, social, intellectual, and artistic life in the years of
Eisenhower's Presidency.

IV

Affluence and Anxiety

FOR the American people as a whole, the two salient, overriding features of life in the decade of the 1950s were "affluence and anxiety," as the historian Carl Degler has phrased it. Never had Americans—never had any people—been so generally and spectacularly prosperous. On all sides were the evidences of widely distributed wealth and enormous national power. In the midst of their unparalleled abundance, however, Americans also had to get used to the constant threat of nuclear annihilation. They had to learn to live with perilous and frequent international crisis, with radioactive fallout from nuclear weapons tests in the atmosphere, and with a steady barrage of scientific doomsday prophecies. However much they might dim their consciousness before their television sets, travel to places their parents had only dreamed of seeing, increase their consumption of alcohol and other drugs, or otherwise engage in the collective pursuit of pleasure, the American people could never really escape the reality that their country could be largely destroyed within a matter of an hour or so. Yet if the specter of total destruction could not be completely banished, Americans could still find some solace in the mounting array of goods and gadgets available during this time of wealth unprecedented in the nation's history.

I

The United States had experienced periods of widespread prosperity before, notably during the 1920s and under the full-production economy of the Second World War. Not until the

1950s, however, did the nation truly arrive at what John Kenneth Galbraith has called "the affluent society." By the fifties the American economy seemed to have overcome man's historic struggle to secure the basic necessities of life—food, clothing, shelter. Despite the persistence of substantial poverty, the pertinent question no longer seemed to be whether America could feed, clothe, and house its citizens, but how it could sustain the steady advances in living standards under way since 1945. By 1956 American business corporations were paying out some $12 billion a year in dividends. Economists pegged the net worth of all Americans at $875 billion, and people were saving at the rate of 7½ percent of their incomes. Average personal income, figured after taxes and at 1956 prices, had grown to $5,050, up $530 since 1947. By 1960, although unemployment remained at about 6 percent of the work force, a record 66½ million Americans held jobs. Gross national product (GNP) had climbed from $322 billion in 1947 to more than half a trillion. Inflation, after slowing down considerably with the end of the Korean war, continued to nibble at the purchasing power of the dollar; nonetheless, real income had increased 29 percent since 1947. Because corporations had come to finance their expansion primarily out of profits rather than from stock sales, the stock market was no longer the key business barometer it had once been. Still significant, however, was the fact that late in 1954 stock averages finally regained their 1929 peak of 381.

Whereas before World War II the commonly used measures of economic health had been the volume of employment and industrial productivity, by the mid-1950s many economists had come to place primary emphasis on the rate of overall economic growth, measured in terms of increases in GNP. To be sure, the Eisenhower administration, little influenced by Keynesian economic theory and generally inclined toward fiscal conservatism, was less concerned with growth rates than would be the succeeding Democratic administrations in the 1960s. Under Eisenhower little effort was made to manipulate federal fiscal policy as a way to stimulate economic growth; from 1953 to 1960 GNP grew at a modest annual rate of 2.9 percent, considerably below the increments of the 1920s or the period 1879–1919. Yet if the rate of overall economic expansion was generally sluggish in the post-Korean period, there could be little doubt that the United States was still experiencing the greatest peacetime prosperity in its history.

One of the key factors behind the economic surge of the 1950s was public spending. The decade saw no notable rise in federal transfer payments (expenditures for Social Security benefits, unemployment compensation, veterans' benefits, and the like) in relation to the rest of the national budget. Under a Republican administration the momentum toward the welfare state generated in the thirties and forties by the New Deal and Fair Deal, while by no means reversed, did slacken somewhat. Even so, state and local expenditures, particularly for public services, rose steadily —from 7 percent of GNP in 1950 to 9.4 percent by 1960. More importantly, because of continuing huge outlays for military purposes, overall federal expenditures remained at a high level despite the end of the Korean war and the Eisenhower administration's dogged pursuit of balanced budgets. Defense Department allocations accounted for more than half the total national budget each year of Eisenhower's Presidency.

Another key to the boom was the rapid expansion of private credit, which made it possible for Americans to buy a great deal more of almost everything with relatively less in the way of savings. For example, while family homeownership rose from 40 percent to 60 percent and disposable income increased 3½ times between 1939 and 1955, mortgage and installment indebtedness grew fivefold. Early in 1953 only about 6 percent of all Veterans Administration loans were secured without down payments, as opposed to nearly 40 percent two years later. By 1955 some 60 percent of all automobile purchases, usually cited as the single most important element in the consumer economy, took place under credit terms, which were often as generous as $100 down and three years to pay. Such terms, along with the drastic depreciation characteristic of the automobile market, commonly made it more advantageous for buyers to let their cars be repossessed than to pay them off. By the mid-fifties installment indebtedness in the United States had reached $27 billion, ten times what it had been in the 1920s. Although total personal indebtedness was still only 12 percent of total personal income, indebtedness was growing considerably faster than income.

Unprecedented private indebtedness, freely entered into and often casually borne, was one of the most important economic realities of the fifties—as was the appearance of a sizable new industry whose concern it was to investigate, report, and maintain files on the credit rating of individuals. Frequently secured at the expense of personal privacy, a good or at least passable standing with the credit agencies might be worth more than an individual's capital assets. Credit-buying made it possible for the great majority of Americans to share at least to some degree in the material abundance of the fifties. By 1956, 81 percent of American families had managed to acquire television sets, 96 percent had refrigerators, nearly 67 percent had vacuum cleaners, and almost 89 percent had washing machines. Only in the United States did such luxuries seem essential. At the end of the decade nearly 74 million automobiles were in operation in the United States, while millions more rested in junk heaps along the streets and highways of the country.

In short, the American economy had completed a fifty-year process of transformation—first recognized in the 1920s and then obscured by the Great Depression and the Second World War—from a production economy in which the primary task was to meet basic human needs, to a consumer economy which presupposed that basic needs were already being met and that the primary task was constantly to expand consumption in order to push profits to higher and higher levels. In the new consumer economy, advertising played an indispensable role in convincing consumers that they had numerous—in fact theoretically unlimited—"unconscious needs" which must somehow be satisfied. Another feature of the consumer economy was the ephemerality of goods, whether because of planned obsolescence or because mass production for mass consumption inevitably meant less durable products.

Still another feature was the relative decline in the number of people working to produce goods, and the employment of greater and greater numbers of Americans to sell, distribute, and maintain what factories and plants turned out. By the 1950s, for the first time, the "service industries" employed more than half of all wage-earners. This changeover resulted not only from the emergence of the consumer economy but also from the increasing automation of industrial processes. Labor leaders and some economists worried that automated production methods would displace great numbers of workers; other economists, as well as business leaders, believed automation would mean safer and better work, more leisure time, and an actual increase in jobs.

Accompanying the boom was a literature of praise for the American capitalist system which was strikingly similar to the self-congratulatory outpourings of the twenties. The major difference was that those who eulogized the new economy of abundance generally accepted the emergence since the thirties of the "umpire state" to promote, police, and mediate between economic interests. Among those leading the applause was David E. Lilienthal, once damned by right-wingers as a mortal enemy of private enterprise when he was a Director of the Tennessee Valley Authority and subsequently, as the first Chairman of the Atomic Energy Commission, accused of being soft on Communism. Now Lilienthal wrote lyrically that big business had entered a "new era" of maturity, responsibility, and public service, an era in which the stereotypes of the depression years had become irrelevant. In the thirties the economist Adolph A. Berle had been a sharply critical observer of the concentration of corporate power in the hands of a managerial elite; now he described the modern corporation as "a social institution" whose "aggregate economic achievement is unsurpassed." "Taking all elements (including human freedom) into account," proclaimed Berle, the corporation's "system of distributing benefits, though anything but perfect, has nevertheless left every other system in recorded history far behind." Having once written a perceptively critical history of the confident and complacent twenties, Frederick Lewis Allen had become convinced by 1953 that the United States had built "an orderly and successful substitute" for socialism and Communism. Americans were blessed with "a system which not only helps the underdog, and brings about a dynamic redistribution of income in his favor, but also maintains the freedom of business enterprise and other private institutions, in all their fruitful diversity, to compete, invent, experiment and create . . . ."

Why did the system work so well? According to John Kenneth

Galbraith, it worked because of American capitalism's built-in "countervailing power"—the economic and political interaction of such massive elements as corporate producers, sellers, and buyers; labor unions; organized agriculture; and government itself to balance and block the abuse of power. And what about poverty? Galbraith and many other experts freely acknowledged that it still existed. The usual judgment, however, was that offered by Galbraith in 1958 in *The Affluent Society:* Not a "massive affliction," poverty in America was "more nearly an afterthought." Galbraith also insisted that even vestigial poverty in the midst of plenty was a "disgrace." His prescription for eliminating poverty was a moderate, "qualitative" extension of the social welfare directions taken under the New Deal and Fair Deal but slowed under the Eisenhower administration. Others contended that the "problem" could be "solved" by new federal policies designed to accelerate economic growth, which would in turn sweep up the poor in the overall process of expansion.

Yet for all the glowing statistics attesting to the undeniable material well-being of most Americans and all the self-congratulatory paeans in behalf of the new capitalism, the American economic system revealed a number of fundamental shortcomings and weaknesses in the 1950s. For one thing, the American people went on something of an ecological binge, blissfully and wastefully expanding across the national landscape with little concern for the injury they were doing to their physical environment or for the accelerating depletion of their energy resources. It would remain for a succeeding generation to assess and work to remedy the ecological damage Americans had systematically wrought throughout their history, but especially under the heedless boosterism of the fifties.

Even in the midst of this obsessive growthmanship, the economic system still was not able to maintain unbroken prosperity. The business cycle remained a fact of American economic life. To be sure, certain structural changes in the economy—notably the rise of big government spending and massive government intervention—served to cushion the impact of economic downturns. At the same time, the economic history of the Eisenhower years suggests how sensitive the economy had become to fluctuations in the federal budget. A rather sharp recession followed the drop in military expenditures accompanying the end of the Korean war in 1953, although the economy had generally recovered by the middle of the next year. A more severe recession came in 1957–1958, this one following substantial budget cuts during the "budget battle" of 1957. Unemployment, which had hovered around 4 percent of the civilian labor force since the 1954 recovery, climbed to 7½ percent by mid-1958, the peak for the fifties. Recovery was again well under way by the end of 1958, but two years later unemployment still stood at 6 percent. Thus each recovery period after the Korean war left a higher proportion of the work force without jobs than had been true before the downturn.

Those who had jobs were more likely than ever to be working for someone other than a business employer. Whereas in 1929 only 15 percent of the labor force had worked outside private enterprise, by the early 1960s about one-third of all jobholders were employed by government, in education, or by nonprofit organizations. In the midst of effusive claims that American capitalism had eliminated the threat of massive unemployment, private enterprise in the years 1950–1960 was able to account for only one-tenth of all the new jobs generated in the economy.

Accompanying the relative decline in private-sector employment was a drop in the amount of wealth produced by American business corporations alongside other elements in the economy. The growth in national income attributable to corporations reached a peak at 55.8 percent in 1955 and then began a slow decline to the 1948 level of 53.8 percent. Nevertheless, the trend toward the concentration of corporate power, which had been under way since the last decades of the nineteenth century, continued apace during the fifties. Between 1947 and 1958 the 200 biggest industrial firms increased their proportion of total manufacturing output from 30 percent to 38 percent, while the 50 biggest upped their share from 17 percent to 23 percent. By 1961 the 100 biggest corporations had come to control 31 percent of all industrial wealth in the United States.

On the surface, it is true, concentration seemed to be shrinking in about as many industries as it was increasing. This paradox is explained by the spectacular appearance in the post–World War II period of the business conglomerate, marking a new phase and offering a new instrument in the historic movement to centralize economic power in America. Unlike earlier forms of business combination, which had sought to consolidate producers within a single industry, the conglomerate featured industrial and mercantile diversification. Ostensibly the conglomerate seemed not to threaten the existing competitive situation because it did not aim to monopolize a particular industry or segment of trade. Actually it made fewer and fewer parent firms more powerful than ever by extending their operations into areas of the economy having no apparent relation to each other. Thus one conglomerate of businesses might be involved in manufacturing numerous different products, in operating resort hotels, in mining and lumbering operations, and in various other ventures.

On the whole, the Department of Justice was not disposed to interfere with conglomerate mergers. As a consequence, between 1950 and 1961 the 500 largest corporations in America merged with and absorbed a total of 3,404 smaller companies operating in a bewildering variety of areas of manufacturing and merchandising. Meanwhile the 50 biggest corporations acquired 471 firms, all without objection from the Justice Department. Two main arguments were used to justify or at least mitigate the increasing centralization of corporate power. The first was the longstanding one that concentration was inevitable and in the long run productive of order, efficiency, and better service to the consumer. The second argument was initially advanced in rudimentary form in the twenties and then refurbished and elaborated in the post–World War II years: The modern corporation, according to its defenders, had taken on a new sense of "public conscience" and a new obligation to serve the public interest even, so the rhetoric of both corporate managers and lay advocates seemed to suggest, at the expense of turning a profit.

Yet turning a profit remained the raison d'être of American business, and during the Eisenhower years there were repeated instances showing the conflict between the incessant pressure for private profit and power and the vaunted public conscience of corporate management. The most dramatic was the scandal in the electrical manufacturing industry which was uncovered in the last year of the Eisenhower administration. Officials of the General Electric Corporation, a firm hailed by Adolph Berle and others as almost a paragon of corporate responsibility, conspired with executives of twenty-nine smaller companies making electrical machinery to set prices on a wide range of products, from turbine generators to kilowatt-hour meters. In 1960 the Department of Justice prosecuted the price-fixing companies for violating the antitrust laws and overcharging customers by several billion dollars. Of twenty indictments secured, GE officials were named in nineteen. Ultimately seven executives, including a GE vice president and two general managers, served short prison terms. Eight other GE officials received suspended sentences; five more were fined individually. The federal courts imposed nearly $2 million in fines on the 30 offending companies, of which GE paid $437,500.

Another example of the dubiousness of the corporate conscience—though in this instance not involving illegal practices—was the conduct of the Ford Motor Company during the Eisenhower administration's campaign to halt the drain on United States gold reserves in the fall of 1960. With the country experiencing a deficit in its balance of payments for the first time in the post–World War II period, the administration moved to cut down overseas spending by ordering home dependents of military personnel at the rate of 15,000 a month and by trying to economize the operation of its military installations abroad. The Mutual Security Administration and the Defense Department also required countries getting economic aid and defense support money to spend more in the United States. Meanwhile Secretary of the Treasury Robert Anderson and Undersecretary of State Douglas Dillon vainly sought to get Chancellor Adenauer of West Germany to take on more of the costs of stationing American troops in his country. At this juncture, in November 1960, Ford determined to go ahead with its plan to pay out $360 million to European stockholders for the public shares in its British affiliate, in which it already had a controlling interest. Although Anderson

personally urged Chairman of the Board Henry Ford II to hold
up the stock purchase, the company's leadership refused to cooperate with the administration, the purchase went through, and
that week the United States' gold reserves dropped another $204
million.

Such episodes should have helped discredit the carefully nurtured image of the benevolent corporation dedicated to serving
the public interest. Similarly, even a rudimentary knowledge of
the realities of taxation should have been enough to puncture the
myth that the United States had an equitable, graduated income
tax system. For example, in 1959, of nineteen Americans with incomes of more than $5 million, five paid no federal taxes at all,
and not one of the nineteen paid taxes at the nominal legal rate.
By the 1950s the federal tax system had become so complex, so
full of loopholes, and so geared to encourage property ownership and capital investment that the more money a person made
the smaller the percentage of his income he was likely to pay in
federal taxes. In 1960 the Chase Manhattan Bank published some
statistics on the discrepancies between legal and effective tax
rates for various income levels. A person with an income of less
than $3,000, for instance, had a scheduled income tax rate of 20
percent and paid at the rate of 19 percent. A person in the income
range $50,000–$99,999, however, was supposed to pay at a rate of
55 percent and actually paid at 39 percent. In the range between
$200,000 and $499,999 a year, tax payments should be made at 80
percent but were actually made at 42 percent. And the average
payment of people making a million dollars or more a year was
but 38 percent of their incomes, as opposed to the nominal rate of
87 percent.

The economic history of the fifties also should have shown the
hollowness of the claim that poverty in America was either in-
significant or was in the process of evaporating. Far from being
swept up in the expansionary surge, poverty remained one of the
stubbornest features of American life. Living conditions, income
levels, and employment opportunities were generally bad among
four groups: the rapidly growing number of black people living
near the center of cities; white, commonly "old-stock" Americans

in the Appalachian coal regions from western Pennsylvania to northern Georgia; mill workers in the declining industrial towns of New England; and rural people, both white and black, in the southern states. Of course it is true that economists used different measures of poverty, and that even the poorest Americans were in better shape than much of the world's population. But it was cold comfort for a black ghetto resident to be told that his standard of living was higher than that of the average European, when from every side he was bombarded by reminders that as Americans he and his family were supposed to have all sorts of things he simply could not afford, and that he should be working regularly, when some 30 percent of black city dwellers were unemployed. By any measure it was clear that many millions of citizens lived far below the general level of material affluence.

Michael Harrington would not publish his influential account of the American poor, *The Other America,* until 1962. Yet for those who wanted to listen, there was plenty of information available by the late fifties on the nature and extent of poverty in the United States. One could have found out, for example, that since 1944 one-fifth of American families had received only 5 percent of total national income, while the wealthiest fifth of the population had accumulated some 45 percent. Various studies showed that about 20 percent of all Americans lived in conditions below what should be considered a minimum standard of subsistence. In 1960 the federal Bureau of Labor Statistics set $3,000 as the minimum annual income with which an American family of four could live decently, $4,000 for a family of six. Some 40 million Americans, according to the Bureau, lived below these income levels. Leon Keyserling, chairman of the Council of Economic Advisers during the Truman administration, pointed out in the late fifties that another 39 million or so Americans, though above the poverty line, found themselves in a condition of "deprivation." Keyserling enumerated some of the items a family in such circumstances might be able to afford by stringent budgeting: no more than three new dresses a year, no more than one movie and a one-ounce drink of whiskey every two weeks, a $100-a-month

apartment, a vacuum cleaner every fourteen years. Clearly, for
nearly half the people in the United States the affluent society was
still mostly a hope, not yet fully a reality.

II

On one matter, however, there was general agreement in the
1950s: The average American industrial workingman was better
off than he had ever been. Pay was higher and hours were shorter
than during any previous period. Workers had been protected by
law in their right to organize and enter into collective bargaining
with employers since the 1930s. One of the major legacies of the
New Deal–World War II years, "big labor," seemingly possessed
great economic leverage, even though the 1947 Taft-Hartley Act
had restricted certain kinds of union activity, had outlawed com-
pulsory union membership before employment (the closed shop),
and had sanctioned state "right-to-work" laws prohibiting com-
pulsory union membership after employment (the union shop).

Big labor became even bigger in February 1955, when the
American Federation of Labor (AFL) and the Congress of Industrial Organizations (CIO), archrivals since the rise of the CIO in the
mid-thirties, merged their combined memberships of 15 million.
The merger did not entirely end jurisdictional disputes between
AFL craft unions and CIO industrial unions, but organized labor
could now function better than ever to gain regular wage increases, greater job security, and even profit-sharing agreements.
The United Auto Workers (UAW) won a landmark victory in the
summer of 1955 in the form of new contracts with Ford and
General Motors which guaranteed UAW members incomes of at
least 60-65 percent of the wages they were then receiving. Over
the years other unions came to use the UAW agreements as models
in negotiating new contracts in other industries.

Strikes continued, mostly limited to one geographical area but
occasionally extensive enough to cause serious dislocations in the
national economy. Despite protracted strikes by the steelworkers
in 1955 and 1959 and walkouts in a few other major industries,
labor-management relations were considerably more tranquil under Eisenhower than under Truman. The steadily higher wages

gained by workers—characteristically passed on by companies in the form of higher prices—usually kept pace with or exceeded the relatively modest inflation rate, which averaged around 2.5 percent a year during the period 1953–1960.

All the same, the United States was still a long way from being a workers' utopia. Hard questions might have been asked—and usually weren't in the fifties—about the character of work, which for great numbers of jobholders was monotonous, unsatisfying, often trivial. Another matter usually not discussed was the extent to which the welfare of the industrial work force had, like much of the rest of the economy, come to be bound up with military spending. Throughout the fifties sharp dips in industrial employment regularly followed cuts in military funding. The correlation between military outlays and employment levels doubtless partly explains the tendency of many labor leaders to be ardent cold warriors. At the end of his Presidency Eisenhower would warn of the growing power of the "military-industrial complex"; he might have referred more descriptively to a "military-industrial-labor complex" tied closely to the perpetuation of a semi-wartime economy.

Something economists did often suggest by 1960 was that organized labor seemed to be approaching its growth limits. After reaching a peak of nearly 18½ million in 1957 (27.1 percent of the total civilian work force), union membership began a gradual but steady decline, a trend that would continue through the next decade. The economic expansion of the fifties took place mostly in areas—the South and Southwest—where unionism had traditionally been weak and where right-to-work laws were the rule. Meanwhile, in those regions and industries where labor had traditionally been strong, technological changes steadily reduced the number of available jobs. Between 1947 and 1961 about two-thirds of the jobs in bituminous coal mining disappeared; in railroading, about 40 percent; in steel, copper, and aluminum production, about 17 percent. Those sectors of the economy expanding most rapidly—like finance, real estate, retail sales, and government employment—proved generally inhospitable to union activity. In 1956, for the first time, the total number of white-collar workers exceeded blue-collar workers. Assuredly, organized labor

was big and strong, but by 1960 it was questionable whether
labor really had as much countervailing power as Galbraith and
others claimed.

For labor leaders, who had become almost as concerned as corporate executives about their public image, a succession of revela-
tions of corrupt behavior on the part of union officials and tie-ins
between unions and criminal elements proved acutely embarrassing. The most publicized union malpractices involved the International Longshoremen's Association (ILA), dominant on the Atlantic
coast, and the International Brotherhood of Teamsters, the
country's biggest union. In 1953 the New York State Crime Commission disclosed that the ILA was controlled by racketeers who
systematically terrorized workers on waterfronts in the New York
City area. The AFL moved quickly to expel the ILA and to set up
a new longshoremen's union, but on three occasions the dock
workers voted down the AFL's alternative. Meanwhile the ILA
called a crippling strike, which ended only after President Eisenhower invoked the Taft-Hartley Act.

Four years later a Senate select committee, with John Mc-
Clellan of Arkansas as its chairman and young Robert F. Kennedy
as its zealous chief counsel, found that Teamsters President Dave
Beck and other officers had made no effort to follow democratic
procedures, and had misappropriated union funds to invest in
personal stock accounts and in a string of gambling casinos,
whorehouses, and bars in the Pacific Northwest. The AFL-CIO
executive council voted in December 1957 to expel the entire
Teamsters membership of 2½ million. By 1959 Beck was in federal
prison and James R. Hoffa, his defiant successor, was himself involved in a protracted legal battle which would end with his
conviction and imprisonment. The AFL-CIO tried further to put
its own house in order by toughening its code of ethical practices
regarding the uses of union funds and the handling of union
elections. Nevertheless, in 1959 lopsided congressional majorities
passed legislation which required unions to account publicly for
the disposition of funds and to make financial reports to the
Secretary of Labor, guaranteed free elections, and further restricted secondary boycotts. At the end of the decade the stereotype of the "labor racketeer" was doubtless fixed even more firmly

in the public consciousness than the earlier stereotype of the "labor radical."

III

If one happened to be black, the rise of big labor meant little in the way of a better standard of living—and might even mean the loss of a job. For the most part the craft unions affiliated with the AFL systematically excluded blacks from the skilled trades; by 1960, according to some estimates, there were fewer black carpenters, bricklayers, painters, and other tradesmen in the country than there had been at the beginning of the century. The pattern of exclusion in the craft unions in combination with generally discriminatory hiring and pay practices on the part of employers put promising, good-paying jobs beyond the reach of the vast majority of black people. The result was that after 1952, for the first time since the depression era, overall black income began to decline in relation to white income. Between 1937 and 1952 black income had grown 80 percent faster than white, and the median income of black families had climbed to 57 percent of white families. By 1962, however, median black family income had dropped back to 53 percent of that of whites.

Economic discrimination was only part of the catalog of injustices, indignities, and oppressions suffered by black Americans. Black people were victimized not just by being mostly at the bottom of the economic class structure but also by the fact that in America class interacted with a historic system of caste, which made blacks almost a pariah element in the population. Of course the caste system operated most viciously and with the strongest legal foundation in the southern states, where a vast array of laws and ordinances decreed the rigid separation of blacks and whites in virtually every area of social life. From the Chesapeake Bay to the Rio Grande at El Paso, from the Oklahoma panhandle to the Florida keys, from the Ohio River to the Gulf of Mexico, legally enforced racial segregation was the universal practice. While the federal courts had struck down the most obvious legal devices which had prevented blacks from voting, discriminatory application of existing statutes, together with violence, economic coercion, and other forms of extralegal intimidation, kept the great majority of black southerners disfranchised. In eleven southern states in 1957, only 25 percent of the black population of voting age was registered, as compared to 60 percent of the whites. Some three million black citizens were denied the ballot.

Even with voting rights and an absence of laws mandating racial segregation, blacks outside the South also remained second-class citizens—underpaid and underemployed, limited to the least desirable jobs, crowded into rundown schools in the decaying central cities, blocked by restrictive covenants from securing better housing even when they could afford it, and in their day-to-day contacts with whites alternately ignored, abused, and feared. Two incidents from the Eisenhower years typify what commonly happened when northern blacks tried to leave the ghetto and settle their families in more attractive circumstances. In November 1953, after four black families moved into Trumbull Park Homes, a publicly owned apartment project in Chicago, white occupants smashed their windows and stoned and spat on them. Chicago police had to establish 24-hour patrols to keep order at the project and protect the black residents in their new homes. Four years later a black family bought a house in the suburban development of Levittown, Pennsylvania. Local whites greeted them with a barrage of rocks and insults, and formed a Betterment Committee to try to evict them. Another group of white residents managed to calm the area and eventually get grudging acceptance of the newcomers. One Levittowner expressed characteristic feelings of northern whites about residential integration when he said that the black father was "probably a nice guy, but every time I look at him I see $2,000 drop off the value of my house."

The United States had always been a white-man's country, and so it remained during the Eisenhower Presidency. Yet in these same years the cracks in the American caste system which had opened during the Truman period widened considerably. The Eisenhower administration moved less than zealously to combat racial injustice, but in some ways it did move. The President carried through with the Republican party's 1952 pledge to complete the desegregation of the armed forces begun under the Truman administration. Under insistent pressure from Representative Adam Clayton Powell, Eisenhower had Secretary of the Navy Robert Anderson personally take a hand in ending segregation at the naval bases at Norfolk, Virginia, and Charleston, South Carolina. Other military installations across the country were quietly desegregated, as were public schools at such installations and 47 Veterans' Administration hospitals. Meanwhile the White House and the Justice Department pressured operators of hotels, theaters, and restaurants in the District of Columbia to integrate their establishments; and officials of the District integrated its parks, swimming pools, and fire department. Although he opposed a federal fair employment law, Eisenhower did appoint a committee headed by Vice President Nixon to consider ways to curb widespread discrimination on work done under federal contracts. Proceeding very cautiously, the committee did little to end discriminatory practices nationally, but it was instrumental in getting District bus companies to lift their ban on black drivers and in desegregating telephone company business offices in the District.

These actions were as far as the Eisenhower administration was willing to go on its own in altering the national pattern of race relations. Even in interstate transportation, a matter clearly within federal jurisdiction, southern segregationist practices remained undisturbed.

Then, on May 17, 1954, the United States Supreme Court ruled unanimously in the case of *Brown* v. *Board of Education of Topeka* that racial segregation in the nation's public schools was contrary to the Fourteenth Amendment of the federal Constitution. In so ruling the Court not only agreed with the contention of the plaintiff, a black father who had sued the Topeka, Kansas, school officials, but also with the brief filed the previous November by Attorney General Herbert Brownell, who had entered the case as *amicus curiae* (friend of the court) after overcoming Eisenhower's strong misgivings. Segregated schools, the Court said, were "inherently unequal"; there was "no place" for the "separate but equal" doctrine laid down by the Court in 1896 and used thereafter to justify educational facilities in the South that were usually grossly unequal.

At one stroke the Court had theoretically outlawed a historic system of educational segregation—legally mandated in 17 states, optional in four others, and also practiced in the District of Columbia. From the white South came the cry that the Court had tyrannically interfered with the region's age-old customs and traditions and had created a situation bound to produce "miscegenation" and "mongrelization." Yet the practical consequences of the *Brown* decision were neither immediate nor momentous. A number of school districts with few black students, mainly in the mountain South and western Oklahoma and Texas, dropped their racial barriers, and Eisenhower quickly ordered public schools desegregated in the District of Columbia. But most of the white South replied "Never!" to the Court's ruling and steeled itself to offer "massive resistance." In 1955 the Court made plain that it expected no sudden overturn of existing practices when it placed responsibility for implementing its decision on local authorities, who, under the supervision of the federal courts, should go forward with desegregation plans at "all deliberate speed." The general interpretation of this phrase in the South, and especially in those states with the largest black populations, was that state and local officials could procrastinate and practice evasion for an indefinite period.

Although he had acted to achieve speedy compliance with the *Brown* verdict in the District of Columbia, Eisenhower otherwise showed little interest in using his powers to enforce the Court's wishes. He took no action early in 1956 when University of Alabama officials expelled Autherine Lucy, the first black person admitted to the institution, on the grounds that her presence threatened public order. He remained similarly passive when racial disturbances broke out at the opening of school that year in Mansfield, Texas, Hoxie, Arkansas, and Clinton, Tennessee. Questioned in a news conference at the time about his feelings on the *Brown* decision, Eisenhower replied, "I think it makes no difference whether or not I endorse it. What I say is the Constitution is as the Supreme Court interprets it; and I must conform to that and do my very best to see that it is carried out." In his memoirs Eisenhower wrote that "there can be no question that the judgment of the Court was right." Arthur Larson, however, quotes him as saying in 1957, "As a matter of fact, I personally think that the decision was wrong." One of the President's oft-repeated statements echoed the contention of white people throughout the South: "I don't believe you can change the hearts of men with laws or decisions." Clearly, Eisenhower had strong reservations not only about the wisdom of the *Brown* judgment but also about the broader issue of the status of black people in America. Larson's conclusion is that "President Eisenhower, during his presidential tenure, was neither emotionally nor intellectually in favor of combating segregation in general."

Despite the lack of presidential leadership in the field of civil rights and the white South's determined resistance to the abolition of its codified racism, the *Brown* decision slowly became a powerful galvanizing symbol for southern blacks as well as a turning point in the history of all black Americans. The National Association for the Advancement of Colored People (NAACP), which had worked tirelessly for decades to get judges to desegregate public facilities in the South, continued its traditional patient pursuit of change through the federal courts. But in the meantime younger black organizations and leaders began to consider more direct and dramatic tactics for challenging the American caste system. The first instance of such direct action came in Montgomery, Alabama, beginning late in 1955. The events in Montgomery thrust into national prominence a twenty-seven-year-old black Baptist minister named Martin Luther King, Jr.—a man of great oratorical gifts and charismatic personality who was to remain at the center of public life for more than a decade and then, after his assassination in the spring of 1968, continue to haunt the American consciousness.

What happened in Montgomery began with a single unplanned act—the refusal of a black woman to give up her seat to a white man on a city bus, as she was required to do by state and local law. After the woman was arrested and indicted, local black leaders convened a mass meeting at Dexter Avenue Baptist Church, where King, freshly graduated from Boston University Divinity School, had assumed the pastorate. Under King's leadership the assemblage voted to form the Montgomery Improvement Association and to boycott the Montgomery bus system. Word of the boycott and willingness to participate spread quickly among the city's blacks, who made up most of the bus company's customers. For more than eleven months an effective network of car pools got many black people to work, while others walked rather than ride the buses. The boycott cut bus patronage by a third. Meanwhile NAACP lawyers challenged the state and local public transportation laws in the federal courts; in November 1956 the Supreme Court ruled the Alabama laws unconstitutional.

Integrated seating on Montgomery's city buses was not won—perhaps could not have been won—without the traditionally unspectacular work of the NAACP. National attention, however, focused on the handsome young leader of the boycott rather than on the prosaic legal maneuvering. Lerone Bennett, King's biographer, contends that King had not thoroughly worked out a philosophy and strategy of nonviolent protest when the Montgomery boycott began, but that he did so in the course of the boycott after intense meditation on the teachings of the Indian revolutionary pacifist Mahatma Gandhi and after profound soul-searching when a bomb exploded on the front porch of his home. In any case, King came out of the Montgomery experience preaching a systematic doctrine of massive but peaceful resistance, based on universal love and a willingness to suffer in order to touch the compassionate spirit which King perceived in all mankind. Perhaps the most succinct statement of his outlook came at the height of the boycott, when he told his Dexter Avenue congregation: "Blood may flow in the streets of Montgomery before we receive our freedom, but it must be our blood that flows and not that of the white man. We must not harm a single hair on the head of our white brothers."

The nonviolent tactics of King's Southern Christian Leadership Conference (SCLC), founded in the wake of the Montgomery victory, set the pattern for black protest in the South for the next decade. Early in 1960 students from all-black North Carolina Agricultural and Technical College sat down at a lunch counter at the Woolworth store in Greensboro and remained on their stools after being refused service. The incident triggered a campaign of "sit-ins" aimed at desegregating restaurants, theaters, and other public facilities across the South. Sometimes sit-ins were sponsored by the Congress of Racial Equality (CORE), which had operated mostly in the North for the past two decades, but usually they were initiated by local groups of young black people. During 1960 such demonstrations involved some 50,000 blacks and white supporters (of whom perhaps 3,600 were jailed), and led to the partial or total integration of public accommodations in 126 southern cities. Sit-ins and other kinds of passive civil disobedience would continue into the mid-sixties under the organizational aegis of SCLC, CORE, and the Student Non-Violent Coordinating Committee (SNCC), until formal segregation in public establishments had mostly disappeared from the South.

The much-publicized attack on legal segregation, together with the ultimately successful drive for federal action to insure black suffrage, could go far toward securing basic civil rights for a people long deprived of even the trappings of citizenship—and could win the sympathies of great numbers of northern whites. Yet such efforts rather quickly reached their effective limits. The tactics which worked in tearing down formal racial barriers in the South could have little effect on the complex, extralegal pattern of discrimination in jobs, housing, educational opportunities, and law enforcement plaguing black Americans throughout the nation. In other words, the dramatic struggle for civil rights in the South long obscured the lack of significant progress toward the fulfillment of those black aspirations for which little sympathy and understanding among whites had ever existed. Though not generally realized at the time, at the end of the Eisenhower years conditions were already ripening for the eruption of the black-power and black-nationalist movements and the great urban riots of the mid- and late sixties.

IV

The 1950s, particularly the last half of the decade, thus brought intensifying activity in behalf of civil rights for southern blacks. At the same time, there seemed to be comparatively little concern, except on the part of the American Civil Liberties Union and a few other organizations, about the preservation of civil liberties—those freedoms presumably shared by all Americans but always in need of protection from overzealous government acting in the name of national security and public safety. Public opinion polls indicated that a large majority of Americans favored strong curbs on the Communist party and other suspect radical groups, if not their outright repression. One might argue, of course, that America's increasingly urbanized and impersonal society was more tolerant than ever of diverse personal life styles. Yet it is also true that the cold war atmosphere of the fifties produced steady erosion in the freedom to dissent and carry out radical protest against the existing political and economic system. Evidently most Americans had scant regard for the historic libertarian proposition that repressing the free expression of one imperiled the liberties of all. Under a barrage of federal, state, and local laws and rulings aimed at restricting the range of allowable dissent, political radicals and civil libertarians looked mainly to the United States Supreme Court to protect the freedoms set forth in the Bill of Rights. The response they got from the Court was mixed and inconsistent in the Eisenhower period. There were signs, however, that the Court was moving toward the thoroughgoing commitment to civil liberties it assumed during the 1960s.

In September 1953 President Eisenhower named Earl Warren, California's three-term governor, to succeed the late Fred M. Vinson as Chief Justice of the Supreme Court. One of the major ironies of recent American history is that Warren, who as attorney general of California had urged the forced internment of Japanese-Americans after Pearl Harbor, came to preside over a Court subsequently both hailed and cursed for its civil libertarianism and its expansion of popular democracy at the state level. In Warren's sixteen-year tenure the Supreme Court, more than at any time since the days of John Marshall, was identified almost reflexively with its Chief Justice. Warren's influence on his fellow justices was less a matter of intellectual prowess than of his persuasive and politic manner. Although there is some evidence that Eisenhower later regretted the Warren appointment, in fact the success of both men—of one as general and then as politician, of the other as politician and then as jurist—was attributable to many of the same qualities of personality and temperament.

Warren's influence showed as early as the *Brown* verdict, the unanimity of which resulted largely from his patient efforts. No other judgment handed down during the era of the Warren Court had quite the blockbuster effect of *Brown*, but in a number of cases in the field of civil liberties the Court's rulings dismayed and inflamed right-wing elements across the country.

The Court moved cautiously enough under Warren in 1954–1955. The majority, including Warren in each instance, held evidence gained through electronic surveillance to be admissible in jury trials (*Irvine* v. *California*); upheld the professional suspension of a New York physician after he was convicted of contempt of Congress for refusing to turn over records of a left-wing organization to the House Un-American Activities Committee (*Barsky* v. *Board of Regents*); and affirmed the constitutionality of the Immunity Act of 1954, which Congress had passed to try to force witnesses to testify about Communist connections (*Peters* v. *Hobby*).

In 1956–1957, however, the Court, again with Warren joining the majority, broadened the immunities and protections available to political dissenters. The Court in April 1956 (*Pennsylvania* v. *Nelson*) held that Congress—by passing the Smith Act of 1940, the Internal Security Act of 1950, and the Communist Control Act of 1954—had preempted the field of sedition from the states. This ruling, which invalidated portions of all existing state sedition laws, brought from the *Dallas Morning News* the declaration that "The Supreme Court thus becomes a threat to state sovereignty second only to Communism itself." In two other cases that same month, the Court overturned the firing of a Brooklyn College professor who had taken the Fifth Amendment before a congressional committee (*Slochower* v. *Board*), and invalidated actions taken by the federal Subversive Activities Control Board (sacb) on the basis of perjured testimony (*Communist Party* v. *Subversive Activities Control Board*).

Even more inflammatory to militant anti-Communists were the 1957 decisions in *Yates* v. *United States, Watkins* v. *United States,* and *Sweezy* v. *New Hampshire*. In *Yates* the Court, reversing the convictions of California Communist party officials prosecuted under the Smith Act, drew a distinction between advocating the "abstract doctrine" of political revolution and advocating a specific course of action to overthrow the government of the

United States. Right-wingers clamored that the Court had given Communists sanction to carry on revolutionary activity. In *Watkins* the Court reversed the conviction for contempt of Congress of a labor union official who, in testifying before HUAC, had refused to name others as Communists. Now, said the Court's critics, congressional committees would be hamstrung in their hunt for Reds. And in the *Sweezy* case the Court again struck at state action against alleged subversives, in this instance overturning the contempt conviction of the well-known economist Paul Sweezy. Sweezy had refused to answer questions put to him by New Hampshire's Red-baiting attorney general, Louis Wyman, who had questioned the content of Sweezy's lectures at the state university and his earlier activities in the Progressive party.

After 1957 the Warren Court appeared to backtrack before growing public criticism ("Impeach Earl Warren" billboards had already appeared in various parts of the country) and efforts in Congress to limit the Court's appellate jurisdiction. In *Barenblatt* v. *United States,* involving circumstances almost identical to those in the *Watkins* case, the Court renewed HUAC's "hunting license"; and in *Uphaus* v. *Wyman,* another case stemming from the activities of Louis Wyman, the Court essentially reversed the *Sweezy* judgment. In these decisions Warren and Justices Hugo Black, William O. Douglas, and William Brennan (like Warren an Eisenhower appointee) found themselves in the minority. The Court also upheld the constitutionality of the Smith Act provision making it a crime to belong to an organization that advocated the overthrow of the government, and sustained SACB's requirement that the Communist party register as a subversive "action group."

In the areas of criminal procedure and freedom of expression, the Court was no more eager to expand civil liberties. For example, in 1958 (*Crooker* v. *California*) the Court rejected the appeal of a man whom police had forbidden to see his lawyer before he gave them a written confession. Again the vote was 5-4, with the Chief Justice again one of the minority. The controversial *Escobedo* and *Miranda* decisions restricting police procedures were still some years in the future. And while the Court did unanimously legalize showings of the film version of D. H. Lawrence's *Lady Chatterley's Lover* (after a lower federal court had lifted the ban on the unexpurgated novel itself), the nine justices offered six separate opinions and thus left clouded the perhaps impossibly complex question of what really constituted obscenity.

In short, despite its image as the most liberal of the three branches of government, the Court functioned like everybody else in the context of cold war anxiety, concern over the rising rate of crime, and residual Victorian moral and social strictures. Liberal the Warren Court may have been in the Eisenhower years, but it was hardly a bastion of libertarianism.

V

If the American people as a whole seemed little dedicated to winning and protecting constitutional freedoms for blacks, dissenting minorities, and suspected criminals, they were certainly dedicated to the frenzied pursuit of material accumulation and upward social mobility. Social mobility in America had always been closely linked to geographical mobility. But whereas that had once meant the steady push of the population westward and the accelerating migration of rural people to towns and cities, by the middle decades of the twentieth century social mobility usually meant escape from, not to, an urban existence. By 1960 about 70 percent of all Americans lived in urban areas. Even more notable, though, was the fact that approximately half the population lived not in the inner cities but in peripheral suburban regions.

The flight from the inner city became epidemic in the fifties, as rising personal incomes and easy home financing enabled tens of millions of families, mostly middle-class and almost entirely white, to move into treeless, monotonous housing developments recently scraped out of the rural landscape. Left behind were most working-class whites, anxiously awaiting the time when they too could afford a house in the suburbs, and the vast number of urban blacks, forced by economic necessity and social discrimination to crowd into old and usually deteriorating tenements and neighborhoods near the city's central business district. A number of the older cities—New York, Chicago, Boston, Philadelphia, Detroit—actually lost population during the fifties.

Of course there was nothing new about the movement to the suburbs; Americans had been steadily expanding urban residential boundaries since the advent of streetcars late in the nineteenth century and commuter trains after 1900. But what was particularly striking about the urban exodus of the fifties was that it came at a time when demands on city government for better law enforcement, sanitation, schools, and other services were steadily mounting. Thus the migration of so many prosperous citizens stripped the cities of much of their tax bases just when they needed them most. Moreover, suburban proliferation coincided with and largely contributed to declining revenues and services in public transportation, so that state, county, and city governments had to spend enormous sums on highway networks—in particular the rapidly obsolescent and ironically named freeways and expressways—to carry the swelling tide of suburbanites into the cities to their jobs in the morning and back home at night.

Obviously what was needed was comprehensive planning to coordinate governmental services and anticipate and avoid the chaotic and heedless urban sprawl. Efforts at metropolitan planning, however, usually ran up against the rivalries of a multiplicity of governmental units—city, county, state, and federal. Besides that, suburban areas insisted on incorporating themselves, and rural-dominated legislatures were characteristically unwilling to grant power to local planning authorities.

In the midst of the gathering crisis of the cities, the response from Washington was less than heartening. The Eisenhower administration's announced policy was to interfere as little as possible with urban affairs in the interest of limiting federal power. Neither the administration nor a majority of Congress was willing to move against racial discrimination in employment practices and housing. The social and economic barriers ringing the black ghettoes receded somewhat but remained as unassailable as ever for most black people. Congress did try to come up with an alternative to the destructive consequences of the housing act of 1949, which had made available "redevelopment" money with which city governments had evicted inner-city residents, torn down slum housing, and built new projects often beyond the means of the urban poor. Under a program known as "urban renewal," established by Congress in 1954, local housing authorities received federal funds to restore salvageable buildings and raze only the worst housing. Even under this program, though, the process of dislocation and resettlement went forward on a massive scale. Urban reformers watched with dismay as new public housing projects rose, opened with appropriate ceremonies, and then quickly became run-down and crime-infested when occupied by people who felt no sense of proprietorship and no obligation to maintain these huge, impersonal piles of brick, steel, and glass. By 1960 the central residential areas of most American cities were already in a condition of marked decay; they would get even worse during the succeeding decade.

The most common reasons suburbanites gave for leaving the central city were that they needed more room and wanted a better physical, social, and educational environment for their children. These reasons suggest the vital interconnection between spreading affluence, spreading suburbs, and another arresting development of the fifties—the "baby boom." Under the force of the Great Depression, the national rate of births per 1,000 people had fallen during the thirties to 19, the lowest point in the nation's history to that time. The Second World War brought a substantial rise in the birthrate, but demographers still predicted that over the long run the population would continue to decline or at least would stabilize. To their amazement, the surge of births continued far into the postwar period, reaching a peak at more than 25 per 1,000 in the mid-fifties before finally beginning a gradual decline. In the year 1957 alone 4.3 million babies were born, one every seven seconds. Between 1950 and 1960 the baby boom, coupled with continuing medical advances, most notably in curbing diseases of infancy and childhood, produced a startling increase of 29 million people living in the United States. Geographically, population expansion, like economic expansion, was most pronounced in the Southwest and West, where cities like Houston, Lubbock, Albuquerque, Tucson, and Phoenix doubled, tripled, and sometimes quadrupled between 1950 and 1960. Los Angeles moved ahead of Philadelphia as the country's third-largest city; one-fifth of all national population growth took place in California.

Sociologically, the most interesting thing about the spiraling birthrate was that the middle class—which had been, in America as in Europe, the class most inclined to limit family size in the interest of higher living standards—was having more children than at any time since before 1900. As one economic historian said, "Americans began to behave as if they preferred the extra baby to the extra unit of consumption." Closely related to the baby boom was the temporary reversal or at least retardation of the long-term movement of women into the job market. Decades later, feminists would look back on the fifties as a bleak period, one in which tens of millions of women willingly abandoned their own educations and career prospects, worked hard to put husbands through college, and then, cheerfully accepting the role of homemaker, settled down to a life of child-rearing and housekeeping. Rising wages and employment and the distance between the suburbs and central cities made domestic help more and more difficult to come by. Husbands may have had more leisure time than ever; the average work week fell from 44 hours in 1940 to 41.5 hours by 1956. But housewives, especially those in the suburbs, found themselves busier than ever, mainly because they had more children to care for and because they had to spend much of each day driving to and from shopping centers and attending to a multiplicity of child-related activities. At the same time, they were constantly hearing from psychologists, marriage counselors, and the advertising media that they should strive to maintain their youthfulness and sexual appeal, else their mates might become dissatisfied and stray.

Perhaps the most significant short-term consequence of the baby boom was the strain it imposed on the country's educational system. College and university enrollments continued to grow steadily during the Eisenhower period because Congress gave GI bill benefits to Korean war veterans as it had to veterans of World War II, because family income continued to rise, because employers expected more and more in the way of formal education, and because military conscription, which caused many young men to enter college to win draft deferments, remained in force. For most institutions of higher learning, the enrollment losses following the graduation of World War II veterans were restored in the mid- and late fifties. By 1960 a record 3.6 million people were pursuing college degrees. Yet because of what happened in the next decade—skyrocketing enrollments, headlong expansion of faculties and physical plants, an upsurge of student political activism and an epidemic of violent campus disorders— in retrospect the 1950s look like a placid, relatively uneventful time in the history of American higher education.

Such was hardly the situation in national pre-college education. Besides the trauma of incipient racial integration in the schools of the South, the years spanned by Eisenhower's Presidency brought crisis both in the practical operation of elementary and secondary systems and in educational theory. In the decade 1946–1956 enrollment in the first eight grades of the public schools jumped from 20 million to 30 million. The soaring postwar birthrate, combined with the slowdown in school construction during the depression years and the virtual moratorium on plant expansion during World War II, made for overcrowded classrooms, a teacher shortage, and administrative and financial confusion in school districts across the country. By the mid-fifties educational leaders estimated that the United States needed 300,000 more classrooms and that low salaries were driving 75,000 teachers into other occupations each year.

Because local property taxes varied wildly from district to district and tended to be particularly inadequate in urban areas, harassed local school authorities had little choice but to submit frequent bond issues to unhappy property owners and look to Washington for help. The Eisenhower administration was willing to subsidize school construction in order to relieve the classroom shortage, but beyond that it was reluctant to go. Even this limited approach made little headway. In 1953 Congress did authorize federal grants for construction of school facilities in "impacted areas," those towns and cities subjected to extraordinarily rapid population growth following the location of new military installations or defense plants. From 1955 onward, however, broader education bills proposed in Congress repeatedly got snarled in controversies over whether federal funds should be used to induce racial integration and whether they should go to parochial as well as public schools. By the time Eisenhower left office, the federal government still had done relatively little to alleviate the financial maladies of the nation's school systems.

Paralleling the financial crunch in the schools was a swelling debate over the goals and direction of American public education. By the fifties the body of concepts and theories known as "progressive education" dominated teacher-training programs in colleges and universities and strongly influenced the nation's vast educational bureaucracy. Progressive educational theory was multifaceted, taking its inspiration from the voluminous writings of John Dewey and a host of other thinkers. Its three basic precepts were that education should be an open-ended process, approximating actual life experience as closely as possible; that the subject should learn through discovery, thus fulfilling his whole personality and developing methods of adaptation to and self-realization in society; and that the school, besides reflecting the social environment in which it functioned, should answer the changing needs of modern America.

Such ideas had served quite effectively in challenging the dreary rote-learning methods imposed on children in the nineteenth century. In fact, however, progressive theory had never been fully implemented in the American public schools, but had received its fullest application in small private schools and there mainly in the education of preadolescents. Progressivism's main significance was in giving a kind of intellectual sanction and respectability to developments that had stemmed inevitably from the American passion for giving every boy and girl at least twelve years of free schooling. Progressive theory by itself had produced no revolutionary transformation. Rather, the condition of American public education was a consequence of its efforts to educate everyone, regardless of level of intelligence, socioeconomic background, or personal interests. Thus the curriculum of the public high school typically ranged from fender repair to calculus, from personal grooming to biology, from driver education to world history. Straining to give every youth—whether college bound, job bound, army bound, or marriage bound—both the rudiments of traditional education and some attention to individual needs, the schools had assumed an array of responsibilities they simply could not fulfill.

By the mid-twentieth century the American people had come to focus their hopes and frustrations largely on their educational system. Because they expected so much—entirely too much—from their schools, Americans tended to hold them responsible for many of the country's shortcomings. And while progressive theorists and educators were only partly responsible for the character of the educational system, they got most of the blame for the national embarrassment which followed the launching of the "sputniks," the first two artificial satellites of Earth, by the Soviet Union in the fall of 1957. The dramatic Russian space successes precipitated a wave of national soul-searching and intensified an attack on progressive influence in the schools which had been mounting since the early fifties. As early as 1953, in his widely read *Educational Wastelands*, Arthur Bestor, a professional historian at the University of Illinois, had denounced the "retreat from learning" in the public schools. Terming the progressive emphasis on "life adjustment" a "parody of education," Bestor called for more rigorous standards, academic freedom and involvement in professional scholarship for teachers, and a liberal rather than vocational curricular orientation. That same year Albert Lynd even more vehemently assailed alleged progressive dominance, which he charged had led to "quackery in the public schools."

After the orbiting of the sputniks the educational controversy took on a more urgent tone. Critics like Admiral Hyman Rickover, designer of the atomic submarine, and study groups subsidized by the Rockefeller Brothers Fund warned that the sputniks proved the Russian schools, with their heavy emphasis on science and mathematics, were producing a generation of young people who would be able to give the USSR scientific and technological superiority. Meanwhile the United States would remain stuck in what *Life* called "the debris left by 40 years of the progressive educationists." America had neglected its gifted students, went the reformers' argument, while it exalted mediocrity and offered boys and girls an eclectic mishmash of subjects aimed more toward social skills than intellectual development. In mid-1958 the educational report of the Rockefeller Brothers Fund urged the American people to engage in a "pursuit of excellence." While acknowledging that the present educational system featured a "tug-of-war between excellence and equality," the report went on to deny that there was any necessary conflict between fully culti-vating the talents of the gifted and educating young people within the framework of democracy.

One of the less strident voices raised in behalf of reform in the post-sputnik period was that of James Bryant Conant, former president of Harvard University and former High Commissioner in occupied Germany. Conant had been at the center of govern-ment-scientific and government-educational activity for nearly two decades. In a study financed by the Carnegie Corporation and published early in 1959 as *The American High School Today,* Conant proposed a list of twenty-one needed changes, of which the foremost were consolidating small schools into larger, pre-sumably more efficient units and developing a multilevel cur-riculum geared to individual intellectual ability and the student's post–high-school intentions. The trend toward consolidation had been under way for several decades, and a considerable number of the larger high schools had already instituted differentiated paths of study—what came to be called "tracking." But the atmosphere of educational crisis after 1957 accelerated both trends. A Gallup poll taken in the spring of 1958 revealed that one-quarter of the public schools had made changes in their curricula since the previous fall.

At the end of the decade Charles Silberman, a close observer of the movement for educational change, was able to announce that "where we are going is toward a major overhaul of U.S. education." After visiting schools across the country and finding such innovations as grouping by aptitude, team teaching, tougher science and mathematics requirements, and more provision for independent study, Silberman was convinced that "American society has embarked on an effort to lift the quality and change the direction of its schooling. . . . Nearly all of the change and experimentation now apparent turns around a central idea: the pursuit of intellectual excellence."

The post-sputnik self-analysis and innovation may actually have improved the quality of public education available to many boys and girls. Yet educational change appeared to have gone furthest in the suburbs, where the concern for quality schooling had been most evident all along. Tracking and grouping may have made sense in the pursuit of excellence, but they often resulted in apathy toward the approximately 50 percent of the high school students who would not enter college. The reformist impulse of the late fifties and early sixties had little to offer such youths, characteristically poor and disproportionately black. It remained for a later group of very differently inclined educational reformers, appalled by the persistence of poverty and racial injustice in America, to call attention to a very different kind of neglect—the neglect of the vast numbers of young people effectively excluded from the job market unless they had high school diplomas, yet offered little in the way of meaningful educatior while they waited out their twelve-year confinement.

VI

The charge that American public education had exalted the mediocrity of the mass and stifled the talents of the gifted few was part of a broader complaint coming from a number of stu-. dents of American society, especially sociologists and social psychologists. America, so the argument went, had once been a land of exciting diversity and new beginnings—a magnet for the adventurer, the dissenter, the free individual. But now Americans had come to worship the cult of conformity, to settle comfortably for a homogenized existence, to carry on an obsessive quest for personal security. David Riesman's *The Lonely Crowd,* published in 1950, was probably the best-known effort to describe such changes in the American character. Riesman posited an archetypal "inner-directed" American, a product of an age that had idealized self-denial and thrift. Holding to an internalized set of values, the inner-directed man had achieved a high degree of emotional self-sufficiency. This traditional American, according to Riesman, had steadily given way to the "other-directed" man of modern urbanized, bureaucratized, and consumption-oriented society. Instead of following his own internalized life goals, the archetypal American of the mid-twentieth century continually adapted and readapted his personality and behavior to the changing collective aspirations, life styles, and idea patterns of peer groups and society as a whole. Riesman warned against the destruction of individual personality by "groupism," but he seemed generally pessimistic about chances for escaping the pressures for conformity.

Two other key works published in the fifties also explored the transforming effects of modern mass society on the individual: C. Wright Mills's *White Collar*, appearing the year after Riesman's book, and William H. Whyte's *The Organization Man* (1956). Mills grimly described how the rapidly multiplying number of white-collar employees—typically people who worked within a complex, impersonal corporate setting—had to repress their true feelings and engage in constant posturing and self-deception to make their way in the organizational maze, or even to keep their jobs. Whyte, like Riesman, dealt in historical and contemporary archetypes, contrasting the traditional American conformity to the Protestant Ethic, which had emphasized hard work, sacrifice, and personal responsibility, to the new "Social Ethic" of the organization. Whyte defined the Social Ethic as "that contemporary body of thought which makes morally legitimate the pressures of society against the individual." The modern organizational creed taught the individual that he had no identity apart from the "team," which alone gave him a sense of "belongingness." Under the earlier Protestant Ethic, Whyte observed, the boss had demanded only the sweat of his employees, whereas the new leader of the organization "wants your soul."

The historical accuracy of the sweeping archetypal generalizations made by Whyte, Riesman, and others was debatable, as were other aspects of their methodologies. Moreover, what they had to say was scarcely new, except insofar as it came from professional social scientists rather than lay critics. Some 120 years earlier the Frenchman de Tocqueville had similarly described the strong pressures for ethical conformity operating on Americans. The lamentations about the erosion of individual personality in the prosperous fifties were also reminiscent of protests against suffusive materialism and moral tyranny voiced in the prosperous twenties—although it is ironic that then the villain had often been the same determined, power-seeking traditional American whose passing Riesman, Whyte, and their followers seemed to regret.

One new feature of the social criticism of the fifties was its focus on the expanding suburbs. A host of social scientists, popular writers, and novelists turned their attentions to the manners, mores, and anxieties of the inhabitants of "suburbia." Suburbia was supposed to be the breeding ground of other-directedness, the locus of the Organization Man, the place where the troubled careerist in Sloan Wilson's best-selling novel, *The Man in the Gray Flannel Suit*, slept and spent his weekends. Of course not all suburban areas were architecturally monotonous, choked with children, settled by rootless, driven adults. Suburbs could and did vary considerably in age, appearance, and the life styles of their inhabitants. Still, there remained much truth in the stereotype of suburbia and its people. Suburbia was where nearly everyone either already lived or seemed to want to live. A house in the suburbs had become the chief symbol of success for many millions of Americans. That success—translated as a comfortable income, job security, perhaps a chance for advancement—increasingly was achievable only within a bureaucratic framework. Americans were in fact becoming organization men, and organization women as well.

Even when they supposedly put aside material concerns to observe the Sabbath under a bewildering variety of religious affiliations, the American people still could not escape the cult of conformity and the bane of other-directedness. So contended Will Herberg, whose *Protestant-Catholic-Jew* (1955) was a landmark contribution to the sociology of American religion. Herberg applauded the prevalent spirit of tolerance and freedom in the nation's religious life. Yet accompanying the decline of religious prejudice had been a decline of piety and zeal, and the rise of a bland, overarching "religion of religion" and "faith in faith." According to Herberg, Americans characteristically de-emphasized the particular content of religious belief while they insisted on some kind of belief. Thus in a nation historically dominated by Protestantism, there had emerged the concept of the three great faiths—Protestantism, Roman Catholicism, Judaism. Each faith, Herberg said, "tends to regard itself as merely an alternative and variant form of being religious in the American way." Americans thus sought not absolution for their sins, not an understanding

of divine mysteries, but peace of mind, adjustment, and normality
—"a spiritual anodyne designed to allay the pains and vexations
of existence."

Herberg wrote this commentary at a time when church
attendance was climbing to record levels; when the Reverend
Billy Graham, a young Baptist evangelist from North Carolina,
was effectively exploiting modern organizational techniques and
communications technology to bring his "crusades" to millions;
and when religious popularizers like Bishop Fulton J. Sheen, a
Catholic, and the Reverend Norman Vincent Peale, a Protestant,
were becoming national personalities through their simple, reas-
suring lectures on how to be at peace with oneself. The fifties was
also perhaps the richest period in American religious thought—
particularly Protestant theology—since the time of Jonathan Ed-
wards in the eighteenth century. In the major Protestant
seminaries the decade saw the ascendancy of the body of ideas
variously termed neoorthodoxy, crisis theology, or Christian realism. Influenced greatly by the European-born thinkers Paul Tillich
and Karl Barth, but perhaps even more by the American Reinhold
Niebuhr, neoorthodoxy had first begun to win adherents in the
United States during the thirties, although its teachings did not
become firmly entrenched until after World War II. Repudiating
liberal Christianity's belief in human progress through love,
compassion, and the growth of social morality, neoorthodoxy
restored the traditional Protestant emphasis on original sin and
urged a recognition of man's finiteness, of his inability to achieve
a moral social order, and of the sovereign otherness of an ultimately unknowable God. For Niebuhr, a staunch political liberal,
the major task of man in this life was to work for "proximate
justice" in society, realizing all the while how little human nature
could actually achieve in the way of social betterment. In the
Christian Existentialism of Tillich (who had immigrated to the
United States in the thirties), the task in the modern era of dread
and despair was to attain the "courage to be" in the midst of
human tragedy.

The Protestant theological revival paralleled similar stirrings
in Catholic and Jewish thought. The new intellectual ferment in
religion, together with swelling church rolls, Billy Graham's

mass conversions, and greater outward displays of religious feeling (such as the addition of the words "under God" to the Pledge of Allegiance), seemed to point to a great spiritual rebirth in the United States. Such an assumption was highly questionable. In fact formal theology—more and more an academic discipline pursued in seminary studies—had little direct bearing on religious practice in America. The apex in church attendance followed that of the birthrate by a few years, and then churchgoing, like the birthrate, began a slow decline. The American people, like the rest of Western society, continued to move from theism toward secularism, from the spiritual toward the material. Herberg was probably right when he said that for most Americans religion had become "a religiousness with almost any kind of content or none, a way of sociability or 'belonging' rather than a way of reorienting life to God."

An exception to the homogenization of belief and the decline of piety was the rapid expansion of radical sectarianism or "third-force Protestantism," in the form of such groups as the Churches of Christ, the Assemblies of God, the Seventh-Day Adventists, and the Jehovah's Witnesses. By 1958 the membership of the radical sects was approximately six million in the United States, an increase of some 600 percent over the previous fifty years. Henry Van Dusen, president of Union Theological Seminary, suggested that "Peter and Barnabas and Paul might find themselves more at home in a Holiness service or at a Pentecostal revival than in the formalized and sophisticated worship of other churches, Catholic or Protestant."

VII

Those who worried about conformity, standardization, and other-directedness commonly blamed the mass media—the popular press, advertising, television, radio, motion pictures—even more than public education for what was wrong with American life. By pandering to the lowest common denominator of public taste in an incessant drive for profit, the media had supposedly perverted and debased the fine arts and molded an unthinking and unfeeling mass mind. Much of this criticism had to do with the media's failure to fulfill their responsibility for informing the populace on public issues. The liveliest controversy, however, centered around the effects of the media on creative cultural expression.

Intellectual awareness of what had come to be called "mass culture" or "popular culture" dated from the middle decades of the nineteenth century. By that time improvements in transportation and communication, the growth of cities, the spread of literacy, and the emergence of a sizable middle class had created a mass market for commercial entertainment. By the mid-twentieth century there had accumulated a huge body of material analyzing, attacking, and praising those forms of expression geared to a mass audience. In the fifties, however, the rate of accumulation increased greatly as more and more cultural commentators, social scientists, and journalists struggled to understand and explain the pervasive, transforming consequences of the mass media for American society and culture.

Broadly speaking, the focus on mass culture was only part of the spreading concern over the putatively coercive, enervating effects of modern mass society. There was, though, a more specific reason why after 1950 more words were spent in discussion of mass culture than ever before—the arrival of television as a central fact of American existence. The availability of cheap electricity and the affluence of the period enabled the great majority of Americans to acquire television sets much sooner than they had radio in the twenties and thirties. During the Korean war the Federal Communications Commission froze the number of licensed television stations at 108. By 1956, however, more than 500 stations were in operation, serving some 40 million homes. Nearly all local television stations were affiliated with the three networks—CBS, NBC, and ABC—which had previously dominated radio and had quickly come to control television. By mid-decade advertisers were paying out a billion dollars yearly to the TV networks and their affiliates, twice as much as was going to radio.

Americans exulted in, argued about, and were generally more fascinated by the images on the small glowing screens in their homes than they would ever be again. Except for the drab offerings of the publicly owned stations usually connected with colleges and universities, television programming depended on profit considerations. Among other things, that meant that both networks and local stations followed the pattern of pre-1950 radio programming, presenting a potpourri of soap operas, children's features, newscasts, quiz shows, variety (basically music and comedy) programs, dramatic series, and sports events. Most of what appeared on the picture tube either repeated the stale formulas of radio or plumbed new depths of inanity and tastelessness.

All the same, some people would later look back on the fifties as television's golden age. Television drama, centered in New York City and usually broadcast live from the network studios, was frequently excellent. Such series as "Goodyear-Philco Playhouse," "Studio One," "U.S. Steel Hour," and later "Playhouse 90" first brought recognition to playwrights like Paddy Chayefsky, Horton Foote, and Tad Mosel; to directors like John Frankenheimer, Arthur Penn, and Sidney Lumet; and to actors like Paul Newman, Rod Steiger, Kim Stanley, and Geraldine Page. The early fifties was also the time of the gifted comedy of Sid Caesar and Imogene Coca, of Edward R. Murrow's vivid explorations of public issues on "See It Now," and of the imaginative, wide-ranging "Omnibus" series. The scheduling of "Omnibus" and several other public affairs and cultural programs on Sunday afternoons caused that programming period to be termed TV's "intellectual ghetto."

Television overshadowed all aspects of mass culture in the fifties, yet it was apparent that significant alterations were under way in various other forms of popular expression. Radio, for example, was radically changed by the ascendancy of television. By 1960 network radio had essentially returned to the skeletal condition of the twenties. Radio's daily fare once again consisted almost entirely of music, newscasts, and weather reports originating mainly at the local station level. Seldom given concentrated attention, radio served mostly as a backdrop for daily activities, including the increasing amount of their time people spent in automobiles.

The musical sounds heard on radio in the fifties were often new and strange. Both jazz, which had won critical recognition and mass acceptance in the thirties, and the sentimental, heavily melodic music generically known as "Tin Pan Alley," which had traditionally accounted for most record sales and radio time, lost much of their popular appeal, especially among teen-agers and young adults. Jazz became less danceable, more complex and intellectualist, no longer "hot" but now mostly "cool"—in short, a self-conscious "fine art" attracting cognoscenti all its own. Supplanting jazz and Tin Pan Alley as the music most favored by an unprecedentedly big and affluent youth market was rock 'n' roll. Combining elements of jazz, blues, Tin Pan Alley, and country music, rock 'n' roll featured extraordinarily strong (though not intricate) rhythms and lyrics that were frequently unintelligible. By 1956 America's foremost rock 'n' roll idol was Elvis Presley, a white youth from Mississippi whose raucous singing and pelvic gyrations worked hysterical effects on his young audiences—and caused religious leaders and parents to worry.

For some observers Presley, his music, and the whole phenomenon of rock 'n' roll testified to the bored, restless mood of the nation's youth. For others rock 'n' roll was still more evidence of America's moral and spiritual decay. More important than value judgments, however, was the paradoxical cultural situation presented by the rise of rock 'n' roll. Mass culture, by definition, may have to seek the public's lowest common denominator. But it is also true that by the fifties mass culture had become fragmented and specialized, and now there were many entertainment publics. Rock 'n' roll reached a specialized market; so, in varying degrees, did comic strips and comic books, country music, detective fiction, historical romances, or soap operas. Only spectator sports and the popular magazines—*Look, Life, Reader's Digest*—seemed to reach across generational, economic, and educational lines.

Motion pictures, still one of the most popular forms of mass diversion, were subject to the same process of cultural fragmentation and specialization. After reaching an all-time peak of nearly 100 million weekly customers right after World War II, attendance at movie theaters began to plummet with the advent of television and continued to decline through the fifties. The Hollywood studios, after virtually monopolizing American motion picture production for four decades, began to take massive financial losses. Ordered by the federal courts to discontinue the practice of block-booking (which had forced theater operators to lease a succession of second-rate offerings to get one feature attraction) and to divest themselves of the theater chains they owned across the country, the studios were also intimidated by the congressional Communist hunts of the late forties and early fifties. Most of all they were hurt by television. Desperately trying to lure the customers back, moviemakers turned to such innovations as three-dimensional projection, greatly enlarged screens, stereophonic sound, and more lavish and spectacular productions. But the box office receipts continued to fall, as did Hollywood's film output. From 1946 to 1960 the number of pictures produced annually in the United States declined from about 500 to about 200.

Initially Hollywood's reaction to television was hostile; as late as 1954 Jack L. Warner banned the appearance of television sets in all Warner Brothers productions. The very next year, however, Warners followed the lead of Walt Disney Studios and began to make inexpensive TV films (of which the major early successes were the "Cheyenne" and "Maverick" series), thereby tapping a new source of profits which other major studios were also quick to exploit. By 1960 live TV programming was already scarce, and a mass exodus of television industry personnel from New York to Hollywood was under way.

Meanwhile motion picture content supposedly became more mature, certainly more explicitly violent and more frankly sexual. Except for the Walt Disney pictures, Hollywood made few movies for children, who now got most of their visual entertainment from television. Middle-aged and elderly Americans also tended to stay at home before the TV set, so that the remaining audience for movies consisted mostly of adolescents and young adults, for whom movie-going continued to be part of the ritualized mating process. Much of the controversy over censorship in the mass media shifted from movies to television, with child psychologists and parent groups expressing alarm about the amount of TV violence to which children were exposed.

Meanwhile, like jazz music, motion pictures got increasing attention from intellectuals, who studied "the film" not as a medium for mass entertainment but as an established art form. By the late fifties there existed an avid fandom for the pictures of such early American directors as D. W. Griffith and Charles Chaplin and of contemporary foreign directors like Ingmar Bergman, Akira Kurosawa, and Satyajit Ray. The early work of a group of underground film makers centered in New York had also begun to receive critical attention. The last part of the decade brought a proliferation of "art cinemas" showing "classic films" to small but studious audiences, of journals of film criticism, and of books on film history and technique.

Among those responsible for making American students of movies-as-art more aware of their own film heritage and of what was happening in other countries was Dwight Macdonald, who was also, somewhat contradictorily, one of the most vehement foes of mass culture. Macdonald well fitted Harold Rosenberg's description of such disapproving commentators—people "who keep handling the goods while denying any appetite for them." Macdonald was one of that small but influential body of intellectuals, most of whom had been associated with *Partisan Review,* who fused political radicalism, cultural avant-gardism, and a disdain for what they called "kitsch," the superficial, commercialized art of modern mass society. For Macdonald mass culture was not only bad, it was getting worse and was dragging "high culture" down with it. Kitsch was the mass mind's way of escaping from the terrible realities of the contemporary age. Exemplified by *Life* magazine, which might offer a lavish spread on medieval iconography alongside a picture essay on angry mothers at Little League baseball games, kitsch was a "homogenization process that distributes the globules of cream evenly throughout the milk instead of allowing them to float separately on top. It thus destroys all values, since value judgments imply discrimination." By 1960 Macdonald had even isolated a new virus which he called "Midcult" or "high kitsch"—a self-conscious, devitalized version of the fine arts exemplified by "Omnibus," the poetry and fiction of *Atlantic Monthly,* and the social-message films of Stanley Kramer. Midcult offered no resolution to the irreconcilable conflict between the two cultures, "one for the masses and the other for the classes." It was useless, Macdonald insisted, to try to "fuzz up the distinction with Midcult."

At the other end of the critical spectrum was Gilbert Seldes, who not only handled the goods of mass culture but exhibited a robust appetite for them. A close observer of popular entertainment since the twenties, when he had written his pioneering *The Seven Lively Arts*, Seldes broadened and updated his analysis of what he now called the "public arts." Freely acknowledging the meretricious, tasteless content of much popular culture, Seldes also understood well the constraints operating on the public arts. They were, as he pointed out, "also media of communication, and bring up social questions so important that at times it is hard to remember their primary function as entertainment." Even so, Seldes argued, popular culture offered much that was insightful, enriching, even ennobling. Damned for debasing high culture, popular culture's artistic content was often as high and sometimes higher than what was done in the traditional literary, visual, and auditory forms. Since the public arts were an inescapable part of modern life, Seldes believed that the task of the critic was to understand how they worked and to strive to make them better.

The vast majority of the American consuming public—the "great audience," Seldes called it—knew little of the raging controversy over mass culture's virtues and vices carried on by Macdonald, Seldes, and a host of others. Americans as a whole apparently were willing to take what was available from their media of mass communication and entertainment without worrying about intellectual or artistic content. Some people testified before congressional committees, formed organizations to influence public policy, and otherwise labored to rid mass culture of sex, violence, unorthodox political ideas, or other elements deemed injurious to the nation's moral and ethical standards and patriotic values. But most seemed content to be entertained, diverted, deluded, bored, inspired, or affected in myriad other ways by those forms of expression that reached always for larger audiences and larger profits.

Toward the more formalized, more intellectualized, and more difficult arts—toward high culture—the general public attitude

was more nearly confusion, even bewilderment. The chasm between the public and the fine arts—widening for most of the
twentieth century but narrowed somewhat under the politically
and socially conscious artistic moods of the thirties—yawned
wider than ever in the post–World War II years. Techniques in
the traditional arts became more experimental, content less explicit and less concerned with collective issues and experience.
The outlook of the artist—as critics said so often that the remark
became an intellectual cliché—was characteristically that of the
alienated, isolated individual searching for meaning and identity
in impersonal, brutal mass society.

Much of the artistic output of the fifties seemed directly or
indirectly influenced by European and American existentialist
philosophy and theology, which taught the meaninglessness and
absurdity of modern social existence and thus the necessity for
the individual to seek his purpose—even his salvation—within
himself, not in collective values, ideals, or causes. Clearly evident
in much of the fiction, poetry, and theater of the period, such an
outlook often received its most explicit expression in the writings
of people whose own heritage bespoke futility, despair, and
grotesquery. Especially significant in this connection were the
black writers Ralph Ellison and James Baldwin; Jewish novelists
like Saul Bellow, Bernard Malamud, J. D. Salinger, and Norman
Mailer; and the white southerners William Styron, Carson Mc-
Cullers, Flannery O'Connor, Tennessee Williams, and (at least
in his posthumously published works) James Agee.

Even stronger stuff for the general American audience was the
most critically acclaimed visual and aural art produced in the
period. In painting and sculpture the dominant influence was
Abstract Expressionism, which virtually abandoned the repre-
sentation of life in a commonly recognizable manner. Assuming
that the possibilities of representational art had been exhausted
and that artists must strive for a higher, more personally ex-
pressive reality, painters like Willem de Kooning, Jackson Pollock,
Hans Hofmann, and Mark Rothko produced strange arrangements of paint splashes, daubings, and droplets, usually incom-
prehensible to the untrained eye. The same was true of the
sculpture utilizing welded metal blocks and cylinders, twisted

wire, pasted glass and wood, and other new techniques by Alexander Calder (whose fascinating mobiles had first caused a stir in the thirties) and by younger men like Seymour Lipton, David Hare, and David Smith. Critics won over by such avant-gardism —and almost all were, sooner or later—wrote voluminously in an effort to achieve a systematic body of esthetics for the new visual expressions. Musicologists faced much the same task as they sought to analyze the twelve-tone compositions of Milton Babbitt, Ben Weber, or George Rochberg; the bizarre electronic innovations of John Cage; and the "corporeal" music of Harry Partch, who integrated spoken words with the sounds of new instruments he himself invented using bowls, resonating boards, and up to seventy-two strings.

If music was the most abstract art, an art of pure feeling, then architecture was supposed to be the most public art, combining both beauty and collective utility. And if Western leadership in literature, painting, sculpture, and formal music shifted in the post–World War II years from Europe to the United States, as was often asserted, then this was even more incontestably the case in architecture. The nationwide building boom accompanying the decade's rapid economic expansion made the fifties the most dramatic years in the history of American architecture. Functionalism—pioneered in the United States by Chicago-area designers before 1900 and then powerfully affected by European architects in the twenties and thirties—finally triumphed in American commercial, institutional, and residential building. In commercial architecture the major influence was the International Style, identified especially with the Frenchman LeCourbusier and the German architects who had been associated with the Bauhaus art center. Closed by the Nazis in the thirties, the Bauhaus had given such famed designers as Walter Gropius and Ludwig Mies van der Rohe to the United States. Gropius himself contributed one of the most striking designs of the postwar years, Harvard University Graduate Center (1950); while Mies, already celebrated for his austere buildings at the Illinois Institute of Technology, designed the Lake Shore Apartments in Chicago, completed in 1951. Mies then collaborated with Philip Johnson on the Seagram Building in New York City (1958). The leading firm working in the International Style was Skidmore, Owings, and Merrill, which conceived, among its many outstanding designs in the fifties, Lever House in New York City (1952) and the Air Force Academy at Colorado Springs, Colorado (finished in 1960).

Other architects rebelled against the impersonal, severely rectilinear conceptions in steel and glass of the International Style, although they still held to functionalism's basic ethos of habitability, usability, and structural organicism. Edward Durrell Stone put screens and other decorative effects into his design for the United States embassy in New Delhi, India. Eero Saarinen thought not in terms of the glass boxes of the International Style but in cylinders, spheres, concavities, and other nonrectilinear forms. Such conceptions were manifest in Saarinen's auditorium and chapel for the Massachusetts Institute of Technology (1950–1955), his General Motors Technical Center in Detroit (1955), and Dulles International Airport outside Washington (1960). Meanwhile Frank Lloyd Wright unwillingly took on the role of America's esthetic patriarch. Wright's synthesis of nineteenth-century romanticism, Western functionalism, and Asian and pre-Columbian forms—not to mention his turbulent personal life—had made him a center of architectural controversy for fifty years. Besides continuing to offer his aphoristic judgments on American culture and society, Wright produced a succession of brilliant new designs before his death in 1959. Perhaps the foremost were the ingenious Price Tower office building in Bartlesville, Oklahoma (1954) and the Solomon R. Guggenheim Museum in New York City (1959). Although he had designed a number of other famous commercial and institutional structures over the years, Wright's influence continued to be greatest in residential architecture. It obviously took more money than most people had fully to emulate Wright's conceptions, but by the fifties much home building did embody the Wrightian preference for native wood and stone rather than brick and steel, his practice of integrating a structure into its natural setting instead of altering the setting to fit the structure, and his enthusiasm for flowing, undemarcated interiors rather than closed spaces.

The American architectural achievements of the 1950s testified to the enormous national wealth available to foster the arts. The affluence of the decade remarkably increased both passive enjoyment of and active participation in the arts. What took place was often termed a "cultural explosion." By 1959 there were 160 American symphony orchestras, more than five times as many as in the thirties. An estimated 15 million people listened to the Saturday Metropolitan Opera radio broadcasts, which had so stimulated interest in musical drama that 702 other opera groups had formed across the country. Twice as many Americans (about 28 million) played musical instruments as twenty years earlier. Art galleries and museums drew some 55 million viewers annually, far more, cultural enthusiasts were quick to point out, than went to professional baseball games. Americans might devour such abominable fiction as Grace Metalious's lurid *Peyton Place* (1956) or the nihilistic detective stories of Mickey Spillane, but they also bought the major works of Western literature, now available in cheap paperback editions, by the hundreds of thousands. Some might inundate themselves with the hammering rhythms of rock 'n' roll, but others spent many millions of dollars annually on the new long-playing albums of European and American chamber, choral, and symphonic music—from the familiar, standard works to the previously obscure Baroque compositions of Telemann or Vivaldi.

In short, by the 1950s Americans more than ever consumed culture, much as they consumed the other products of their economy of abundance. Abstract expressionist paintings, fashionable if little understood, graced corporate offices; owners of expensive high-fidelity record players listened perplexedly to avant-garde musical arrangements; housewives bought abstruse literary works from paperback stands in supermarkets. Whether the quantitative growth of cultural activity portended an overall decline of standards and performance or marked the beginning of an American renaissance occasioned ardent discussion in intellectual and artistic circles. One thing was obvious: More Americans had more money to spend on everything. By the mid-fifties the American people, for all their individual and collective anxieties, appeared generally satisfied with their economic system, their political leadership, and themselves. They seemed scarcely interested in ideological controversy, in searching analyses of social ills, or in seeking alternatives to the status quo.

VIII

If such was the popular mood during the Eisenhower years, then it was also in considerable measure the mood characterizing American intellectual life. Feelings of resignation, restlessness, even resentment might mingle with the more general attitudes of satisfaction and complacency; but the fifties was hardly a time when any substantial segment of the intellectual class showed a willingness to challenge the prevailing public ethos formed by the cold war and economic abundance. John Kenneth Galbraith, whose books served ironically to fortify confidence in the existing system, complained that "even the mildly critical individual is likely to seem like a lion in contrast with the general mood. These are the days when men of all social disciplines and all political faiths seek the comfortable and the accepted; when the man of controversy is looked upon as a disturbing influence; when originality is taken to be a mark of instability; and when, in minor modification of the scriptural parable, the bland lead the bland."

If it seems in retrospect that Galbraith exaggerated the degree of intellectual stagnation, it is also the case that many of his con- temporaries shared his estimate. The intellectual climate in Amer- ica may have become more dynamic and variegated after 1957, largely as a consequence of the national consternation caused by the Soviet space and missile successes and the growing feeling that the nation lacked direction and purpose. Yet as late as 1960 the sociologist Daniel Bell could still describe the previous decade as marking "the end of ideology." What had happened, accord- ing to Bell, was that twentieth-century American radicalism— inspired largely by Marxian socialism but also greatly influenced by native non-Marxists like John Dewey, Thorstein Veblen, and Upton Sinclair—had lost its idealistic, utopian vision. For Bell, himself once a Marxist, and for numerous other intellectuals not only in the United States but throughout Western society, the historic radical faith in man and man's future had been irrep- arably blighted by the collective disasters of the previous generation: the rise of Stalinism and the extinction of the Marxist dream in Russia, the barbarities of Nazism and the advent of the most destructive war in human history, the postwar emergence of cold war confrontation and the peril of nuclear annihilation. Confusion and desertion had followed on the ideological left, as more and more disillusioned radicals stopped asking fundamental questions and joined the cold war consensus. Thus the fifties had brought, in Bell's words, an "exhaustion of political ideas."

Bell himself saw no reason to lament the passing of ideology. Intellectuals could now look more realistically and also more hopefully at the United States as a place where ideologies were irrelevant, where the overriding considerations were change and growth. The American system of democratic capitalism, Bell said, had given "one answer to the great challenge posed to Western—and new World—society over the last two hundred years: how, within the framework of freedom, to increase the living standards of the majority of people and at the same time maintain or raise cultural levels."

Eight years before Bell wrote his reaffirmation of the American system, and in the same year that Eisenhower first won the Presidency, the cultural quarterly *Partisan Review* had published a three-issue symposium which became a landmark in the intellectual history of the fifties—especially the history of the reconciliation of American intellectuals with American society and their absorption into the cold war consensus. Beginning as a literary organ of the Communist party, then reemerging in the late thirties as the chief voice for anti-Stalinist radicalism, *Partisan Review* had become a highly respected journal of avant-garde fiction, poetry, and artistic and social criticism. After 1945, however, *Partisan Review*'s anti-Stalinism had begun to overshadow its radicalism, or at least the political content of its radicalism. Thus in organizing their 1952 symposium around the theme "Our Country and Our Culture," the editors of *Partisan Review* revealed how much they had themselves become part of the phenomenon of intellectual reconciliation and reaffirmation.

In their rationale for the symposium, editors William Phillips and Philip Rahv proclaimed that "American intellectuals now regard America and its institutions in a new way. . . . many writers

and intellectuals now feel closer to their country and its culture."
While acknowledging some misgivings about the powerful, often
enervating influence of mass culture, Phillips and Rahv also insisted that intellectuals in the United States must seek their
personal creative values in relation to larger American values,
because "these values . . . represent the only immediate alternative as long as Russian totalitarianism threatens world domination." Most intellectuals, Phillips and Rahv were convinced, "want
very much to be part of American life."

The twenty contributors to "Our Country and Our Culture"
displayed a considerable range of political and cultural opinions.
Norman Mailer, for example, was "shocked" that such a symposium should be held, while C. Wright Mills reminded the
magazine's editors that they would have "cringed" at such an
idea in 1939. More representative, however, were the responses
of the philosopher Sidney Hook and the historian Arthur M.
Schlesinger, Jr. Hook, once a Marxist logician but now a severe
critic of Marxist theory, warned his contemporaries in scholarship and the arts against minimizing "the Communist danger in
its total global impact" because of the wild and irresponsible
behavior of Senator Joe McCarthy. What should intellectuals
in the United States do in the midst of the cold war crisis? They
should "criticize what needs to be criticized in America, without
forgetting for a moment the total threat which Communism poses
to the life of the free mind." Hook saw "grim years ahead," a
period in which the West would need the "support, the dedicated
energy and above all, the intelligence, of its intellectuals if it is
to survive as a free culture." Schlesinger added that "the chief
hope of survival lies in the capacity of the American government
and the strength of American society." He agreed with Phillips
and Rahv that writers and artists now felt closer to America.
Under the menace of international Communism, the intellectual
"has changed his mind about American institutions."

Hook and Schlesinger were both active in the Congress for
Cultural Freedom, an international association of anti-Communist
artists and scholars established in mid-1950, appropriately enough
at West Berlin, the global center of Russian-American confrontation. The mission of the congress was to organize Western

intellectuals in opposition to the repression of political, intellectual, and artistic freedom in the Soviet Union and its satellites. From its inception the congress espoused a militant cold warriorism, so much so that the Central Intelligence Agency soon began secretly to subsidize the organization and its British-based magazine, *Encounter.* While loudly proclaiming the virtues of cultural freedom in the West, the congress also tended to rationalize growing restrictions on such freedom. Concerning themselves with the tactics of McCarthyism, not its basic premises, American intellectuals affiliated with the congress wanted to devise a more "rational" brand of anti-Communism.

In its early years the Congress for Cultural Freedom took the position that political distinctions among foes of Communism were of no great consequence alongside the urgent need for united opposition to the threat from the East. Hook, the first chairman of the American Committee for Cultural Freedom (the United States branch of the congress), foresaw "the era when references to 'right,' 'left,' and 'center' will vanish from common usage as meaningless." By 1956, however, the American Committee had become torn between a liberal, anti-McCarthy faction which included Hook, Schlesinger, Daniel Bell, and the literary critic Lionel Trilling, and a conservative group led by journalists John Chamberlain and Ralph de Toledano and the social theorist James Burnham. Lauding the actions of McCarthy and calling for even sterner measures against suspected subversives, the conservatives finally left the American Committee. After that the organization began to move toward a more sophisticated style of cold warriorism, which favored partial détente with the Soviets but continued to favor a hard-line policy on Asian Communism— in short, toward the foreign policy style that would characterize the Presidency of Eisenhower's Democratic successor, John F. Kennedy.

Yet Hook's prophecy that traditional ideological divisions would become less and less significant was largely borne out in the fifties. The spectrum of intellectually respectable and politically acceptable opinion did narrow dramatically, so that radicalism became something of a dirty word in the American political lexicon. Emerging almost to monopolize admissible thought and practice on the American political left was the New Liberalism, distinctly a product of the cold war environment. The New Liberalism prided itself on its lack of respect for radical ideological constructs, on its tough-mindedness, "realism," and "pragmatism." Articulators of the New Liberalism like Schlesinger, Bell, Max Lerner, Seymour Lipset, and Irving Kristol read the history of the preceding twenty-five years in terms of the tragic failure of mass movements founded on a belief in progress and human improvability. Within the New Liberalism there was a tendency to distrust all mass movements and to see in "populism" the seeds of fascism and other forms of collective paranoia. Banishing their utopian dreams, New Liberals occupied themselves with the moral complexities, ironies, and ambiguities operating to limit what could be accomplished through politics. Bell wrote that his generation had gained "its wisdom in pessimism, evil, tragedy, and despair. So we are both old and young before our time." What liberals must do, Schlesinger had contended as early as 1949 in a major statement of the New Liberalism, was to seek the "vital center" of political life, shunning both mindless reaction and utopian radicalism.

The Protestant theologian Reinhold Niebuhr was unquestionably the most powerful single stimulus behind New Liberal thought. In his personal evolution from qualified Marxian socialism in the early thirties, to vehement antifascism by 1940, and then to militant anti-Communism after World War II, Niebuhr had mapped the way for numerous other American intellectuals. In 1947 Niebuhr was one of the founders of Americans for Democratic Action, which soon became the main organizational focus of the New Liberalism. Through the fifties Niebuhr continued to work to synthesize his neo-Calvinist theology with his democratic liberal politics. Central to his thinking were the concepts of irony and tragedy—the irony of man's predicament in striving as a sinner for earthly perfection, the tragedy of his inevitable failure.

The New Liberalism powerfully influenced not only American political thought, but also the presuppositions and conclusions operating in various fields of humanistic scholarship. In political science and sociology, for example, the major concerns of scholars were with power conflicts among political, social, and economic elites, with status consciousness and status symbolism, and with the origins and functions of the alleged popular disposition toward authoritarianism. Historical scholarship was greatly affected by what came to be called "consensus historiography." A sizable portion of the postwar generation of historians, led by Daniel Boorstin, Louis Hartz, and Richard Hofstadter, found the key to the American past not in the historic struggle between the public interest and vested interests, but rather in the relative absence of meaningful conflict and the persistence of a broad consensus among Americans on values and purposes.

Hofstadter described the political battles of the late nineteenth and early twentieth centuries as essentially shadowboxing exercises among factions which were all committed to the preservation of private property and the promotion of progress through the growth of industry and technology. The major political issues of that time were scarcely issues at all, but reflections of the status anxieties of groups caught up in accelerating social change. According to Hartz, Americans had been "born free," without the need to overcome the apparatus of feudalism which had constrained the European masses. Thus Americans had historically partaken of a "liberal tradition" derived mainly from the political philosophy of John Locke and articulated in their Declaration of Independence. Boorstin saw the "genius" of the American political system in its lack of ideological divisions and its common agreement on first principles. The initial volume of Boorstin's grand reinterpretation of American history, published in 1959, was one long paean to the pragmatic, accommodating spirit of the American people.

Much of what such historians had to say—indeed much of the overall content of the New Liberalism—seemed very close to ideas commonly associated with political conservatism. Yet if political liberalism edged away from the left and toward the center, and if President Eisenhower, with his talk of "modern Republicanism," seemed to be trying to stake out the broad middle for himself, the fifties also saw the appearance of a highly vocal New Conservatism resolutely "on the right" and usually uncompromising in its opposition to the directions taken by

American government and society since the Presidency of Franklin Roosevelt. To be sure, there were important differences in the views of those figures most often identified with the New Conservatism. All of them, however, shared a belief in the sanctity of private property, a fear of centralized power in the federal government, and a basic distrust of popular democracy.

Perhaps the most significant harbingers of the New Conservatism were Walter Lippmann, whose *The Good Society* (1937) had equated New Deal economic planning with the trend toward totalitarianism in Europe, and the Austrian economist Frederick A. von Hayek, whose widely read *The Road to Serfdom* (1944) similarly warned that large-scale government interference with the workings of free-enterprise capitalism inevitably brought social regimentation. Lippmann, though, showed that his concept of the good society involved much more than protecting property rights in *Essays in the Public Philosophy* (1955). In this work, which might be taken as the capstone of his political thought, Lippmann returned to a theme he had first dealt with more than four decades earlier: the alienation of the public from its political institutions under modern mass politics. Because of this alienation, because of the absence of a sense of civic duty, politics functioned in a climate of irrationality and government functioned without effective legal and constitutional restraints. Lippmann placed his hopes in the emergence of an intelligentsia who would assume the role of Plato's philosopher kings, leading society toward an invigorated "public philosophy" based on natural law—those principles "upon which all rational men of good will, when fully informed, will tend to agree."

Lippmann feared big government not just because of its economic power, but also because it tended toward militarism, warmaking, and the repression of civil liberties. In this critical respect he differed from the New Conservatives, most of whom, in their obsessive fear of Communism, called for a bigger military establishment and either rationalized or praised McCarthyite excesses. Among Senator McCarthy's staunchest defenders was William F. Buckley, Jr., who in 1955, at the age of thirty, founded the biweekly *National Review*. Under Buckley's astute editorship the magazine shortly became both a financial success and the major organ of American intellectual conservatism. Acerbic, quick-witted, a member of a large and wealthy Roman Catholic family, Buckley had first won notoriety in 1951 when he published *God and Man at Yale*, an attack on the liberal, allegedly agnostic academic climate at his alma mater. Three years later he collaborated with L. Brent Bozell on a book-length defense of McCarthy. Although Buckley pretty much controlled the editorial policy of *National Review*, the views of the contributors to the magazine varied widely—from the traditionalism of Russell Kirk, to the moderate conservatism of Will Herberg, to the libertarianism of Wilmoore Kendall.

The New Conservatism looked and sounded like a fresh, vital influence. It seemed to offer an antidote and an alternative to a liberalism that had become stale and shopworn. On college and university campuses across the country, "young conservatives," inspired by reading *National Review* and books like Peter Viereck's *Conservatism Revisited* (1949) and Kirk's *The Conservative Mind* (1953), formed organizations to spread rightist views among their fellow students. A mood of conservatism even found its way into some of the prominent fiction of the fifties, notably the novels of John P. Marquand, James Gould Cozzens, and Herman Wouk. Yet the New Conservatism worked little if any influence on public policy. In fact, most writers identified with the New Conservatism were highly critical of the Eisenhower administration's tacit acceptance and furtherance of the collectivist tendencies established during the Roosevelt-Truman years. Moreover, it became increasingly apparent that the New Conservatism's intellectual contributions were slight. Basically what Buckley, Kirk, Viereck, and New Conservatives in general did was to refurbish and reiterate the attacks on modern mass society, mass politics, and "sentimental humanitarianism" made earlier in the century by the band of cultural critics known as the New Humanists. Kirk, often described as the most important conservative writer of the fifties, really added little to the tenets set forth late in the eighteenth century by his philosophical master, Edmund Burke. For all its voguishness and surface vitality, the New Conservatism, like the New Liberalism, testified to the essential sterility of American public thought during the Eisenhower years.

In this age, which commonly equated ideological radicalism with Communist subversion, little remained of radical political and social criticism. There were, though, some voices raised in dissent from the prevailing outlook of acceptance and acquiescence, consensus and conformity. One was the collective wail of the "Beats" against the materialistic, competitive, patriotic ethos of majoritarian America. As the prosperous twenties had had its alienated, world-weary Lost Generation, so the prosperous fifties had its Beat Generation, less a movement than an aggregation of mostly young people centered in San Francisco and New York's Greenwich Village. The Beats took their appellation from "beatitude," the state of spiritual peace some of them claimed to have found in Zen Buddhism and other Eastern religions. Having "dropped out" of conventional society, the Beats flaunted their disdain for the "square world" by growing beards and long hair, affecting bizarre clothing styles, exalting sexual freedom, and experimenting with drugs.

The Beats—or "beatniks," as less liberated Americans called them—proclaimed total disinterest in ideology, programs, or causes. Their most commonly expressed attitudes were of despair, detachment, boredom. Thus their fondness for the subtle and complex rhythms of "cool jazz." The term "beat," in fact, might well have connoted fatigue as much as Buddhist bliss. The self-description of the poet Lawrence Ferlinghetti caught the essence of being Beat: "I was a wind-up toy someone had dropped wound up into a world already running down."

The Beat Generation was thus a protest of resignation and inaction. It did produce a rather substantial body of writing, of which the best examples were the poetry of Ferlinghetti and Allen Ginsberg and the novels of Jack Kerouac. Even so, the Beat phenomenon affected American thinking only indirectly and by way of contrast, as the manifestation of a radical alternative to existing values and life styles. Its main significance was not in the small number of converts it made in the fifties, but rather in the fact that it served as a precursor of the much larger and more challenging cultural rebellion which was to appear throughout the United States in the middle and late 1960s.

Besides the Beats, a handful of professional scholars and nonacademic intellectuals managed to remain outside the New Liberal–New Conservative dichotomy and work in the spirit of radical criticism. One was the philosopher Herbert Marcuse, whose *Eros and Civilization* (1955) was an impressive if abstruse effort to synthesize Freudian psychology and Marxian sociology into a full-scale critique of American political, economic, and social institutions. Marcuse would be one of the major sources of wisdom for the New Left movement of the sixties. So would Paul Goodman, who in *Growing Up Absurd* (1960) explained both the Beats and the rising number of juvenile criminals as products of a society that could offer little to its young people in the way of meaningful education, employment, or standards of behavior.

Perhaps an even more prophetic figure was the sociologist C. Wright Mills, who analyzed not only the predicament of white-collar Americans but also the locus and function of power in the United States. When Mills published *The Power Elite* in 1956, many of his fellow social scientists were writing in praise of the balance, order, and efficiency of the American economy and the stability and durability of the political system. Mills, however, focused on what he saw as quite different realities in American economy and government. For Mills the American political system was not democratic, nor was economic and political power balanced and restrained at the national level. In fact, major national decisions were invariably in the hands of a "power elite" of corporate, military, and political leaders. As a result of the Second World War and the persistence of a semi-wartime economy in the postwar period, this elite had come to hold the "command posts" in American society and to constitute its "power structure." Mills described the power elite as "an intricate set of overlapping cliques [which] share decisions having at least national consequences." Below the power elite were the "middle powers"—labor unions, consumer groups, most politicians, professional associations, and organized property owners. Only at this level did the theory of a pluralistic system of checks and balances actually operate—and then usually to stalemate the various middle powers. At the bottom of the power scale were the great majority of Americans, not a public in the traditional sense, but masses of fragmented, apathetic, vaguely discontented people. Unlinked and powerless, they could exercise no real influence on the decisions that most vitally affected their lives.

The writings of Marcuse, Goodman, and Mills would be frequently quoted (and sometimes misquoted) in the sixties by ardent young advocates of "participatory democracy," "relevant education," and greater personal freedom. In 1956, however, such radical analyses were far too avant garde; not even college students showed much desire to challenge the existing bases of power and authority or the assumptions of the cold war. At the apex of the Eisenhower equilibrium, insofar as they had any interest at all in systematic political thinking, Americans found more congenial those writers who offered reassurances that the system worked basically as it was supposed to work in distributing material goods, responding to popular demands, and generally providing the good life. The Eisenhower crusade had evolved into the Eisenhower equilibrium. In the presidential election of 1956 a big majority of the American electorate would make manifest their endorsement of that equilibrium.

V

Equilibrium Endorsed

THE first half of the year 1956 marked the high point of the Eisenhower equilibrium of the mid-fifties. The surface warmth generated by the Big Four summit conference in Geneva the previous summer could still be felt in Europe and America. President Eisenhower, apparently fully recovered from his heart attack, had announced that he would be willing to run for re-election, and there seemed little doubt that he could again defeat Adlai Stevenson or any other Democrat. At peace and in the midst of a record economic boom, the country appeared generally satisfied and complacent. The journalist Marquis Childs summed up the essentials of what he perceived to be the national mood: "no American boy was being shot at anywhere, our taxes had been cut, and we were on our way to making eight million automobiles in a single year."

I

By 1956 there had developed a widely held notion that mid-century economic abundance was rapidly breaking down class divisions and creating one vast class of comfortably fixed Americans. For the political journalist Samuel Lubell, this "struggle for unification toward the middle class" was the central feature of contemporary American politics. Lubell perceived a "revolt of the moderates" against the rhetoric and symbols which had dominated politics since the New Deal, and which had depicted a sharp clash between the working class and big business. This moderate revolt was particularly advantageous to the Republican party. According to Lubell, the GOP could expand its popular base by bringing together the older middle class, formed mostly in the 1920s and generally Republican already, with the newer middle class emerging out of those segments of the population that still had grim memories of the Great Depression, generally had supported the Democrats, but in their present affluence were losing interest in the hoary issues of the thirties.

In short, there was now a rich opportunity for the Republican party to recapture much if not all of the national popularity and power it had lost as a consequence of the Great Depression. That was the implicit message of Arthur Larson, whose *A Republican Looks at His Party*, published in the spring of 1956, gave him some standing as the ideologist of the GOP in that election year. Larson was a former dean of the law school at the University of Pittsburgh and since 1954 had been Undersecretary of Labor; at the end of 1956 he would head the United States Information Agency. Larson's views closely represented the "moderate" or "liberal" wing of the GOP, which had won the presidential nomination for Eisenhower in 1952 and now found itself in effective control of the party hierarchy.

President Eisenhower, Larson proclaimed, was building a "New Republicanism," which eschewed both the standpattism of the earlier GOP and the extreme welfare statism of the New Deal and Fair Deal. For the New Republicanism the central reality of the times was the economy of abundance. While intervening when necessary to see that all shared in that abundance, the federal government must not interfere with the innovative, expansive, and creative impulses of private enterprise. Thus the key to the New Republicanism of the Eisenhower administration was balance. The President had placed himself at the "authentic American center," the meeting ground for the majority of citizens who formed the "American Consensus."

In the early months of 1956, despite his heart attack the previous fall, Dwight Eisenhower gave every appearance of a man who was eager to reap the harvest of Larson's American consensus. The President was at the peak of his personal popularity, having easily surmounted a succession of potentially damaging situations which might have meant considerable trouble for a less overwhelmingly admired leader. By far the most serious of these situations was the hotly controversial Dixon-Yates affair.

The Dixon-Yates controversy arose from a combination of two factors: the expanding electrical power needs of the Atomic Energy Commission for its operations in the Tennessee River Valley region and the general animus of the Republican party and the Eisenhower administration toward the Tennessee Valley Authority (TVA), the federal corporation established in the early New Deal period to provide power to the valley. The Atomic Energy Commission obviously had to have more power, whether from TVA or some other source. In a series of statements in the summer of 1953, the President denounced "creeping socialism" and made it clear that what he had in mind was TVA's effort to extend its power monopoly by building a steam plant at West Memphis, Arkansas. Alternatively, the administration favored partnership arrangements between Washington, the states, and private interests in providing electrical power and other kinds of essential services. In September 1953 Adolphe Wenzell, an investment firm executive hired by the Bureau of the Budget to study TVA, proposed that private power companies, not TVA, supply whatever additional electricity AEC needed. At this juncture President Edgar Dixon of the Middle South Utilities Corporation and President Eugene Yates of the Southern Company formed a combine to seek a government contract for the West Memphis steam plant. They planned to supply power to both the city of Memphis and AEC, thereby obviating any further TVA expansion. Wenzell's First Boston Corporation would provide the capital for the Dixon-Yates project.

In June 1954 Eisenhower followed the recommendation of Budget Director Rowland Hughes and instructed AEC to negotiate a contract with Dixon-Yates. Almost as soon as the contract was signed in October, public power advocates went on the attack. Republican William Langer of North Dakota spearheaded a Senate investigation, while Democratic Senator Lister Hill of Alabama uncovered Wenzell's dual role as a government consultant on power development and a member of the firm that was to finance Dixon-Yates. The Democrats, playing on the slogan "Nixon, Dixon, and Yates," used the issue with some effect in regaining control of Congress in 1954.

Eisenhower had not known beforehand of the conflict of interest involving Wenzell. After eight months of embarrassing delay, the President finally found a way out when Memphis officials, afraid that they would have to pay higher electrical rates to Dixon-Yates, announced that the city would build its own generating plant. Claiming that such local initiative exemplified the kind of partnership he had wanted all along, the President in July 1955 ordered AEC to cancel the Dixon-Yates contract. Subsequently AEC used the Wenzell matter in arguing successfully against the Dixon-Yates combine's federal suit to force AEC to pay its expenses while the contract was in force.

The two major issues raised by the Dixon-Yates affair were the conflict of interest between private employment and public service, and the conflict of philosophy between advocates of hydroelectric power development by private interests and advocates of government ownership of power sources. Conflict of interest came up again during the first Eisenhower administration in the case of Secretary of the Air Force Harold Talbott, who had to resign in August 1955 when it became known that he had used his influence to win business for an engineering firm in which he was a partner. The philosophical conflict over power development manifested itself again in the controversy over the Hell's Canyon site on the Snake River boundary between Oregon and Idaho.

Spurred by rapid industrial and population growth and frequent electrical brownouts in the Pacific Northwest, the Truman administration had planned federal construction and operation of a high dam and generating complex at Hell's Canyon. The private Idaho Power Company contended vigorously that it could do the job better with three smaller dams. Although Eisenhower favored private development from the beginning as part of his partnership approach, it was August 1955 before the Federal Power Commission (FPC) granted a fifty-year license to Idaho Power. Organized advocates of public power like the National Hell's Canyon Association and the National Rural Electric Cooperative Association protested to FPC that the three-dam plan would be inadequate for the Northwest's power needs. Eventually a federal appeals court turned down their suit to annul FPC's decision. They also failed to get through Congress bills authorizing a federal project at Hell's Canyon. At least for the Snake River region, the Republican partnership philosophy remained in force.

Eisenhower's personal popularity suffered little if any because of the Dixon-Yates episode, the Talbott case, or the Hell's Canyon decision. Nor did two notable vetoes in the first part of 1956 hurt his prospects for reelection. The first killed a bill exempting the price of natural gas shipped through interstate pipelines from control by FPC. Pushed by representatives from the gas-producing states of Texas and Arkansas, the bill had passed the House in 1955 behind a coalition of southern Democrats and midwestern and western Republicans. Northeastern representatives, both Democrats and Republicans, had opposed it because they feared higher prices for gas consumers. In the deliberations in the Senate on the natural gas bill, Republican Francis Case of South Dakota disclosed that a lawyer for the gas interests had offered him a $2,500 bribe. The bill nevertheless passed the Senate by a substantial margin. Although Eisenhower had originally favored the measure, by the time it reached the White House the Case disclosure and press accounts of other pressure tactics by the gas interests had persuaded the President that the bill was a product of "arrogant" lobbying methods. On February 17, 1956, he sent it back to Congress with a stinging veto message. Pro-Eisenhower sentiment nevertheless remained preponderant in the Southwest, especially in Texas.

The second veto had more serious political implications. In the spring of 1956, with farm income declining and agricultural surpluses still piling up in government storage facilities, the Democratic majority in Congress was able to pass a new farm bill which restored the 90 percent parity level for major commodities. Heeding the counsel of Secretary of Agriculture Benson that the bill was extravagant and unsound, Eisenhower sent it back to Congress, which sustained his veto. The President's action was a bold move in an election year. Alarmed farm-belt

Republicans looked to the administration for some kind of alternative that would enable them to go into their campaign with their heads up. What the administration offered was no alternative at all, but only a reworked version of a section in the original bill fathered by Senator Hubert Humphrey. Humphrey had proposed that the government make cash payments to agricultural producers who would let portions of their land lie fallow. This proposal now became the basis of the administration's Soil Bank plan, which passed Congress in June with bipartisan support. The Department of Agriculture would have $750 million a year to pay producers for putting acreage into the Soil Bank, while another $450 million a year would go to encourage the use of untilled acreage for conservation purposes.

The Soil Bank Act allayed some discontent in the major grain, cotton, and tobacco producing areas, but it proved no more effective than any of the other legislation passed since 1929 in curbing farm surpluses. Family farm income continued to be generally lower than that of the rest of the population. In political terms, however, what was most important was that Eisenhower remained essentially immune to farm discontent, almost all of which centered on Secretary of Agriculture Benson. For the eight-year duration of Eisenhower's Presidency, the ultraconservative, bluntly spoken Benson served quite effectively as a lightning rod on agricultural policy.

II

Early in June, while the Democrats were thrashing through a succession of hard-fought presidential primaries, Eisenhower suffered another physical setback. This time an attack of ileitis, a severe inflammation of the lower intestine, necessitated emergency surgery for the President. Again he proved to have remarkable recuperative powers. Eisenhower quickly let GOP leaders know that he still intended to seek another term, and an examination by Paul Dudley White's team of specialists showed that his heart was in good shape.

Of course no Republican would dare challenge Eisenhower's claim on the presidential nomination. The Vice Presidency, though, was another matter. Next to Henry Wallace, Roosevelt's wartime Vice President, Richard Nixon had been the most active Vice President in the country's history. Besides performing several important assignments for the President and campaigning vigorously in the 1954 congressional elections, he had won praise from the press, many of his fellow Republicans, and even some Democrats for the circumspect but effective way he had carried on during Eisenhower's convalescence in the fall of 1955. All the same, the relationship between Nixon and Eisenhower, though cordial, never became close. Eisenhower, according to Emmet John Hughes, once said privately that Nixon "just hasn't grown up," and that he could not believe Nixon was "Presidential timber." The President seems to have favored Deputy Secretary of Defense Robert Anderson for his running mate in 1956. Moreover, Sherman Adams and John Foster Dulles, the two people closest to Eisenhower within the administration, evidently had suspected Nixon's motives during the period immediately following Eisenhower's heart attack. These men and others around Eisenhower viewed Nixon as an opportunist. They had been perfectly willing for the GOP to benefit from Nixon's continuing exploitation of the Communism-in-government issue, but they found his Red-baiting personally distasteful. One of the strongest arguments they had used in urging Eisenhower to run again was that Nixon would likely be the party's choice to succeed him.

Eisenhower's remarks in his first press conference after his February 29 announcement hardly constituted a ringing vote of confidence in the Vice President. No one could tell him to "dump somebody," Eisenhower said, and he hadn't tried to tell Nixon what to do. He had only asked him "to chart his own course and tell me what he would like to do." By this time Eisenhower had suggested to Nixon that he might want to become Secretary of Defense after the resignation of Charles Wilson, who had let Eisenhower know that he wished to leave the administration after the election. At this point, however, the only course which interested Nixon was continuing as Vice President. Eisenhower's unwillingness to give him an explicit endorsement so distressed Nixon that he would later write of this period as one of the "six crises" of his public career.

For all his annoying ambiguity, Eisenhower had enough political acumen to see that Nixon would again help his candidacy. Now on better terms than ever with eastern moderates in the GOP, Nixon still retained strong ties to the Republican right. Any effort to replace him with someone closer to the President might revive the Taftite fervor of 1952. So argued Senate Minority Leader William Knowland, GOP National Chairman Leonard Hall, and key figures on the Republican National Committee. Although for several more weeks Eisenhower talked about leaving the vice presidental choice to the Republican convention in San Francisco, he finally let Nixon announce on April 26 that the President wanted him on the ticket.

That seemed to settle the matter—but not quite. In July Harold Stassen, formerly Mutual Security Administrator and at the time Eisenhower's Special Assistant for Disarmament Studies, mounted a one-man campaign to deny Nixon the nomination. Stassen was a somewhat anomalous figure in the Eisenhower administration. Once a young and popular governor of Minnesota, then a delegate to the charter session of the United Nations in 1945, and still later president of the University of Pennsylvania, Stassen had become a perennial aspirant to the Presidency, and he still had strong ambitions for national leadership. Idealistic and outspoken, thought eccentric by many people in Washington, Stassen favored a more flexible foreign policy than the administration had pursued, pushed hard for more peace initiatives, and ardently supported the UN. Stassen personally disliked Nixon; beyond that, citing the results of his own private poll, he argued in a conference with Eisenhower that Nixon's presence on the ticket would diminish the President's national support by as much as 6 percent. In place of Nixon, Stassen advanced Governor Christian Herter of Massachusetts.

Again to Nixon's chagrin, Eisenhower did nothing to stop Stassen from holding a press conference to announce his dump-Nixon campaign. The President even began to talk once more about an open convention at San Francisco. Stassen intensified his efforts, claiming that Herter could give the national ticket the broad appeal it must have to win in 1956. Yet it became increasingly apparent in the weeks before the Republicans convened on August 20 that Stassen spoke for hardly anyone but himself. Congressional Republicans and the party hierarchy continued to back Nixon, and Eisenhower finally abandoned his caginess shortly before his own renomination on August 22. Following another conference with Stassen, the President announced that his Special Assistant for Disarmament was convinced the majority of delegates wanted Nixon.[1] That night Herter placed Nixon's name in nomination for the Vice Presidency, urging the delegates not to "break up that winning team." Stassen seconded the nomination.

The flurry caused by Stassen's persistent but quixotic efforts to dump Nixon provided the major excitement at San Francisco's Cow Palace. The President was in undisputed control, and the GOP platform clearly expressed his middle-of-the-road views. Above all the platform was a safe document. It lauded the administration for bringing prosperity without war, for resisting Communism at home and abroad, and for showing a budgetary surplus ($1.75 billion) at the close of fiscal year 1956. The Republicans pledged to continue opposing the admission of Communist China to the United Nations, to aid farmers and small businessmen, and to support statehood for Alaska and Hawaii. The platform said only that the GOP "accepts" the Supreme Court's 1954 school desegregation ruling in the *Brown* case; there was no explicit endorsement. The Republicans also promised to work for passage of the civil rights program proposed by the administration earlier in the year but thus far stalled in Congress.

In his acceptance speech on the night of August 23, Eisenhower invited independents and "discerning Democrats" to "come in and help" Republicans give the country four more years of peace and prosperity. At the same time, he admonished members of his own party to stop quarreling over the past and concentrate on present and future questions. While acknowledging that government must serve the public good, the President repudiated the idea of "a tight federal monopoly on problem-solving." As for civil rights, the President spoke proudly of steps taken in his administration to desegregate the armed forces and public facilities in the District of Columbia. Not once, however, did he mention

---

1. Eisenhower had agreed to meet with Stassen only if Stassen agreed to endorse Nixon.

the *Brown* decision, nor did he say anything about voting rights for southern blacks or federal responsibility to move against racial discrimination in employment, housing, and interstate transportation. Vague, even evasive, yet also brimming with confidence, Eisenhower's acceptance speech basically offered more of the same. As the Democrats would soon learn, however, that was plenty for the majority of Americans in 1956.

If anything, the task confronting the Democratic party that year was tougher than in 1952. Meeting in Chicago the week before the GOP's San Francisco gathering, the Democrats had again chosen Adlai Stevenson. Putting aside the Hamlet-like role he had played before the 1952 Democratic convention, Stevenson had begun his drive for the renomination the previous fall. Again his major rival had been Senator Estes Kefauver of Tennessee. Meanwhile Governor Averell Harriman of New York had bided his time, hopeful that Stevenson and Kefauver would neutralize each other or that one of them would drop out.

Beginning in New Hampshire in March, Stevenson and Kefauver had joined battle in a series of grueling, often bitter presidential primary campaigns. Kefauver made a strong early showing, winning handily in New Hampshire and Minnesota. In April, however, Stevenson polled some 700,000 votes in Illinois, his home state, while Kefauver's write-in campaign produced only about 28,000 votes. Stevenson went on to defeat the Tennesseean in the New Jersey, Oregon, and Florida primaries before crushing Kefauver's hopes by gaining 68 delegates in California's primary early in June. Unable to gather significant backing in states where delegates were chosen in state party conventions and deserted by Democratic leaders even in his own state, Kefauver finally gave up and endorsed Stevenson. At that point Harriman announced his candidacy. His most important support came from former President Truman, still angry over the reluctance of Stevenson and his managers to invite him into the 1952 campaign and convinced that Stevenson would make an even weaker candidate now than four years earlier.

In 1956, as in 1952, the Democrats refused to take a strong stand in favor of civil rights out of fear of provoking another 1948-style southern walkout. Kefauver wanted a platform that called for full enforcement of the Supreme Court's school de-segregation decision, while Harriman advocated withholding from states with segregated systems any funds Congress might appropriate for educational purposes. Stevenson, on the other hand, favored a gradual approach to desegregation. The report finally submitted by the Platform Committee and adopted by the convention did not even go that far. It merely stated the monu-mental truism that the *Brown* decision had "brought consequences of vast importance to our nation as a whole and especially to communities directly affected."

Most of the rest of the 1956 Democratic platform was equally mild. The Democrats did denounce Republican favoritism toward big business and, in what had become something of a party ritual, advocate repeal of the Taft-Hartley Act. Parity guarantees for farmers should be returned to the levels of the Truman years, and people in the lower income brackets should get tax relief. Otherwise the Democratic platform proposed no major breaks with existing policies, foreign or domestic.

Despite Truman's endorsement of Harriman and the general skepticism about whether Stevenson could do any better than he had in 1952, the convention gave the former Illinois governor the presidential nomination on the first ballot. Abandoning the tradi-tional practice by which the presidential nominee picked his own running mate, Stevenson decided to throw the choice of a vice presidential candidate before the convention. In so announcing, Stevenson pointed out that seven Vice Presidents had succeeded to the Presidency when the elected chief executive died in office, thus inferentially raising the question of Eisenhower's health.

What followed was the most exciting political event of the whole year, as Kefauver, Senator John F. Kennedy of Massachus-etts, and several other contenders scrambled to secure delegates. Kennedy, though a Roman Catholic and a moderate liberal, had the support of most southern delegates. At the end of two ballots he had a substantial lead over Kefauver. Before the final second-ballot tally was announced, however, Senator Albert Gore, Ke-fauver's fellow Tennesseean, withdrew in favor of Kefauver. The Tennessee, Oklahoma, and Missouri delegations then switched their votes, giving Kefauver the nomination by a narrow margin.

The combination of the moderately liberal Stevenson and the more consistently liberal Kefauver seemed to give the Democrats an extraordinarily strong ticket. But Eisenhower and the Republican leadership knew better. The Stevenson-Kefauver ticket, Eisenhower later wrote, "was probably the weakest they could have named." For the Democrats to have any chance at all in 1956, they somehow had to match Eisenhower's ability to appeal to voters across class, regional, and ethnic lines. Perhaps no Democrat could have significantly undercut the President's enormous popularity. Certainly the Stevenson-Kefauver ticket, repugnant to much of the white South and to conservative Democrats in general, was not suited to the task.

Stevenson's campaign was hardly the kind that would win over undecided voters. On the advice of the party professionals, he left off trying to educate the electorate, as had been his style in 1952, and tried to be more plainspoken and gregarious. Worn down by the long preconvention struggle with Kefauver, Stevenson seemed to become sluggish, even bored as the campaign ground on. Meanwhile Eisenhower appeared vigorous and ebullient. After undergoing another thorough physical examination in October, the President heard from his physicians that he was in excellent health.

Stevenson's efforts to generate voter interest sometimes led him into inconsistencies and contradictions. On various occasions he charged that the administration's New Look policy had weakened the nation's overall defense capability; NATO, he said, had been allowed to drift and decay. Terming the 1954 Geneva settlement on Indochina "a debacle," Stevenson grimly observed that fully half the region was now a "new Communist satellite." In general the administration had missed chances to "exploit weaknesses" in the Communist bloc.

Yet before a highly unsympathetic audience at the American Legion convention in Los Angeles, Stevenson advocated ending the military conscription program and establishing an all-volunteer army. He followed in October with a proposal that the United States enter into agreements with the Soviet Union and Great Britain to halt hydrogen bomb tests. On-site inspections, Stevenson maintained, were not absolutely necessary because test-ban violations could be detected by seismographic and other means. Eisenhower retorted that any test-ban agreement unaccompanied by adequate inspection safeguards would be a "design for disaster." The whole discussion involved technical questions which confused many people, a fact that worked to the advantage of the Republicans, who could remind voters that Eisenhower knew best when it came to military matters.

Afraid to attack the President directly, the Democrats had to resort to questioning his health at the same time that they trained their fire on his "heir apparent," Vice President Nixon. Could America afford a "part-time President?" asked Stevenson. The untrustworthy Nixon, a "man of many masks," would be waiting to take over the Presidency from a sick Eisenhower. On election eve Stevenson even predicted that if Eisenhower were reelected Nixon would likely assume the Presidency within the next four years.

The effort to make Eisenhower's health a campaign issue probably damaged Stevenson's chances more than it helped.[2] Newspaper photographs and television coverage in the weeks before the election continued to show the President as vigorous and in good spirits. Meanwhile Nixon, mostly abandoning the vituperative rhetoric that had marked his earlier career, carefully cultivated an image of moderation. Nor were Democrats able to capitalize much on the quite evident unhappiness of agricultural producers with Secretary of Agriculture Benson. Stevenson did pick up a modest amount of support in the Great Plains, but such gains were more than offset by a considerable shift among black voters to Eisenhower. Representative Adam Clayton Powell, Jr., who had pressured the administration into desegregating southern military bases, spoke in Eisenhower's behalf, and most of the leading black newspapers backed the President.

IV

In the final phase of the campaign Stevenson and the Democrats hammered away at John Foster Dulles and Republican

2. Ironically, Eisenhower, though ten years older, would outlive his two-time opponent by three and a half years. Stevenson would die in 1965—of a heart attack.

foreign policy. Here they seemed on surer ground, for the week
before the election brought almost simultaneously two diplomatic
crises, the severest the country had faced since the Formosa
Strait face-off with China in 1954–1955. Both gave the Democrats
a chance to charge that the administration's policies were confused, misdirected, even, as Stevenson said, "bankrupt."

One crisis had been building since late the previous July, when
President Gamal Abdel Nasser of Egypt had ordered the nationalization of the previously British- and French-dominated Suez
Canal. By seizing this commercial lifeline of Europe, Nasser had
brought on a perilous situation in which the British and French,
despairing of restoring their control over the canal through
negotiations, had undertaken military action against Egypt in
connivance with the state of Israel. The assault on Egypt by
Great Britain, France, and Israel in the last days of October and
the early part of November severely jeopardized the relationship
between the United States and its major allies, raised the prospect
of a Soviet-American confrontation over the Middle East, and
called into question the whole basis of American policy in the
area.

The essential feature of that policy was to try to maintain a
balance of power among the Arab states and between the Arabs
and the Israelis in the interest of preventing the growth of
Soviet influence. The balance-of-power approach represented a
significant departure from the Truman-Acheson Middle Eastern
policy, which had been to provide military and political support
for Israel and to safeguard British and French economic interests.
By contrast, the Eisenhower administration, especially after the
Iranian coup d'état in the summer of 1953, aimed to dissociate the
interests of the United States from those of Great Britain and
France and to cultivate Arab friendship by taking a neutral stance
in the Arab-Israeli conflict. Eisenhower and Dulles brought to
their offices a strong distaste for what was left of Anglo-French
colonialism in the Middle East and elsewhere. And while they
always had to consider the powerful emotional ties American
Jews and many non-Jewish sympathizers had to Israel, whose
creation in 1948 the United States had sponsored, the President

and Secretary of State also wanted to get the Arabs to band together to resist Russian designs on the Middle East.

Before 1956 the Eisenhower administration's policy seemed to be working fairly well. In an effort to build good relations with Egypt, the administration had urged the British to reach an agreement with President Nasser on the evacuation of British troops from the huge Suez military base. Though resentful of such pressure, the British finally agreed to pull out in the fall of 1954. Dulles then revived a scheme originally proposed in 1951 for a Middle Eastern defense alliance, aimed at the Soviets. By October 1955 Dulles had managed to get Turkey, Iraq, Iran, Pakistan, and Great Britain to sign a treaty setting up a Middle Eastern Treaty Organization, commonly called the Baghdad Pact. Though not a formal signatory of the treaty, the United States would give military aid to the Baghdad Pact countries and otherwise support the new alliance system.

Nasser refused to cooperate with the pact, which he considered a threat to Arab solidarity. Although Egypt had already outlawed the Communist party, Nasser drew a firm line between his domestic and foreign policies, and seemed to be forming closer ties with the Soviet bloc. Early in 1955 a destructive Israeli raid against the Gaza Strip, an Egyptian-controlled territory serving as a base for Arab guerilla operations against Israel, demonstrated the weakness of Egypt's military forces. Trying to shore up his defenses, Nasser secured a large quantity of armaments from Czechoslovakia in exchange for a shipment of Egyptian cotton. Dulles reportedly went into a tirade on hearing of the Egyptian-Czech arms deal; the Eisenhower administration nevertheless refused to fill Israeli orders for additional military equipment to balance the Egyptian buildup. Instead, Dulles held out to Nasser the prospect of American financial and technical assistance in fulfilling Nasser's plans for a vast dam and hydroelectric plant at Aswan on the Nile River, about 800 miles south of Cairo. The Aswan Dam project was the central feature in Nasser's long-range program for developing his country's industrial and agricultural capabilities; Aswan had also come to symbolize his emerging leadership in the Arab world. Early in 1956 the

Egyptian president indicated that he was ready to conclude an agreement whereby the United States would put up an initial $56 million to finance the dam, with the British providing another $14 million.

The administration soon ran into trouble on Capitol Hill. Congressmen with large Jewish constituencies were naturally reluctant to commit American money toward making Israel's principal foe even stronger. Southern congressmen feared that the increased Egyptian cotton production made possible by irrigation from the Nile's waters would still further shrink the South's share of the world cotton market. Others complained about the cost of the Aswan project. Eisenhower and Dulles themselves began to have second thoughts in the spring, after Nasser stepped up his trade with the Soviet bloc countries and then, withdrawing recognition from Chiang Kai-shek's Nationalist Chinese government, established diplomatic relations with the mainland Communists. The latter move particularly angered Eisenhower. Meanwhile the British began to hedge on their contribution to the Aswan loan.

During meetings with the National Security Council held the second week in July at his Camp David, Maryland, mountain retreat, the President revealed that he had decided to withdraw the Aswan offer. The decision was essentially Eisenhower's, and Nasser probably knew that he was going to be turned down even before Dulles announced the cancellation of the loan on July 16. Yet Dulles personally took almost all the blame for what looked at the time like an abrupt, even capricious shift of policy. Although the initiative for the reversal on Aswan came from Eisenhower, the Democrats, the national and international press, and even lower-echelon officials within the administration immediately assumed that the cancellation of the loan was another instance of the Secretary of State's moral posturing and messianic anti-Communism.

The administration was determined to make Nasser choose between having his dam or continuing his arms buildup and his campaign to unite the Arab states against Israel. Nasser, however, surprised the United States and its allies by neither abandoning the Aswan project nor immediately seeking a loan from the

Russians. What he did do, within ten days after Dulles's announcement, was order the seizure of the Suez Canal. By this move the Egyptian leader not only restored his prestige in the Arab world but also gained control over the annual profits of some $25 million derived from canal tolls. Nasser proclaimed that the canal revenues would go toward building the Aswan Dam.

The effect of Nasser's action on the British and French governments was little less than traumatic. Convinced that the Egyptians lacked the technical skills to operate the canal and fearing that Nasser would close the waterway and thus deprive them of the oil shipments they had to have, the British and French began discussing military moves against Egypt. British Prime Minister Anthony Eden warned Eisenhower that Britain might have to resort to force. Retaining their composure with some difficulty in the aftermath of the takeover, Eisenhower and Dulles proposed the formation of an international users association to insure free access to the canal. Neither the British, the French, nor the Egyptians would have anything to do with such an arrangement.

As months of futile negotiations dragged by, London and Paris became increasingly impatient with the American leadership. In the American view there was no justification for force as long as the canal remained open to Western shipping. From the vantage point of Great Britain and France, however, the longer Nasser kept control of the canal the greater the danger that he would close it. Equally disturbing was the direct challenge Egypt had raised to waning British and French power and the dangerous precedent for nationalizing their vestigial colonial assets embodied in the canal seizure.

Besides preventing war in the Middle East, the Eisenhower administration's main objectives were to avoid alienating Nasser any further and to protect American oil interests in Iraq and Saudi Arabia, countries whose hitherto friendly policies Nasser might be able to change. Moreover, Eisenhower and Dulles did not completely trust the motives of America's allies in the Middle East. While their positions as colonial powers had been severely eroded since the Second World War, the British and French retained extensive economic interests in various Arab countries, interests that sometimes conflicted with those of the United States. The administration's Middle Eastern policy thus combined traditional American anticolonialism with a highly solicitous attitude toward American oil companies and a transcendent fear of the expansion of Russian influence.

By October the British and French had completely lost patience with both the United States and Egypt. A pretext for moving against Nasser finally came on the twenty-ninth, when the Israeli army, in an effort to put an end to eight years of Arab guerilla harassment, drove into the Sinai Desert and toward the canal. The next day Great Britain and France officially warned the Israeli and Egyptian governments to keep the fighting at least ten miles away from the canal. As the Israelis blasted their way across the Sinai and as Egyptian forces took up positions on either side of the canal, British and French aircraft began bombing Egyptian air bases. On November 3, Anglo-French troops landed at Port Said on the Mediterranean and began fighting their way inland toward the nearby canal. The Egyptians retaliated by blocking the canal with sunken ships, while the Syrians blew up pumping stations along the oil pipelines leading from Iraq to the Mediterranean coast. Although the British and French pretended to be acting only in defense of their interests at Suez, there is every evidence they knew beforehand that the Israelis would attack and carefully coordinated their military operations with Israel's. Meanwhile they kept the Americans totally ignorant of their plans.

The reaction in Washington was one of initial befuddlement, followed by shocked outrage. Having only recently reported "good news from Suez," Eisenhower was privately furious. Publicly he declared that "there can be no law if we were to invoke one code of international conduct for those who oppose us and another for our friends." The President and Secretary Dulles sadly discussed the American predicament of having, as Dulles put it, "to choose between following in the footsteps of Anglo-French colonialism in Asia and Africa, or splitting our course away from their course." Britain thought it "simply *had* to react in the manner of the Victorian period," Eisenhower disgustedly wrote a friend. Canceling a windup campaign tour of the South, the

President stayed at the White House to keep in close touch with the mounting crisis. To compound his troubles, on November 2 Dulles, just back from the United Nations debates in New York, entered Walter Reed Hospital with intense stomach pains. Exploratory surgery showed that he had a malignant growth in his abdomen. His surgeons removed as much of the cancer as they could, and the White House, without revealing the true nature of the Secretary's illness, announced that the operation had been successful. Undersecretary of State Herbert Hoover, Jr., temporarily assumed Dulles's duties.

As early as October 30 Ambassador Henry Cabot Lodge had put before the UN Security Council a resolution urging the major powers not to use force and calling on the Israelis to evacuate Egyptian territory. One of the strangest scenes of the cold war era followed. Both the French and British delegates vetoed the resolution, while the Soviet Union voted with the United States. Lodge, joined by Secretary Dulles, then took the American case before the UN General Assembly under the Uniting for Peace Resolution, adopted in 1950 as a device for circumventing the Russian veto in the Security Council. On November 2 the General Assembly voted 64-5 to demand a cease-fire and Israeli withdrawal. The administration followed up its moves in the UN by embargoing oil shipments to France and Britain.

Meanwhile the Russians proposed joint Soviet-American action to halt the Anglo-French-Israeli "aggression" against Egypt. Eisenhower termed such a step "unthinkable" and warned that the United States would use force to prevent Russian interference in the Suez war. In turn Nikita Khrushchev, who had emerged as the dominant figure in the Soviet government, warned the leaders in London and Paris that unless the Anglo-French forces stopped their advance on the canal, the USSR's new long-range missiles would destroy them. This threat did what American admonitions and UN resolutions had not been able to do. On November 6, with the canal almost within their grasp, the British and French governments agreed to a cease-fire and began pulling back their troops. The embittered Israelis soon agreed to do the same.

The Suez imbroglio was a dreadfully embarrassing experience

for both the United States and its foremost allies. Although the Western Alliance had not been ruptured, it had been subjected to the most rigorous strains of the post–World War II period. To the British and French, Dulles was the villain of the whole messy affair, the man responsible for the ill-conceived Aswan loan, for canceling the loan and precipitating Nasser's seizure of the canal, and then for formulating America's hypocritical response after the outbreak of the Suez war. At home the Democrats made the same accusations in the last days of the presidential campaign. Moreover, they were able to couple their charges of bungling over Suez with denunciations of Dulles and the Republicans for the American government's helplessness during the other great crisis in the fall of 1956, that brought on by the Hungarian rebellion against Soviet domination. If the Suez crisis embarrassed American policy, what happened in Hungary was—for a party and an administration that had come to power proclaiming the goal of liberation for Russia's eastern European satellites—an international humiliation.

The Hungarian revolt was a direct consequence of the loosening-up process within the Soviet empire which had begun after the death of Stalin early in 1953, and then had accelerated in 1956. The crushing of the East German uprising in the summer of 1953 should have removed any doubts about Moscow's determination to maintain ultimate control over its satellites. Outwardly, though, Russian policy appeared to continue to soften. In February 1956, at the Twentieth Congress of the Russian Communist party, Nikita Khrushchev delivered a long recapitulation of the "crimes of the Stalin era." While insisting on the inevitable triumph of "socialism," he also reiterated what he and Nikolai Bulganin had said in a joint declaration with Tito the previous spring in Yugoslavia: That different countries might choose "separate roads to socialism." Finally, Khrushchev suggested that further relaxation of the tight internal and external restrictions of the Stalin period was in the offing. The speech was supposed to remain secret, but in succeeding months reports of its contents filtered into the West. In June the State Department published what seemed to be a bona fide text.

In the satellite countries, especially Poland and Hungary, anti-

Russian elements quickly became militant. In June an outbreak of riots in the Polish city of Poznan brought not intervention by Russian armor but the arrival of Russian emissaries willing to talk about compromise. By October 21 Khrushchev had agreed to the installation of Wladyslaw Gomulka, an independent, as head of the Polish Communist party. While Poland continued to be governed by the Communist party, remained in the Warsaw Pact, and professed its friendship toward the USSR, the Poles had won a degree of control over their own affairs unknown in the rest of the Soviet empire.

In Hungary events moved much faster and further, and ended not in partial victory but in bloody defeat. On October 23 fighting began in the streets of Budapest, the Hungarian capital. Bands of students and workers attacked government buildings, captured and shot members of the Communist police, and destroyed statues and portraits of Stalin and Lenin, Russian flags, and every other symbol of Soviet rule they could find. At first the rebels demanded that Imre Nagy, an imprisoned Communist moderate, be brought back to head the government. This concession Khrushchev was willing to permit. But as the disturbances continued in Budapest and then spread over the country, what had begun as a revolt became a revolutionary movement which aimed to overthrow Communist rule and end the Russian presence in Hungary. By October 28, yielding still further, Krushchev had ordered the withdrawal of Soviet tanks to the outskirts of Budapest.

In this supreme test of the doctrine of liberation, the American response was cautious and vague. On hearing of the outbreak of fighting early on the morning of the twenty-third, Dulles is supposed to have said excitedly, "The great monolith of Communism is crumbling." But publicly the administration, while praising and encouraging the Hungarian "freedom fighters" in general terms, carefully avoided the question of possible American intervention. There had, in fact, never been any time since they came into office when Eisenhower and Dulles had seriously considered using military force to break the Russian grip on the satellite countries of Europe. Speaking to the UN General Assembly less than three months after the 1953 East German revolt,

Dulles had stated that American policy "does not call for export-
ing revolution or inciting others to violence. Let me make that
emphatic. . . . We put our hopes in the vast possibilities of
peaceful change." In a speech in Dallas four days after the
beginning of the Hungarian revolt, the Secretary of State did
offer economic aid to countries that threw off Russian domination, but he went on to say that the United States did not regard
such countries as potential military allies. The American leaders
knew, as did nearly everyone else, that American military action
in eastern Europe would almost certainly mean World War III.
After a Republican rally in New York on the night of October 25,
Eisenhower confided his dilemma to the journalist C. L. Sulzberger: "Poor fellows, poor fellows, I think about them all the
time. I wish there were some way of helping them."

During the Hungarian rebellion the State Department's Voice
of America propaganda outlet in Europe generally followed the
circumspect administration line. The nominally private, CIA-
financed Radio Free Europe (RFE), however, began broadcasting
militant calls to arms into Hungary as soon as it received news of
the uprising. Not content with Nagy's assumption of the premiership, RFE's powerful transmitters repeatedly urged the Hungarians
to fight on until Communism was totally destroyed. Help from
the West, RFE insisted, was on the way.

Radio Free Europe's reckless exhortations apparently helped
embolden many Hungarians into trying to transform their rebellion into a revolution. In any case, the Soviets finally reached the
limits of what they would tolerate. On October 30—the same day
the British and French governments warned the Egyptians and
Israelis to keep away from the Suez Canal—Moscow radio broadcast a declaration that the USSR was willing to withdraw all its
forces from the eastern European countries if they so wished.
The statement drew no comment from Washington. The next day,
as the British and French began their attacks on Egyptian air-
fields, Nagy announced that Hungary would pull out of the Warsaw Pact. That was too much for Khrushchev and his generals,
now faced with the prospect of the dissolution of the whole
eastern European empire the USSR had built so carefully and so
ruthlessly after 1945. Taking advantage of the confusion and

acrimony in the Western capitals over the Suez war, Khrushchev on November 4 ordered Soviet armored units to move back in and crush the Hungarian "fascists." Some 30,000 Hungarians and 7,000 Russians died in the bitter conflict that followed. Another 200,000 Hungarians managed eventually to make their way to western Europe and the United States. Nagy was captured and taken to Moscow, where a Russian firing squad executed him in 1958.

As the fighting raged in the streets of Budapest and in the countryside, the United States could do little more than protest. The UN adopted an American resolution deploring the Soviet intervention and calling for withdrawal, while Eisenhower personally appealed to Bulganin, still titular head of the Soviet state, to let the Hungarians alone "in the name of humanity and in the cause of peace." Bulganin replied that Hungary was none of the United States' business. To the end the rebels sent out teletyped messages pleading for American help. As the dream of revolution died in Hungary, so also finally died the Republican myth of liberation.

V

On election day, November 6, the mopping-up process was still under way in Hungary, while in Egypt the British and French troops had begun to pull out. The Democrats had scored some telling rhetorical points against Eisenhower-Dulles foreign policy at the end of the campaign. Yet in 1956 the American people, as they had on previous occasions in their history, showed a disposition to stay with the existing national leadership at a time of acute international tension. Eisenhower doubtless would have won anyhow, but it seems clear that the twin crises in the fall of 1956 turned what would have been a fairly easy victory into a landslide for the President. Winning every state but seven, Eisenhower amassed 457 electoral votes to Stevenson's 74. Although the President lost Missouri, which he had carried in 1952, he won Louisiana, the first Republican to do so since the Reconstruction period. Eisenhower's total popular vote was nearly 35,600,000, Stevenson's slightly more than 26 million. Nearly 58 percent of the voters chose the President. Again Eisenhower showed great strength in the cities and among ethnic minorities. He also made substantial gains among black voters. Adam Clayton Powell's Harlem district gave Eisenhower 16.5 percent more votes in 1956 than in 1952, the President's vote increased 11 percent in the biggest black congressional district in Chicago, and overall his support among blacks was up 5 percent, to some 47 percent of all black voters.

Yet the 1956 election also demonstrated once more that Eisenhower's popularity was far greater than his party's. The Democrats held their 50-46 margin in the Senate and won 233 House seats to the Republicans' 202. When the Eighty-fifth Congress convened in January 1957, a President beginning a new term would face opposition majorities in both houses for the first time since 1848. Moreover, the Democrats won half the governorships at stake in 1956.

The year 1956 had begun with Eisenhower still semiconvalescent and with the country doubtful about his political future. When it ended he was about to begin his second term, having been overwhelmingly reelected. At the beginning of the year America's international relations had been relatively quiet. Twelve months later its alliance with Great Britain and France was in disarray, its objectives in the Middle East had been frustrated, and the Soviet Union's bloody suppression of the rebellion in Hungary had given the lie to the crusading rhetoric behind the administration's foreign policy. Yet despite Dixon-Yates, despite the continuing slump in the agricultural economy, and despite the fundamental doubts raised by the Suez and Hungarian debacles, most Americans were still willing, as the Republican slogan urged, to "trust Ike." At the close of 1956 the Eisenhower equilibrium remained intact.

The next two years, however, would bring rapidly multiplying troubles both abroad and at home. The Eisenhower administration would never be able to get the Middle East back to the status quo ante Suez. Again the United States and China would skirt war over the offshore islands. In Berlin the Soviets and the Americans would move toward their most dangerous confrontation since 1949. At home there would be recriminations and soul-searching over Soviet space successes, mounting anxiety over the alleged gap between Russian and American missile capabilities, and the President's agonized decision to use federal troops to integrate a Little Rock, Arkansas, high school. Eisenhower's relations with the Democratic congressional majorities, generally amicable in 1955–1956, would become increasingly difficult. The President's closest subordinate, Sherman Adams, would have to leave the administration after still another conflict-of-interest disclosure. Meanwhile the economy would slide into a full-scale recession, and the 1958 congressional elections would bring the worst defeat the Republican party had suffered since 1936. At the halfway point of Eisenhower's second term, little would be left of the Eisenhower equilibrium.

VI

Breakdown of the Eisenhower Equilibrium

DWIGHT Eisenhower's first presidential term ended on January 20, 1957, although the formal inauguration of his second term was not scheduled until the next day. In taking the oath of office in closed ceremonies at the White House on the twentieth, Eisenhower became the first President affected by the provisions of the Twenty-second Amendment to the Constitution, submitted by a Republican Congress in 1947 and ratified by the required three-fourths of the states in 1951. Intended to prevent a repetition of the four terms won by Franklin Roosevelt, the amendment prohibited anyone from being elected President more than twice. In general the second terms of previous Presidents had been more strife-ridden and less successful than their first, and one might have supposed that Eisenhower's second four years would follow this historical pattern. Yet there was also speculation after the election of 1956 that the constitutional limitation itself would be enough to make the next four years an inconclusive lame-duck period. Not only Democrats but also perhaps right-wingers in the President's own party would feel free to work openly against his policies in the assurance that, whatever happened and however popular Eisenhower remained, they would not have to contend with him after 1960.

If such speculations bothered Eisenhower, he gave no sign of it. Implicit in his inaugural address, delivered on January 21 to a smaller and more subdued crowd than he had faced in 1953, was his intention to continue strong leadership in foreign affairs. After repeating the swearing-in procedure with Chief Justice Earl Warren, the President solemnly urged his countrymen to be willing to make the sacrifices and bear the burdens of leadership in the ongoing struggle between Communism and the "free world." Not total victory over Communism, but "peace with justice," was the way Eisenhower described the goal of his administration. The United States must stand ready to "help others rise from misery, however far the scene of suffering may be from our shores." Even though the rhetoric continued to be messianic, it was fairly clear that when Eisenhower spoke of uplifting others he no longer had in mind the liberation of eastern Europe, or any other area already under Communist control. Rather, his speech suggested what would be one of the major thrusts of his second term: stepped-up attention and assistance to the "underdeveloped" and "uncommitted" nations of Asia and Africa in an effort to block the spread of Soviet and Chinese influence.

I

There could be little question of the strength of Russian ambitions in the Middle East, where American policy was in deep trouble in the aftermath of the Suez war. While the United States had strongly condemned the Anglo-French attack on Egypt, the Russians could claim, with considerable justification, that they had actually compelled the Allied withdrawal from the Suez area. Rapidly expanding their naval power, the Soviets were in a position to establish an increasingly potent presence in the eastern Mediterranean. Short of military confrontation, there was not much the United States could do to thwart the USSR's drive toward the warm-water regions. American policy should, however, operate more effectually toward the Arab countries themselves.

Both Russians and Americans tried to exploit Arab nationalism. The Soviet aim was to persuade the Arab leaders that they must drive out the Western "imperialists," while the Americans sought not only to align as many Arab governments as possible against the threat of Russian "aggression" but also to convince them that their policies should remain independent of Gamal Abdel Nasser's Egypt and Egypt's ally Syria. In the fifties both the United States and the USSR produced most of the oil they consumed; of the relatively small quantities the United States imported, little came from the Middle East. Western Europe, however, was heavily dependent on Middle Eastern oil. Ultimately, Western policy makers feared, the Russians might be able to wield enough influence in the Arab world to effect a squeeze on Europe's oil imports, split the NATO countries, and force major changes in the European power arrangements.

The Suez war virtually destroyed what little influence the French had managed to retain in the Middle East after World War II, while the British position was greatly weakened. The United States, as a result of the Aswan loan cancellation and its refusal to countenance force against Britain, France, and Israel in the Suez war, had incurred the long-term enmity of Egypt and Syria. The American government remained on good terms, however, with Lebanon and Jordan, and with the major oil-producing states of Iraq and Saudi Arabia. In January 1957 Eisenhower, breaking diplomatic precedent, went to the airport to greet King Ibn Saud of Saudi Arabia when he arrived for a state visit. After being lavishly entertained for several days, the king agreed to continued American use of the air base at Dhahran in exchange for pledges of substantial military aid.[1]

The United States still refused to become a formal member of the Baghdad Pact on the grounds that such a step would antagonize most of the Arab states. Eisenhower and Secretary of State Dulles did move, however, to commit the United States more deeply in the Middle East and also, as in the Formosa Strait crisis two years earlier, to secure greater presidential authority for military action without consulting Congress. On January 5 Eisenhower asked Congress to approve a joint resolution authorizing him to use up to $200 million in economic and military assistance to preserve "the independence and integrity of the nations of the Middle East," and also to use American armed forces in support of any Middle Eastern state facing "overt armed aggression from any country controlled by international communism."

---

1. Eisenhower also assured Ibn Saud that the United States would station no Americans of Jewish ancestry at Dhahran.

Quickly dubbed the "Eisenhower Doctrine," the President's proposal came under much closer scrutiny and critical examination than had the Formosa Resolution. Both the Senate and House held protracted hearings, which brought out considerable criticism of Secretary Dulles and the administration's whole Middle Eastern policy. The most effective point made by the administration's critics was that there was little danger of a Soviet military blow in the Middle East; the threat, they argued, was really Communist subversion and infiltration, about which the Eisenhower Doctrine said nothing. Dulles answered in the congressional hearings and before the press that the United States could not make agreements to protect countries against Soviet political penetration without becoming involved in local disputes, that there was in fact a danger of Russian overt armed aggression, and that the Soviets would be hesitant to move either openly or subversively in the Middle East if they knew beforehand that they faced prompt and vigorous American counteraction. Dulles proved a most persuasive advocate, while the Democratic congressional leadership again swung into line behind administration foreign policy. Early in March the Senate (72-19) and the House (350-60) approved the Eisenhower Doctrine with minor modifications. The President signed the joint resolution into law on March 9.

The Baghdad Pact nations—Great Britain, Turkey, Iraq, Iran, and Pakistan—fully backed the Eisenhower Doctrine, but of the other Arab states only Lebanon formally endorsed it. Israel also announced its support for the new policy declaration, although Eisenhower and Dulles, again trying not to rile the Arabs, had carefully excluded the Israelis from the doctrine's provisions. It was of course Israel—or rather the unwillingness of the surrounding Arab countries to tolerate the existence of the Israeli state—that accounted for most of the difficulty American policy encountered in the Middle East. However much the Eisenhower administration might blame the Russians for the unsettled condition of Middle Eastern affairs, as long as American policy included the preservation of the state of Israel, the administration's goal of a united Arab front to resist Russian penetration remained fanciful. With every demonstration of Israeli power, such as the

Gaza Strip raid and the Suez war, the Egyptians and Syrians moved closer to the USSR, while Arab governments friendly to the West found it that much harder to keep down rising pro-Nasser emotions among their peoples.

In the immediate post–Suez war period the Israelis aggravated matters by their procrastination in giving up the Egyptian territory they had overrun after October 29. At the beginning of 1957 Israel still held the Gaza Strip and key positions on the Gulf of Aqaba to the south. The administration tried as best it could to pressure the Israelis into full withdrawal, but its means were limited since American aid to both Egypt and Israel was already suspended. Eisenhower and Dulles considered, and finally rejected, a suggestion for a UN resolution against the raising of private financial contributions for Israel; according to the Treasury Department, American citizens were annually sending about $40 million to the Jewish state and buying an additional $50–$60 million in Israeli government bonds. The President finally went on national television and radio to call on the Israelis to get out of Egypt. Both Senate Majority Leader Lyndon Johnson and Minority Leader William Knowland publicly disagreed with the President's stand. Meanwhile the Lebanese UN delegate proposed economic sanctions against Israel, and other nations called for an Israeli withdrawal. In the face of growing international opposition, Israeli UN Ambassador Golda Meir announced early in March that her country's forces would pull back to their boundaries in exchange for the stationing of UN personnel to police the Egyptian-Israeli cease-fire. With the Israelis out, the Egyptians began dredging operations to free the Suez Canal of the ships Nasser had ordered scuttled to block it the previous fall. Remaining under Egyptian control, the canal reopened to the traffic of all countries except Israel.

Another urgent matter before the administration early in 1957 was patching up relations with its two foremost allies. The French never really forgave the Americans for taking sides against them during the Suez intervention. After Charles de Gaulle came to power in 1958, he would use the events of the fall of 1956 as an object lesson illustrating the necessity of France's conducting its foreign policy independently of the United States and developing its own nuclear capability. Britain, on the other hand, seems to have drawn from its Suez adventure the lesson that it was no longer a first-class power. After 1956 the British tacitly accepted a role of dependence on the United States in both foreign policy and defense.

Meeting in Bermuda in March 1957, Eisenhower and Harold Macmillan, successor to the ill and harassed Anthony Eden in the aftermath of the Suez fiasco, greeted each other warmly and gave every indication that Anglo-American relations were again in good order. The two leaders agreed that the United States would build rocket bases in England and Scotland and supply the British government with Thor intermediate-range (1,800-mile) ballistic missiles. The missiles would both extend the forward nuclear striking power of the United States and, according to official pronouncements, give the British the capability to stand up to threats such as the Soviets had made during the Suez crisis. Back at home, however, Dulles assured congressional leaders that the United States would keep absolute control over the warheads and firing mechanisms.

As Eisenhower and Macmillan refurbished the Anglo-American alliance, as the Israelis began to evacuate their remaining positions in Egypt, and as the Eisenhower Doctrine became operative, the Arab kingdom and former British protectorate of Jordan became the new Middle East trouble spot. Yielding to the demands of ultranationalists within his country, Jordan's young King Hussein ended his alliance with Great Britain. In April pro-Nasser Jordanian army officers demanded Hussein's abdication. Although Eisenhower and Dulles quickly assumed that Egypt and Syria were behind the unrest in Jordan, they obviously lacked grounds for invoking the Eisenhower Doctrine. The President nonetheless ordered the Sixth Fleet to move from the French Riviera into the eastern Mediterranean and pledged Hussein an initial $10 million in military aid. Backed by this American show of force, the king was able to put down the dissidents. The next month another $20 million for military purposes came from the American government, which now assumed the British role of watching over Jordan.

Shortly after the situation in Jordan stabilized, Syria, still professing "positive neutralism," received a large arms shipment from the USSR together with hundreds of Russian military instructors and technicians. In August militantly anti-Western army officers took over the Syrian government and expelled three officials of the American embassy accused of subversive activities, whereupon the Eisenhower administration sent the Syrian ambassador home. More airlifted American military equipment arrived in Jordan as well as in Turkey, Syria's northern neighbor and the United States' NATO and Baghdad Pact ally. In the UN Syria's foreign minister warned that Turkish troops were massing along its border, while in Moscow Nikita Khrushchev proclaimed that the Soviet Union would intervene if Syria were invaded. On October 14, in a show of solidarity, a detachment of Egyptian troops landed on the Syrian coast. The situation became very tense indeed three days later, when Dulles stated explicitly in a press conference that the United States would retaliate directly against the Soviet Union if the Russians moved against Turkey. Then, on October 28, Khrushchev attended a reception at the Turkish embassy in Moscow and said to the assembled diplomats that "there will be no war." After that the Middle East again quieted down somewhat.

The Syrian-Turkish crisis—if it could be called that—not only dramatized the depth of Russian and American commitments in the Middle East, but also helped polarize power arrangements in the area still further. On February 1, 1958, Egypt and Syria formed the United Arab Republic (UAR), a single state with Nasser as president. One of Nasser's first acts was to outlaw the sizable Syrian Communist party, the only political faction in Syria opposing the merger with Egypt. In fact, as the Central Intelligence Agency reported to Eisenhower, the Syrian army had pushed for the union with Egypt to counter growing Communist influence. In the confused world of Middle Eastern politics, here was a sharp reminder—usually lost on cold war policy makers and military leaders in the United States—that the basis for Egyptian and Syrian ties to the Soviet Union was not a liking for Communism but a search for outside support in furthering intensely nationalistic ambitions.

Within two weeks after the formation of the UAR, the pro-

Western kings of Jordan and Iraq, with Washington's strong approbation, federated into the Arab Union. Thus by the spring of 1958, instead of an Arab consensus in opposition to the Soviets, there had emerged two rival blocs—one supported by the USSR, the other by the United States. Although the governments of the oil-rich states were still friendly to the West, they also remained unremittingly hostile toward Israel. And in every Arab country anti-American sentiment appeared to be growing.

II

If the American position in the Middle East was shaky in 1957, at home Eisenhower's relations with the Democratic-controlled Eighty-fifth Congress were even shakier. The first half of the year witnessed what journalists called the "great budget battle"—a curious spectacle in which a President who had worked hard for less costly government and had accused the Democrats of fiscal profligacy found himself having to fight to save his budget from meat-ax cuts by both Democrats and Republicans. Even more than the volatile situation in the Middle East, where growing Soviet-American rivalry had severely undermined the partial East-West detente of 1955–1956, the abrasive quarrel between Eisenhower and Congress over the budget promoted the rapid breakdown of the Eisenhower equilibrium.

The early part of 1957 marked the high point of what Eisenhower, in his election-night remarks the previous November, had called "modern Republicanism." A week after his victory the President defined modern Republicanism as "the political philosophy that recognizes clearly the responsibility of the Federal Government to take the lead in making certain that the productivity of our great economic machine is distributed so that no one will suffer disaster, privation, through no fault of his own." The $71.8-billion budget for fiscal year 1958, which he sent to Congress in January, embodied the essential features of middle-of-the-road Republicanism. The biggest budget ever drawn up in peacetime, it contained generous provisions for federal school-construction grants, for the development of water resources, and for the expansion of existing social welfare programs. The Defense Department and the foreign aid program, while still accounting for close to 60 percent of all federal expenditures, got only moderate increases. The total budget exceeded that of fiscal 1957 by almost $3 billion, but the President anticipated that continuing prosperity and record peacetime tax revenues would leave a $1.8-billion surplus, which should go toward retirement of the national debt.

At this point Eisenhower's fear was that the "spenders" in Congress would disregard his goal of a balanced budget and pile on lavish new appropriations. He was especially concerned about the annual appearance of the Joint Chiefs of Staff during the congressional budget hearings, supposedly to defend the specified spendings levels but actually to plead for more money for their individual services and projects. While preparing the fiscal 1958 budget, Eisenhower remarked sourly that the Chiefs "don't know much about fighting inflation. This country can choke itself to death piling up military expenditures just as surely as it can defeat itself by not spending enough for protection." As he later admonished the Republican congressional leadership, "There is no defense for any country that busts its own economy."

In a news conference on January 16, the same day the budget went to Capitol Hill, Secretary of the Treasury George Humphrey described the administration's spending requests as "a terrific amount" and bemoaned "the terrific tax take we are taking out of the country." If the government continued to spend at present levels for a long period, Humphrey predicted, "you will have a depression that will curl your hair." When asked about Humphrey's prophecy, Eisenhower properly pointed out that he and the cabinet had helped Humphrey prepare the statement, and that Humphrey had not said a depression was inevitable but only that one could happen if present expenditures continued on a long-term basis. But then he added that he was sure the congressional committees could "find some place where [we] might save another dollar." It was, he said, Congress's duty to do so.

Frustrated by his inability to hold down spending in the face of rising costs and the Pentagon's constant demands for more money, Eisenhower honestly wanted Congress to consider the budget carefully and make prudent cuts where they seemed appropriate. What he and Humphrey had done, however, was to prompt more charges of divided and muddled thinking within the administration, and in effect to invite Congress to hack away. Joined by Republican rightists who had never been happy with the administration's tacit acceptance of welfare statism, the Democratic congressional leadership prepared a full-scale assault on the budget.

From Speaker of the House Sam Rayburn, from House Minority Leader Joseph Martin and Senate Minority Leader William Knowland, from Chairman Harry F. Byrd of the Senate Finance Committee, and from various other leading figures on Capitol Hill in both parties came claims that the budget could be reduced by as much as $6.5 billion. Rayburn talked of a tax cut as well. The economizers went after the foreign aid and overseas propaganda allocations with particular vengeance. Senate Majority Leader Johnson sarcastically quizzed Arthur Larson, the new director of the United States (formerly International) Information Agency, as an expert witness on the subject of modern Republicanism.[2] Both Democrats and Republicans attacked the Eisenhower administration's foreign aid program as wasteful and mismanaged. Even Pentagon spending came in for sharp criticism and some fairly substantial trimming.

By the spring the administration had become alarmed over what was happening to the budget. On April 18, in a formal letter to the House of Representatives, the President warned that "in these times a cut in current expenditures for national security and related programs would endanger our country and the peace of the world." In conferences with congressional leaders and in numerous telephone calls to Capitol Hill, the President and the White House staff pleaded for restraint. Eisenhower made two television appearances in May to defend his overall budget and in particular the section on mutual security, which, he argued, was no international giveaway but a practical substitute for bigger American military forces. Again and again he reminded his critics that three-fourths of all the money given other countries went

2. Larson, of course, had used the term "New Republicanism" in his 1956 book, *A Republican Looks at His Party*.

either for direct military assistance or for defense support. Almost all of the arms purchased with American money, he also pointed out, were manufactured in the United States.

Despite the administration's strenuous efforts, the appropriations bill finally passed in August represented Eisenhower's worst setback in his dealings with Congress. Fiscal 1958 appropriations totaled $4 billion less than the President's requests. The mutual security budget of $3.8 billion had been cut by $1.1 billion, while USIA came out with only $90.2 million, 38 percent less than had been originally allocated. The Defense Department's appropriation of $33.7 billion was $2.4 billion less than the administration had budgeted. Even with these reductions, however, there was no accompanying tax cut. By the time Congress finished with the budget, the economy had begun to slump and tax revenues had dropped. Thus the administration now projected a half-billion-dollar deficit instead of a tidy $1.8-billion surplus.

The budget battle was scarcely the sum of Eisenhower's troubles with the Eighty-fifth Congress in 1957. An administration-favored bill for school-construction grants died because it carried a rider banning federal assistance to racially segregated schools. And the administration's civil rights bill, although it passed, came to the President substantially modified. Nonetheless, Eisenhower, the GOP, Senate Majority Leader Johnson, and the northern Democrats could all claim credit for the first legislation in the field of civil rights since 1875.

While Eisenhower had strong apprehensions about the Supreme Court's 1954 school desegregation decision and had no use for those who, as he described them in his memoirs, "believed that legislation alone could institute instant morality," he did feel deeply that every American citizen was entitled to the right to vote. At the beginning of 1956, in his State of the Union message, he had promised to have Attorney General Herbert Brownell draw up civil rights legislation for Congress to consider that session. Not submitted until April, the administration proposal would have outlawed interference with the efforts of black people to vote in federal elections, set up a new Civil Rights Division in the Justice Department, and created a bipartisan Civil Rights Commission to make inquiries and general recommendations.

After passing the House in July, the administration bill went to the Senate Judiciary Committee, chaired by the archsegregationist James Eastland of Mississippi. There it remained when the session ended.

During the 1956 campaign the President had said little about his stalled civil rights program. But at the beginning of the next year—buttressed by his lopsided reelection margin, urged on by Brownell, and facing a new Congress—Eisenhower again sent a civil rights measure to Capitol Hill. This one was considerably tougher and more specific than the 1956 bill. Besides setting up a Civil Rights Division and a Civil Rights Commission, the administration's new bill would have empowered the Justice Department to lodge suits in behalf of blacks denied their rights and would have suspended jury trials for persons held in contempt of federal court for interfering with the civil rights of others.

By 1957 the chances for such legislation had greatly improved, primarily because Lyndon Johnson, leader of the Senate Democrats, had decided that the time had come to use his powers of persuasion and coercion in behalf of civil rights. The previous year Texan Johnson and Estes Kefauver had been the only two southern Senators declining to sign the Southern Manifesto, in which one hundred senators and representatives from the South denounced the Supreme Court's ruling against segregated schools and pledged legal resistance to this "clear abuse of judicial power." All the same, Johnson's image among northern Democrats, both black and white, remained that of an anti–civil-rights southerner. Ambitious for the Democratic presidential nomination in 1960, Johnson knew that he must shake off this stereotype and gain a much greater degree of national identification. The proposed civil rights bill afforded an excellent opportunity. At the beginning of the congressional session he announced to his fellow senators that some kind of legislation pertaining to civil rights would pass that year.

Both contemporary observers and later students of his career have maintained that Johnson was more responsible than anyone else for the Civil Rights Act of 1957. If so, then it is equally true that he was mainly responsible for a succession of compromises

which, while they may have facilitated the bill's passage, significantly weakened its original content. The key compromises had
to do with Section III, which gave the Justice Department the
authority to sue violators not only of voting rights but of other
civil rights as well, and also suspended jury trials in contempt
cases. Trying to convince his southern colleagues in the Senate
that some law was inevitable and also working to accommodate
their strongest objections, Johnson helped muster a 52–38 majority to restrict the Justice Department's sphere of action to cases
involving voting rights. Eisenhower and Brownell resignedly
agreed not to press this point for the rest of the session. It seemed
that the provision for suspending jury trials was about to suffer
the same fate. On this item, however, Eisenhower and Brownell
were more determined. As they were fully aware, if trials were
held with juries recruited from white southerners, it would be
impossible in most instances for federal prosecutors to get convictions. Citing thirty-six different existing laws that denied jury
trials in cases of contempt of the federal courts, they, along with
Senate Minority Leader Knowland, urged the Senate to keep
what was left of Section III.

By early August it seemed that no civil rights legislation at
all would get out of the Senate. The National Association for the
Advancement of Colored People and other leading black organizations and individuals protested that the administration bill
had been gutted. "We disagree," the recently retired baseball star
Jackie Robinson wired the President, "that half a loaf is better
than none. Have waited this long for bill with meaning—can
wait a little longer." At this point the Republican leadership in
the Senate suggested leaving the question of jury trials for de-
fendants in voting-rights contempt cases up to the local federal
judges. Without a jury trial, according to this new proposal, the
maximum sentence would be 90 days in prison and a $300 fine;
with a jury, six months and $1,000. Johnson informed Eisenhower
that he could deliver a majority for a compromise provision
stipulating a maximum penalty of 45 days and $300 in cases where
the judge chose not to empanel a jury. The President agreed.
Johnson's compromise was also acceptable to the House of Rep-

resentatives, which passed the amended bill 279–97. The Senate, by a vote of 72–18, sent it to the White House on August 29.

The complex bill Eisenhower signed into law eleven days later fell considerably short of what he had proposed in January. Even watered down, though, the Civil Rights Act of 1957 was an important step toward full citizenship for black Americans. A six-member Civil Rights Commission did come into being, as did a new Civil Rights Division in the Department of Justice. While the Attorney General lacked the power to initiate suits against suspected violators of blacks' voting rights, the federal district courts were authorized to hear any civil action brought by a person who claimed his rights had been abridged. And at least something of the original jury-trial-suspension clause had been salvaged.

Privately Eisenhower had worked hard for the law and, in his conferences with congressional leaders, had shown a good grasp of the tangled legal issues involved. Yet in this instance, as in the case of the Bricker Amendment and other controversial measures before Congress, his public comments suggested a lack of understanding, even interest. Again Eisenhower had followed his preference for unobtrusive, almost covert procedures in dealing with Congress, and had revealed his distaste for dramatic gestures to rally public support. The value of such strategy was highly questionable. One thing was certain: Lyndon Johnson, not the President and his party, got the major political advantage from the 1957 legislation. Eisenhower had still avoided close personal identification with the civil rights issue.

That same September, however, Eisenhower finally had to act publicly and forcefully where the aspirations of black people were concerned. At Little Rock, Arkansas, he faced the most serious domestic crisis of his Presidency, one that featured a head-on clash between federal and state authority over racial desegregation in the public schools.

Earlier in the summer, when a newsman asked whether he would be willing to use force to implement court-ordered school desegregation in the South, Eisenhower replied, "I can't imagine any set of circumstances that would ever induce me to send fed-

eral troops . . . into any area to enforce the orders of a federal
court, because I believe that the common sense of America will
never require it." At that time the school board in Little Rock was
about to put into effect a plan approved by Federal District Court
for admitting nine black students to the city's all-white Central
High School. Shortly before the school term opened, a group of
local whites brought suit in an Arkansas court to delay imple-
mentation of the desegregation plan. Governor Orval Faubus,
who had refrained from exploiting racial feeling up to that time,
now testified in the state court that the integration of Central
High School would lead to bloodshed. The Arkansas court issued
an injunction against the school board, whereupon the Federal
District Court reaffirmed its order that the board's plan must be
carried out. On the opening day of school Faubus ordered a detachment of the Arkansas National Guard to take up positions outside Central High and block the entrance of the black
students.

Here was the kind of federal-state impasse Eisenhower had
dreaded ever since the *Brown* decision. At Newport, Rhode
Island, on one of his frequent (and increasingly criticized) golf-
ing vacations, Eisenhower received news of Faubus's defiance.
After intense discussions he and his aides invited Faubus to fly
to Newport for a conference. Afterward Faubus claimed that the
President had promised not to use force in the Little Rock situation, while Eisenhower and Sherman Adams contended that the
governor had promised to withdraw the National Guard and
pursue his opposition to integration in the federal courts. Whatever was actually agreed upon, Faubus did remove his troops,
and on September 23 federal officers secretly escorted the black
students into the high school building. An enraged white mob
then gathered outside, while inside the blacks were beaten and
insulted. Within three hours they had been removed.

At last Eisenhower acted. On September 24 he issued a formal
proclamation denouncing the Little Rock disturbances and ordering the mob to "cease and desist" and "disperse forthwith."
When this order was not enough to keep the mass of shouting,
unruly whites from returning to the high school, the President took
two additional steps: He federalized the Arkansas National

Guard, thereby bringing it directly under his command, and ordered a thousand paratroops from the famed 101st Airborne Division to occupy the Central High campus and buildings. Flanked by soldiers with fixed bayonets, the nine black teen-agers entered Central High and, guarded in their classrooms and wherever else they went, began their studies. Outside the crowds continued to gather, shout, and mill around, but they were mostly peaceful. Each day the number of protesters dwindled.

The federal troops remained at Central High throughout Oc-tober and November. Faubus refused to give assurances that he would keep order if the troops were withdrawn, but he and the local segregationist firebrands did quiet down somewhat. By late fall the scene at Central High had become so peaceful that the black students could come and go unguarded. On December 2 Eisenhower sent the National Guardsmen home and removed all but a handful of the paratroops.

School desegregation could come to Little Rock in 1957 only at bayonet point. Despite the efforts of the local daily newspaper and a number of civic leaders to calm the populace, racist emo-tions remained as strong as ever in the city and across the state. In June 1958 the Little Rock school board, fearing a recurrence of the previous fall's strife, secured from Federal District Court an order delaying its integration program for two and a half years. That meant cancelling the enrollment of an additional seven black youths at previously all-white schools. While the NAACP appealed the delaying order to the higher federal courts, Faubus overwhelmed his opponents in the Democratic gubernatorial pri-mary, thus virtually assuring his reelection.

After the United States Court of Appeals overturned the delay granted in Federal District Court, the Little Rock school board took its case before the Supreme Court. In September the Court unanimously rejected the board's appeal and denied that there was any legal basis whatsoever for state defiance of its 1954 rul-ing. Faubus's response was to sign into law a bill just passed by the Arkansas legislature empowering him to close any school in the state, to order the schools in Little Rock to shut down, and to arrange for a local referendum on the integration issue. After Faubus rigged the referendum in such a way as to insure victory for the segregationists, a big majority voted in favor of keeping the schools closed rather than see them integrated. Now the board turned the schools over to a private corporation pledged to maintain segregation.

The experiment with a privately operated educational system proved disastrous not only for the black students whose schools remained closed but also for the whites whose schools were poorly administered and financed. At the end of a year the school board and the local white population as a whole were ready to give up. In September 1959 Central High, as well as four other Little Rock high schools, reopened on an integrated basis.

In the intensity of its racist reaction, Little Rock was typical of the South. Yet it was also among the relatively few places in the region where even token school integration was actually accomplished during the Eisenhower years. By the fall of 1958, more than four years after the *Brown* decision, integrated schools were the rule only in the District of Columbia, West Virginia, Kentucky, Maryland, and Oklahoma; while in Texas an estimated 17 percent of the school districts, mostly in the overwhelmingly white western and southern counties, had begun to implement desegregation plans. In the Deep South states, where the black population was heaviest, almost no racial integration had taken place in the schools or otherwise. A number of school districts in Virginia, following the doctrine of massive resistance, had closed rather than abide by court-ordered desegregation.

Moreover, in the late fifties a wave of bombings, beatings, and murders swept across the South as blacks tried to integrate public facilities and register to vote. Even though a new Civil Rights Act was on the books, the Eisenhower administration, continuing to counsel patience and moderation, was most cautious in enforcing it. In the period 1957–1960 the Department of Justice brought only ten suits to secure voting rights for black people. It soon became apparent that the 1957 legislation was full of loopholes, a fact the Civil Rights Commission pointed out in its first report in 1959. Only about 1½ million of the estimated 6 million potential black voters in eleven southern states had been registered, the commission reported. In Mississippi no more than 5 percent of the adult blacks actually voted.

In 1960 the administration endorsed efforts to put tougher legislation on the books. Despite a nine-day filibuster by southern senators, in May Congress passed a new Civil Rights Act, the success of which was again largely attributable to Lyndon Johnson. Quickly signed by the President, the new statute established stiffer fines and prison terms for persons convicted of interfering with black voting rights, for transporting explosives across state lines with the intent of violating a person's rights, or for sending threats by mail or telephone. The 1960 law also authorized federal judges to appoint referees to investigate voting-rights violations and, if necessary, to supervise the voting process and the counting of ballots.

Yet as black leaders like Roy Wilkins of the NAACP, Martin Luther King of the Southern Christian Leadership Conference, and A. Philip Randolph of the Brotherhood of Sleeping Car Porters continued to insist, what was really needed was a law empowering federal officials to register southern blacks, as well as legislation outlawing discriminatory practices in employment and the operation of public facilities. On these matters both the administration and Congress remained silent. When Eisenhower left office southern blacks had only managed to pry open the door to full citizenship; they had still not got through the door. By 1961 the civil rights movement was still just that—a movement to secure basic constitutional guarantees for southern blacks. Not yet had blacks across the nation begun collectively to struggle against the array of extralegal injustices that bore them down. Only the surface of the American caste system had been broken.

III

Overshadowing all other events and issues at home and abroad in the Eisenhower period was the nuclear arms race, which the United States and the Soviet Union continued to pursue grimly and unrelentingly. Until 1958 both countries steadily poisoned the world's atmosphere with radioactive fallout from their aboveground atomic and hydrogen tests, carried on by the Soviets in Asian Russia and by the United States in its western deserts and in the Pacific Ocean. When Eisenhower left office early in 1961, his government and the Soviets were still uneasily observing a suspension of atmospheric tests. Yet no formal test-ban agreement was in the offing, and within the next fourteen months both countries would resume full-scale nuclear testing. Nor had there been even minimal progress toward reducing either nuclear or conventional armaments.

The administration could point to one accomplishment in a related area, the international use of nuclear energy for peaceful purposes. In October 1956, at United Nations headquarters in New York City, representatives of seventy nations agreed to form an International Atomic Energy Agency (IAEA), thereby largely fulfilling an Atoms-for-Peace proposal Eisenhower had made to the UN General Assembly three years earlier. The IAEA, functioning under UN auspices, was to use fissionable material contributed by the United States, the Soviet Union, and Great Britain for internationally controlled and peacefully directed industrial development projects.

Yet the agreement to create an international pool of fissionable material—while it suggested the enormous potential good in East-West cooperation—brought the United States and the USSR not one step closer to accord on the issues of disarmament and nuclear testing. In his memoirs Eisenhower unctuously attributed the failure to make any progress toward disarmament to "the adamant insistence of the Communists on maintaining a closed society." There is doubtless much truth in the standard American contention that the Kremlin leadership feared the consequences of opening up Soviet society to the free flow of information and ideas from the West. But that was never the major stumbling block in the intermittent and futile disarmament negotiations the United States and the USSR carried on in conjunction with Great Britain, France, and other countries during the 1950s. American and Soviet suspicions were mutually abundant, as were the propaganda motives behind the various proposals and counterproposals the two superpowers exchanged. Each country remained convinced that the other would launch a nuclear attack if the conditions were ever right.

The Eisenhower administration showed little enthusiasm for negotiations leading to full disarmament. Particularly after 1955, the leadership in Washington, aware of America's clear overall superiority in nuclear striking power, was more interested in reaching agreements to limit the stockpiling of nuclear explosives and the expansion of delivery systems. Moreover, the United States was unyielding in its insistence that foolproof inspection procedures must be prerequisite to any arms limitation agreement. The Soviets, on the other hand, fully realized that reducing and stabilizing nuclear arsenals would still leave them with less striking power than the Americans. At the same time, because of their superiority in manpower—not to mention the many millions their Chinese allies could muster—the Russians would obviously benefit from scaled reductions in conventional land forces. Thus they consistently tied phased limitations of nuclear armaments to phased reductions in overall force levels, and they sought to center disarmament negotiations on the question of "general and complete disarmament."

By 1957 there could no longer be any question that the USSR had the capability to inflict a level of physical damage and casualties on the United States which would be, in the parlance of the strategic theorists, "unacceptable." Although the United States had first tested a prototype fusion device late in 1952, it was the Soviets who, three years later, achieved the first successful drop of an actual hydrogen bomb from an airplane. American test teams were not able to do that until May 1956. To be sure, the United States maintained as much as an eight- or nine-to-one preponderance in long-range bombers. By 1956, moreover, the American B-52 superbomber, which was superior to anything the Soviets then had in range and nuclear carrying capability, had become operational and had begun to replace the hundreds of shorter-range and smaller B-47s. Strategic Air Command bases now encircled both Russia and China. In June 1957 General Lauris Norstad, NATO's commander, told a group of visiting United States senators that SAC could launch strikes against the Soviet Union from a 360-degree perimeter, and that it was impossible for the Soviets to knock out all of SAC's bases. The retaliatory might of the United States and its allies would destroy the USSR even if the Russians managed to mass twice as much striking power as the Allies. The West had achieved, in strategic jargon, "maximum deterrence."

Yet even though the Soviets had only a fraction of America's strategic capability, because of the smaller land areas and more concentrated populations of the United States and its western European allies, the USSR had achieved "minimum deterrence." Moreover, since the late forties the Russians had been putting much of their technical resources into missile development; by 1957 they had edged ahead of the Americans in this particular category of military technology. Of course for both East and West the cold war arms race was enormously expensive. But for the Soviets, with a much smaller industrial base, developing and producing ever more complex and costly weapons systems proved especially burdensome. In the period 1954–1956—according to Lincoln Bloomfield and his associates, who have written the best published account of the Soviet side of the arms race—Russian economic and military planners were overly optimistic about the USSR's rate of economic growth and thus its ability to afford escalating military costs. After 1956 this optimism began to fade before the realities of slowing growth rates, aggravated by massive failures in agricultural productivity. By the late fifties, therefore, Nikita Khrushchev and his government had strong reasons for wanting to reach formal agreements enabling the USSR to reduce its military costs.

In the spring of 1956 Premier Bulganin announced that the Soviet armed forces had discharged 600,000 men during the previous year and would muster out an additional 1.2 million by 1957. He added that some 300,000 troops would be withdrawn from East Germany. John Foster Dulles's judgment was that reductions in Russian military manpower only released more workers for the manufacture of hydrogen bombs, but both Secretary of Defense Charles Wilson and Harold Stassen, Eisenhower's Special Assistant for Disarmament Studies, told the President they thought Bulganin's announcement was an encouraging sign. During the following year the Soviets, evidently as part of their strategy of seeking agreements through deterrence, both stepped up their development of an intercontinental ballistic missile and also prepared a new disarmament proposal.

In two presentations in March and April 1957, Valerian Zorin, the Russian delegate to the UN Subcommittee on Disarmament reconvened at London, for the first time put his country on record as endorsing mutual aerial surveillance in order to insure observance of agreements to ban nuclear testing, to curb nuclear stockpiling, to reduce armaments, and to prevent surprise attacks. Specifically, Zorin proposed that the United States carry out photographic missions over eastern Europe, a part of western Russia, and almost all of eastern Russia in exchange for Soviet freedom to conduct overflights of western Europe, the United States west of the Mississippi River, and Alaska. Also for the first time, the Soviets indicated that they were willing to delay the removal of American overseas air bases and to permit the installation of ground inspection stations—at large seaports, railway junctions, and major highways—before the process of disarmament actually got under way. Zorin reiterated the proposed military manpower reductions put forth by the Soviets in their May 1955 disarmament presentation. Finally, he said that the Soviet Union was prepared to negotiate an agreement to ban all nuclear testing; such negotiations should be separated from the broader question of disarmament and settled "immediately and independently."

The Soviets had made historic concessions. The initial American response, however, was to do little more than complain that the indicated inspection zones within the USSR were too narrow. When the Soviets refused to widen the zones, Stassen, the American delegate, decided to bypass the formal subcommittee sessions and talk directly with Zorin and his staff. Among other things, Stassen suggested that the nuclear powers cease stockpiling atomic and hydrogen weapons after 1959. Stassen's conduct upset both the British, who had only recently completed their first hydrogen test and wanted more time for stockpiling purposes, and Secretary Dulles, always resentful of initiatives undertaken without his consent and outside the State Department. Protesting that the Russians were using Stassen to drive a wedge between America and its allies, Dulles persuaded Eisenhower to recall Stassen for consultation. The Secretary of State then flew to London to take over the leadership of the American delegation and get the negotiations back to a formal basis. A chastened Stassen later returned to the talks, but early the next year he left the administration to seek the Republican gubernatorial nomination in Pennsylvania.

It was late August 1957 before the Western powers were ready to present a counterproposal, one that was even more complicated than the Russian offer. Provided that more elaborate ground inspection systems and broader aerial surveillance zones were agreed to, and that progress took place on the reunification of Germany and other "political" questions, the United States and its allies would accept force-level reductions roughly equivalent to what the Soviets proposed. In addition, the Western powers suggested a year's ban on nuclear tests, the ban to be lifted if either side continued to produce nuclear weapons. The Western document also brought up the new topic of banning weapons in the region beyond Earth's atmosphere.

By August 29, when the Western counterproposal came before the Disarmament Subcommittee, the Soviets had decided to break off the talks. Two days earlier Zorin had delivered a ninety-minute diatribe in which he accused the West of procrastination, duplicity, and aggressive intentions. Early in September, after the Soviets demanded that the disarmament negotiations be expanded to include all eighty-two member nations of the UN, the Disarmament Subcommittee again adjourned in failure.

In his public comment on Zorin's August 27 outburst, President Eisenhower pointed out that it followed by only one day an announcement by Tass, the official Soviet news agency, that the USSR had successfully tested a "super long-distance intercontinental multi-stage ballistic rocket." Since the Defense Department had detected as many as six other Russian ICBM firings that summer, it is almost certain that Moscow timed the announcement of its latest successful test immediately to precede Zorin's excoriation of the West. Frustrated in the Disarmament Subcommittee, aware of divided thinking on disarmament among the Western governments and within the Eisenhower administration, and worried that the United States would share nuclear weapons with its NATO partners, the Soviets apparently had concluded that the best strategy, at least for the time being, was to try to overawe the West with their nuclear prowess. To that end, they would of course do nothing to discourage the grim prophecies and wild exaggerations of their missile capabilities abounding in the West in the aftermath of the August ICBM shot and their space satellite launchings that fall.

Despite a total lack of movement in the area of disarmament, there still seemed some possibility of persuading the superpowers to halt the costly and ecologically dangerous nuclear test programs they had conducted at increasingly shorter intervals for the past ten years. For one thing, a considerable number of natural scientists and even some political leaders in the West—doubtless in the USSR as well—had become convinced that adequate technology for detecting nuclear explosions and policing a nuclear test ban already existed. In addition, the late fifties saw the appearance in the Western countries of several relatively small but highly vocal organizations formed to educate the public on the perils of radioactive buildup in the atmosphere and to protest against further testing.

Leading the campaign in the United States for a suspension of nuclear tests was the Committee for a Sane Nuclear Policy, popularly known as SANE. Bringing together philosophical and religious pacifists, advocates of world government, some political radicals, but mostly people who were simply frightened by the prospect of continued atmospheric poisoning, SANE staged peaceful public demonstrations, lobbied in Washington, and otherwise functioned in the traditional manner of organized interest groups to influence policy. Sometimes members of SANE cooperated with the smaller but more activist Committee for Non-Violent Action, which in June and July 1958 tried unsuccessfully to station a shipload of protesters in an area of the Pacific cleared for a new series of American nuclear blasts. SANE probably reached its peak in membership and visibility in May 1960, when it attracted an overflow crowd for a rally in New York's Madison Square Garden. After that, while it remained the biggest American peace organization, SANE lost members rapidly, largely as a consequence of unfounded charges leveled by Senator Thomas E. Dodd and other influential cold warriors that it was Communist-infiltrated.

There is little to indicate that the activities of SANE and similar groups affected official thinking in Washington. Eventually, though, the Eisenhower administration did begin to show an interest in negotiations leading to a permanent ban on nuclear testing. Two major factors—one general, the other specific and immediate—worked to move the American leadership in this direction. Generally, there were mounting protests by leaders of the "nonaligned" nations, whose chief spokesman was Prime Minister Jawaharlal Nehru of India, against the increasing radioactive dangers to all mankind. The more specific factor was the Soviet Union's announcement in March 1958 that it was unilaterally suspending nuclear tests. The Russians urged the United States and Great Britain to join the suspension and called for a formal international agreement to prohibit further tests.

Secretary of State Dulles predictably argued that the Russian overture was no more than a propaganda trick, but Eisenhower felt that the Western powers had to make some kind of positive response. With considerable misgivings, he and British Prime Minister Macmillan suggested that scientific representatives from the Western and Soviet-bloc nations meet in Geneva to study the technical problems involved in developing effective detection systems. The Soviets agreed to such a conference, and in July and August fifteen scientists from eight nations exchanged technical data and held detailed discussions. Their formal report suggested the feasibility and reliability of a worldwide network of detection stations.

Late in August, after the Geneva scientific conference made its report, Eisenhower announced a one-year halt in the United States' nuclear test program effective at the end of October, provided the Soviets did not resume their tests and also agreed to a permanent ban. Accepting the Soviet suggestion for separate and independent negotiations on a test-ban treaty, he proposed that the three nuclear powers—the United States, Great Britain, and the USSR—meet for this purpose beginning October 31 at Geneva. The Soviets quickly agreed to the Geneva meeting, but early in November they went ahead with a brief series of nuclear tests. Eisenhower nevertheless reaffirmed the one-year American moratorium.

The President now found himself in something of a quandary. All along he had shared the view that the dangers from atmospheric contamination were secondary alongside the likelihood that the Soviets would cheat on a test-ban agreement and perhaps score some kind of breakthrough in nuclear weaponry. Now he was confronted with a body of international scientific opinion which held that such cheating could be detected. The United States, he felt, had no choice but to go forward with the negotiations at Geneva. At the same time, however, he listened sympathetically to the many people within and without his administration who opposed a test ban in any form.

At the end of 1958, with the Geneva discussions well under way, Eisenhower received an Atomic Energy Commission report on Operation Hardtack, a series of underground nuclear tests the United States had carried out in Nevada the previous summer. According to these data, an explosion shielded in a huge underground cavern could so reduce the seismic reaction that the blast would be undetectable beyond 250 miles, or beyond the range of any of the detection stations envisioned in the worldwide monitoring network. This information, Eisenhower later wrote, "threw a pall on the conference at Geneva." In March 1959, though, the AEC admitted that it had been mistaken in reporting a 250-mile detection limit on the previous summer's underground tests, and that in fact seismographic .readings had shown up in Alaska, 2,000 miles away. The President nevertheless continued to be more impressed by the argument that a test ban was simply too risky. Among the leading opponents of both the existing American moratorium and the Geneva negotiations were the Joint Chiefs of Staff; Chairman Lewis Strauss of the AEC; Edward M. Teller, a renowned nuclear physicist reputed to be the "father of the H-bomb"; Hanson W. Baldwin, military analyst for the *New York Times;* and Henry Luce, publisher of the enormously popular weekly magazines *Time* and *Life.*

Not wanting to break off the Geneva meetings completely, Eisenhower finally suggested limiting the ban to atmospheric tests. The Russians would have nothing to do with a limited test ban, but they were willing to talk about annual visits by technical teams to conduct on-site inspections in the territory of the nuclear powers. No agreement could be reached on this issue, nor on any other matter of substance at Geneva. Meanwhile France, by exploding an atomic bomb in Algeria, became the world's fourth nuclear power.

The Geneva test-ban conference dragged on through 1959 and into the spring of the next year. At one point late in 1959, the United States delegates abruptly left the conference after the head of the Russian delegation characterized American conjectures about possible ways to conduct undetected tests as being "on the brink of absurdity." Even though the Americans shortly returned, the talks remained deadlocked, finally breaking up in the aftermath of the abortive May 1960 Paris summit conference.

The Americans, British, and Russians continued to observe an informal moratorium on nuclear tests for the next fifteen months. Toward the end of his Presidency Eisenhower became convinced that the United States should start testing again, yet he also thought this decision should be left to his successor. In his meetings with President-elect John F. Kennedy during the winter of 1960–1961, Eisenhower emphasized "my conviction that our nation should resume needed tests without delay."

The Soviets broke the moratorium late in the summer of 1961, beginning a series of fifty atmospheric explosions, including one record blast of 58 megatons. The United States also resumed testing in the atmosphere the next spring. In 1963, however, the two superpowers, along with Great Britain (but not France), finally managed to conclude a treaty prohibiting nuclear tests in the atmosphere. Permitting continued underground explosions and thus embodying the basic approach Eisenhower had put forth in 1958–1959, the treaty marked at least partial realization of the long and intermittent negotiations beginning in the Eisenhower years. Insofar as they had helped clarify issues and viewpoints, the test-ban wranglings of the late fifties had been of some use.

IV

Even if American and Soviet negotiators had somehow been able to come up with a test-ban treaty or an arms-limitation agreement, ratification by the United States Senate would have been most unlikely. Whatever chance there may have been of slowing down the frantic arms race evaporated with the onset of a collective mood of deep anxiety, often bordering on hysteria, among Americans in the late summer and fall of 1957. If the President's budget battle with Congress had undermined the political basis of the Eisenhower equilibrium, then the Soviet announcement of a successful ICBM test and the spectacular Russian satellite launchings largely destroyed the sense of security and complacency that had settled over the country in the mid-fifties.

While it was generally known that both the United States and the USSR were developing long-range ballistic missiles to carry nuclear warheads, Congress, the news media, and the American people had confidently assumed that their country was further along than the Soviets and would gain preeminence in this latest form of advanced weaponry, as it had in other kinds of military technology. In fact, given the history of rocket development in the two countries, it would have been most remarkable if the Russians had not been the first to develop an ICBM, the first to test it successfully, and the first to convert their ICBM into a launch vehicle for space purposes.

What happened in 1957 was a direct consequence of certain basic decisions made by the military planners and governments of the United States and the USSR in the late forties and early fifties, together with the technical constraints under which the Soviets worked. While the United States chose to expand its armada of intercontinental bombers into third- and fourth-generation aircraft which could each carry as much as twenty megatons of hydrogen explosives, the Soviets produced relatively few bombers capable of reaching North America with nuclear payloads. Instead, during the late Stalin era the Soviets determined that long range rocketry offered the quickest, cheapest way to secure a minimum nuclear deterrent. Building on a basic single-stage, liquid-fueled rocket called the T-1, on which they had apparently begun working as far back as 1949, the Soviets went on to develop both intermediate-range ballistic missiles (IRBMs) capable of hitting targets in western Europe and the prototype of a multistage rocket which could, Nikita Khrushchev boasted as early as the spring of 1956, deliver a nuclear warhead to any target on earth.

The multistage Russian ICBM, moreover, had a much greater total engine thrust than the biggest American rocket then under development. That was true because by 1954 American nuclear scientists and engineers, in what became known as the "thermo-nuclear breakthrough," had been able drastically to reduce the ratio between the weight and yield of hydrogen-fusion warheads. It was therefore possible for the Americans to build smaller and lighter thermonuclear payloads still yielding as much as three megatons. To boost such warheads the engine thrust of an American IRBM need be no greater than 150,000-175,000 pounds; of an ICBM, 350,000 pounds. The Soviets made no such breakthrough in warhead weight-yield ratios. Having to deliver much bigger payloads, they had to design much bigger launch vehicles.

Moreover, the pace of military rocket development in the United States was considerably slower than in the USSR. The Eisenhower administration did not put the Air Force's Atlas ICBM project on a crash basis until September 1955. Aware of rapid Russian progress in rocketry, the Defense Department two months later authorized a new Air Force rocket, the intermediate-range Thor, which had been hurriedly conceived for overseas deployment as a stopgap deterrent missile. Secretary of Defense Wilson also gave the Army and Navy joint responsibility for still another IRBM called the Jupiter, designed for both land-based and shipboard firings. Late in 1956 Wilson, in an effort to mitigate the rampant interservice rivalry emerging in the field of long-range rocketry, issued a "roles and missions" memorandum which confirmed the Air Force's sole jurisdiction over development and deployment of ICBMs, also gave the Air Force operational responsibility for land-based IRBMs, assigned ship-based IRBMs to the Navy, and restricted Army missile operations to weapons with ranges up to 200 miles. Shortly thereafter the Navy withdrew from the Jupiter project to concentrate on plans for a new solid-propellant missile called the Polaris, designed for launching from submerged nuclear-powered submarines.

In fiscal year 1957 the United States spent more than $2.8 billion on missile research, development, and procurement—about thirteen times as much as six years earlier. Prime contracts for missile work had gone to some 200 companies, which had then subcontracted with another 20,000 firms. Such financial outlays and corporate involvement, plus the variety of missile projects under way, demonstrate that considerable portions of the American military establishment had become convinced that the ballistic missile, armed with a thermonuclear warhead, would be the ultimate weapon in the decades to come. At the same time, other powerful military leaders—perhaps most notably General Curtis LeMay, commander of sac in the mid-fifties and later Air Force Chief of Staff—argued protractedly and vehemently that the manned bomber should be the backbone of America's nuclear striking force for the foreseeable future. LeMay had strong political allies like Washington's Democratic Senator Henry M. Jackson, in whose state the Boeing Company manufactured both B-47s and B-52s. The split in Air Force thinking indicated that— besides longstanding interservice rivalries, made even more intense by the jockeying for new advantages in the missile age— there were also major differences *within* the services regarding the significance of the new weapons. In the Navy, for example, aircraft carrier devotees downgraded the utility of submarine-based missiles. Meanwhile Army men argued the merits of traditional armored and infantry forces against units equipped with "tactical" nuclear missiles.

Also, as critics of the Eisenhower administration's military policies pointed out again and again in the winter of 1957–1958, the American ballistic missile program suffered from what seemed like an inordinate amount of mismanagement, waste, duplication, and delay. Much of this criticism struck home. Missile development had spawned a plethora of Pentagon committees and a great deal of confusion and both interservice and intraservice squabbling. The administrative history behind the Jupiter project, for example, baffled all but the closest Pentagon insiders. Between 1953 and 1957, eleven major organizational changes pertaining directly to missile programs took place within the Defense Department. "It was just like putting a nickel in a slot machine," recalled the chairman of the board of North American Aviation, a major missile contractor. "You pull the handle and you get a lemon and you put another one in. You have to get three or four of them in a row and hold them there long enough for them to say 'Yes.' It takes a lot of nickels and a lot of time."

It also took a lot of money. In retrospect it is hard to see how the military services and their contractors could have effectively spent much more on missile research and development than the administration allocated after 1955. Nevertheless, in the great public reexamination of the nation's military posture in 1957–1958, the American inclination to believe that more money will always bring faster results again asserted itself. The missile program, so the charge went, suffered from fiscal malnutrition, a consequence of the Republican administration's sustained penny-pinching. The irony of such criticism in the wake of the 1957 budget battle apparently escaped most commentators.

From those Democrats who had warned of a bomber gap in 1955–1956 now came the cry that the country faced a much more perilous missile gap. This time the American public was a great deal more willing to be frightened by such dire prophecies. Opinion surveys indicated widespread popular concern over the state of the country's defenses, while across the political spectrum the press commentary focused on the need for stronger presidential leadership, for a national sense of urgency and spirit of sacrifice, and for the recognition that America would be defenseless before a barrage of Russian rockets.

Then, on October 4, 1957, the Soviets blasted into orbit the first artificial Earth satellite. Called *Sputnik*, a Russian acronym meaning "fellow traveler of Earth," the satellite and its instrumentation package weighed 184 pounds. Some had been skeptical of the earlier Russian claim to have launched an ICBM, but Western astronomical observatories easily picked up and tracked the object orbiting in space. Now there could be no doubt that the Russians possessed a powerful rocket and that they had solved the essential problems of control and guidance necessary to deliver a thermonuclear warhead to its target. An even more dazzling feat came on November 3, when Russian scientists and rocket engineers directed into orbit *Sputnik II*, a space capsule with the startling weight of 1,120 pounds. The second Soviet satellite was big enough to carry a normal-sized dog wired for medical monitoring.

Suddenly there was a "space lag" to add to the missile gap. The initial tendency within the administration was to play down the significance of the Soviet satellites. Four days after the orbiting of *Sputnik II*, however, Eisenhower finally yielded to the clamor in Congress and in the news media for a presidential response to the Russian accomplishments. Speaking over national television and radio, the President acknowledged that the sputniks constituted "an achievement of the first importance. . . ." The Soviets were also ahead in some areas of missile development, he conceded. The fact remained that "as of today the over-all military strength of the free world is distinctly greater than that of communist countries." To prove that the United States was hardly standing still in missile and space research and development, the President displayed a missile nose cone fired to an altitude of 600 miles by an Army test team the previous August and recovered in the Atlantic. Eisenhower went on to announce that he was naming James R. Killian, president of the Massachusetts Institute of Technology, as his Special Assistant for Science and Technology. Steps should be taken, he added, to reorganize the federal government's activities in science, to foster more scientific research in American colleges and universities, and to encourage more young people to enter scientific fields. There was indeed reason for a "high sense of urgency," but "this does not mean that we should mount our charger and try to ride off in all directions at once."

Eisenhower's November 7 speech was probably the most anxiously awaited national address he had made since coming to the Presidency. Given reluctantly and designed more to quiet fears than to inspire support for bold new actions, it satisfied almost none of the critics. Some were disappointed that the President had not made Killian or someone else a "missile czar," with the authority to coordinate and centralize all missile projects. Others called for a crash program in education with the object of turning out vastly greater numbers of scientists and engineers. Still others wanted a full commitment to a "space race," with the United States sparing no effort to wrest supremacy from the Soviets in the nascent field of astronautics.

For the first time a substantial amount of congressional and press complaint began to focus on the President himself. After the first sputnik went into orbit, Eisenhower had pointed out that "our satellite program has never been conducted as a race with other nations." While this was literally correct, in the popular view the sputniks had given the cold war ideological and technological rivalry a new dimension. As far back as 1955 both American and Soviet scientists had announced plans to put into orbit scientific satellites as part of the eighteen-month International Geophysical Year, to begin July 1, 1957. At the outset one of the USSR's leading aeronautical experts had predicted that the Russian satellite payloads would be larger than those described in the American technical literature. The prediction was scarcely a daring one. The Eisenhower administration had already made three key decisions: (1) to assign the scientific satellite project to a Naval Research Laboratory–National Academy of Sciences team; (2) to make publicly available all information relating to the project; and (3) so that the satellite and ballistic missile programs would not interfere with each other and so that militarily related data would remain classified, to develop a wholly new launch vehicle instead of using existing or planned military hardware. Moreover, because of the skill American scientists and technicians had already attained in miniaturizing instrumentation packages, the satellite undertaking, dubbed Project Vanguard, could utilize a relatively small (25,000-pound-thrust) launch rocket.

By the fall of 1957 Project Vanguard, while not far off schedule, was still in its test phase. With the post-sputnik furor mounting, Neil H. McElroy, the new Secretary of Defense, authorized the Army Ballistic Missile Agency at Redstone Arsenal, Alabama, to reactivate its long-dormant plan for converting one of the Army's medium-range Redstone missiles into a satellite launcher.[3] This plan was the one the Eisenhower administration had rejected in 1955 in favor of the Vanguard proposal. Now Wernher von Braun and the rest of the team of rocket scientists and engineers the Army had brought from Germany after 1945 eagerly worked to get an American satellite into orbit as quickly as possible.

Insofar as there is such a thing as American national self-confidence, it very likely reached its nadir for the cold war era in November and December 1957. On November 26 President

---

3. After Charles Wilson's resignation in October 1957, McElroy left the presidency of Procter and Gamble Company to head the Defense Department.

Eisenhower suffered a mild stroke, his third serious illness in little more than two years. Although the permanent effects of the stroke were minor (basically a very slight speech difficulty), Eisenhower disconsolately pondered whether he was still capable of meeting the Presidency's increasingly heavy demands. On December 15 he flew to Paris for a meeting of the North Atlantic Council, which he set as a test of his physical endurance.

At Paris Eisenhower and Dulles pressed the other NATO countries to follow Britain's lead and agree to the stationing of American intermediate-range missiles on their territory. None of the United States' allies were enthusiastic about the offer; missile bases would perhaps anger the Russians and would certainly make the western and southern European nations prime targets in a nuclear exchange. Finally, in return for a reluctant American pledge to support a new foreign ministers conference with the Soviets, to work harder for a disarmament treaty, and to share more scientific and technical information with Europe, the NATO partners agreed to consider individually whether to accept American missiles. As it turned out, only the British, the Italians, and the Turks were willing to take the Thors and Jupiters when they became operational the next year.

While the President and Secretary of State were in Paris trying to sell missiles to their hesitant allies, in Washington Lyndon Johnson again moved to the center of national attention. On November 28 Johnson's Preparedness Subcommittee of the Senate Armed Services Committee had begun a thoroughgoing and highly publicized inquiry into the history, status, and future of the nation's missile and satellite programs. Totally dominated by Johnson, the hearings were, according to Rowland Evans and Robert Novak, "a textbook example of what a Senate investigation ought to be." Taking testimony from a long procession of generals and admirals, officials of the major corporations doing missile work, and astronautical authorities like Wernher von Braun, Johnson's subcommittee was able to publicize the essential facts behind America's lagging missile and space efforts. The hearings were businesslike and decorous except for an emotional appearance by Lieutenant General James M. Gavin, who had recently quit as research and development chief for the Army because of the downgrading of his service's strategic role. Moreover, the hearings did precisely what the Senate Democratic leader wanted them to do: cast severe doubts on the Republican record without challenging Eisenhower personally. By mid-January 1958, when the Preparedness Subcommittee finished listening to witnesses, Johnson had effectively identified himself as the leading spokesman in Congress on missile and space matters. He had also done much to give the Democrats the image of a party pushing for stronger national defense and a more ambitious space program, which would perhaps include sending an American to the moon.

Greatly facilitating Johnson's partisan but careful maneuvers was an embarrassing failure in the Vanguard project, followed by a dramatic success in the Army's revivified satellite effort. On December 6, 1957, before a national television audience, the Vanguard rocket had exploded on its launch stand at Cape Canaveral, Florida. Largely because the White House had erroneously billed the launch as an attempt to orbit a fully instrumented satellite when actually only a test payload was to be used, the Vanguard blowup immediately took on the proportions of a national disaster. Not until January 31, 1958, when the Army rocket team led by von Braun sent into orbit an American satellite called *Explorer I*, did public anxiety ease somewhat. Carrying instrumentation developed for Vanguard by a physicist at the University of Iowa, James A. Van Allen, the 31-pound Explorer scientific payload disclosed the existence of a deep radiation zone girdling Earth, quickly named the "Van Allen belt."

Explorer I was the first of thirty-one scientific satellites the United States would fire into space before Eisenhower left office. On March 17, 1958, the much-maligned Vanguard project fulfilled its purpose by launching a three-pound scientific package into orbit. Nine days later *Explorer II* also began to circle Earth in space. These American accomplishments, together with two successful test launches of the Atlas ICBM over a portion of its 6,300-mile design range, brought a widespread feeling of relief to people across the country, according to public opinion samplings. All the same, in space the Soviets continued to outdo their cold war competitors. In May another big Russian rocket lifted into orbit a satellite weighing nearly 3,000 pounds, or about 56 times as much as the combined weight of the three American satellites. And while the Atlas project was moving forward, the United States' first ICBM would not reach operational status for another year and a half.

Stung by charges that his administration had neglected the nation's defenses and its scientific and technological potential, Eisenhower moved with considerable dispatch during 1958 to remedy much of what his critics claimed was wrong. Segregationist fears of federally coerced racial mixing and Roman Catholic insistence on the right of parochial schools to federal subsidy continued to frustrate the sponsors of general aid-to-education bills. Thus the task of financing the national educational overhauling which seemed in order in the post-sputnik period remained basically a local and state responsibility. But at the President's urging Congress did enact a program designed to improve and expand mathematics, science, and foreign language offerings in the public schools and to encourage more young people to pursue scientific and technical careers. In September Eisenhower signed the National Defense Education Act (NDEA), which set up fellowship and loan programs—partly on a federal-state matching basis—to finance undergraduate and graduate study. NDEA also made available to the public schools a fairly modest $280 million, to be matched by the states, for laboratories and textbooks.

Eisenhower's January 1958 State of the Union message concentrated on the need to fund an accelerated missile program and to reorganize the Defense Department with the goal of curbing interservice rivalry. By that time the same Congress which had exhibited such economy-mindedness the previous year had not only restored all the money cut from the Pentagon's fiscal 1958 budget but had given the President substantial additional spending authority for military purposes. What might be called the "sputnik syndrome" had served to unravel—not just loosen—congressional purse strings, at least as far as the Democratic majority was concerned.

The major complaint against the fiscal 1959 budget the President sent to Congress on January 13 was that it asked for too little. There was, in fact, a strong element of austerity in the new budget. In July George Humphrey had resigned as Secretary of the Treasury, to be succeeded by Robert B. Anderson, a Texas-born financier then serving as Deputy Secretary of Defense. Greatly admired by Eisenhower and every bit as much a fiscal conservative as Humphrey, Anderson had little difficulty selling the argument that increased military outlays would necessitate tightening up elsewhere. Thus the first budget drawn up by Anderson was, as Richard Neustadt has commented, "just the sort of budget Humphrey had desired but had failed to gain before his public outburst a year earlier." In presenting it to Congress, Eisenhower warned that "To amass military power without regard to our economic capacity would be to defend ourselves against one kind of disaster by inviting another." The budget did provide for moderate increases in military spending, but it also featured a ban on new hydroelectric, flood control, and reclamation projects; a reduction in agricultural subsidies; a cut-back on federal grants for hospital construction, urban renewal, and welfare programs; and a higher interest rate on GI home loans. Modern Republicanism, it appeared, had become a casualty of the missile and space age.

Congress gave Eisenhower more than he wanted for both the Pentagon and domestic programs. The effect of the sputnik syndrome, together with a small decline in federal revenues caused by the economic slump of 1957–1958, was to produce a whopping $12.5-billion deficit, far and away the biggest of the Eisenhower presidency. At the same time, Congress was willing to go only part way with the President on military reorganization. Basically what Eisenhower wanted was to give the Secretary of Defense enough authority to control the vast, unwieldy, and rapidly growing military bureaucracy. His reorganization bill, which he mostly drafted himself and sent to Capitol Hill early in April, provided that Congress, instead of making separate appropriations for each branch of the military, would give one unified appropriation to the Secretary of Defense. The three service secretaries and the Joint Chiefs of Staff would be taken out of the chain of command, retaining only administrative and advisory functions; this change would presumably stop the common practice whereby top military officials and their huge staffs bypassed the Secretary of Defense to lobby before congressional committees and with individual congressmen. Finally, Eisenhower wanted to establish the new post of Director of Defense Research and Engineering to supervise all military research and development activity.

Eisenhower got little help from Secretary of Defense McElroy, whose testimony during the congressional hearings on the administration bill was weak and waffling. Powerful opposition came from the service secretaries, the Joint Chiefs, and especially the Army, whose leaders viewed reorganization as another step in the relegation of that service to an inferior strategic role. What the President finally got was far short of what he had called for. The legislation enacted in August somewhat strengthened the powers of the Secretary of Defense and created the Directorate of Defense Research and Engineering, but the services would still be funded separately; and the service secretaries and the Joint Chiefs would keep their positions in the line of authority and thus their lobbying prowess in Congress. For the second time Eisenhower had been unable to convince a congressional majority that there was anything basically wrong with the organization of the country's military establishment.

Besides bigger outlays for missile projects and faster deployment of operational ICBMs, those demanding action in the post-sputnik period wanted the creation of a national space program, both to insure full exploitation of whatever military potential there might be in space flight and to begin to recoup the international "prestige" America had supposedly lost as a consequence of the sputniks. By April 1958 a total of twenty-nine bills and resolutions pertaining to the organization of the nation's space efforts had appeared in Congress.

The administration seemed maddeningly slow in coming up with its own plans for a space program. Never convinced that space flight had either practical or intrinsic value and repelled by the prospect of a space race with the Russians, Eisenhower nevertheless had one overriding concern: Whatever space ventures the United States and the USSR embarked upon must be for the purpose of scientific exploration, not military exploitation. The demilitarization of the region beyond Earth's atmosphere had been one of the points in the American disarmament counter-proposal at Geneva the previous August. And in a letter to Soviet Premier Bulganin on January 12, 1958, the President urged that "outer space should be used only for peaceful purposes. . . . Should not outer space be dedicated to the peaceful uses of mankind and denied to the purposes of war?"

Early in February Eisenhower directed his newly appointed President's Scientific Advisory Committee (PSAC), headed by Special Assistant for Science and Technology Killian, to draw up recommendations for a national program in space science. Within a month Eisenhower had received and approved PSAC's report, the major feature of which was a recommendation for a wholly new agency, to have not only research and development but also managerial and operational responsibilities in astronautics and space flight. The nucleus for the new agency should be the fifty-three-year-old National Advisory Committee for Aeronautics (NACA). Misleadingly named for its governing board, NACA was actually a farflung government research establishment employing some 8,000 people at its Washington headquarters and at labora-tories and test stations in Virginia, Ohio, and California. Little known to the general public, NACA enjoyed great international scientific prestige stemming from its four decades of landmark contributions to military and civilian aeronautics. For a President determined that the nation's space efforts must be free of military control, NACA seemed the logical place to start building a space program.

In April Eisenhower submitted legislation, drafted mainly in the Bureau of the Budget, for a National Aeronautical and Space Agency which would absorb NACA and assume responsibility for all "space activities . . . except . . . those projects primarily asso-ciated with military requirements." The measure went to special committees set up earlier in the year to deal with matters relating to space exploration, chaired in the Senate by Majority Leader Johnson, in the House by Majority Leader John W. McCormack. Over the next three months the administration's bill received sub-stantial reworking in these committees and on the floor of the Senate and House. As finally passed on July 16, the bill upgraded the Space Agency into a National Aeronautics and Space Administration (NASA), headed by an administrator and deputy administrator rather than a single director. The original provision for a large Space Board analogous to the governing Committee of NACA was scrapped in favor of a five-seven member Space Council to advise the President, who was to be its chairman. Indicative of the general congressional concern over the relationship between space technology and national defense was a provision for a Civilian-Military Liason Committee, which was to assure full exchange of information gained in NASA's and the Defense Department's separate programs. Though not entirely satisfied with what Congress had done to his original proposal, Eisenhower was willing to sign the bill into law on July 29.

Henceforth the National Aeronautics and Space Administration would be the focal point of American activities in the exploration of space. Besides NACA's 8,000 employees and $100-million budget, NASA took over the Vanguard project from the Naval Research Laboratory; the Explorer project and other work from the Army Ballistic Missile Agency; the services of the Jet Propulsion Laboratory at Pasadena, California, hitherto an Army contractor; and various Air Force study contracts for satellites and advanced rocket engines. NASA was also to receive $117 million previously set aside in the Defense Department for space ventures.

It remained for the President personally to resolve what promised to be a serious jurisdictional dispute between the new space organization and the Air Force. Since late 1957 the Air Force's Air Research and Development Command had avidly pushed its plans for a manned satellite project. NACA, as it was obligated by statute to do, had worked closely with the Air Force on its designs for a manned space capsule. At the same time, however, NACA researchers, anticipating that the job of putting a man into space would go to the new civilian space agency, had pursued their own studies and tests. Doubtless the Air Force was fully competent to undertake a manned satellite project, but its plans collided with Eisenhower's "space-for-peace" outlook. In mid-August, acting primarily on Killian's advice, the President assigned to the fledgling NASA specific responsibility for developing and carrying out the mission of manned space flight. By the fall NASA had brought into being Project Mercury, a program for orbiting "astronauts" in one-man space capsules launched by modified Atlas ICBMs.

V

Aside from the substantial political damage suffered by the GOP and Eisenhower himself, and the organization of a national space program around NASA, the major consequences of the big missile and space scare of 1957–1958 were to speed up and expand the nuclear arms race and to further the expansion and modernization of American tactical armaments. From 1957 onward the Eisenhower administration was plagued by the accusation that it had allowed a possibly fatal missile gap to develop. The imperative need to strengthen the nation's defenses remained one of the central issues in American national politics through the 1960 presidential campaign, in which John F. Kennedy made much of the alleged parsimony and inflexibility of Republican military policy. The rhetoric of Democrats like Kennedy and Johnson, and even of Republicans like Nelson Rockefeller, tended to gloss over the really critical question: whether there was or ever had been a "deterrent gap." Administration spokesmen were generally willing to concede a temporary Soviet lead in long-range missiles, but they consistently and vigorously denied that there had ever been a time when the United States lacked the capability to deter a Soviet attack.

Here certain essential points should be considered. Not only did the Soviets have a longer lead time, which gave them an initial advantage in missile research and development, but they were able to hold this advantage for a few years because the Eisenhower administration, while accelerating work on liquid-fueled IRBMs and ICBMs after 1955, also decided to base the United States' long-term nuclear deterrent on solid-fueled missiles. If the USSR continued to concentrate on liquid-fueled rocketry —as in fact it did—then there could be a period before the deployment of solid-fueled Polaris IRBMs and Minuteman ICBMs when the Russians had more operational ballistic missiles. By the end of 1958 work was well under way on both the submarine-based Polaris and the Minuteman, designed for launching from nearly invulnerable underground silos, but neither was expected to be operational until the early sixties. Thus administration military planners took a calculated risk in missilery, yet a risk that was greatly minimized by SAC's huge margin of superiority in long-range bombers, which could hit the USSR from bases around the world.

If there was never a deterrent gap under Eisenhower, the question remains, was there a missile gap? In terms of the thrust capabilities of Soviet versus American rockets, obviously there was. Not until the mid-sixties, when NASA's Saturn boosters began to launch prototype three-man Apollo spacecraft, would the United States be able to send into space payloads as heavy as those the Soviets had been launching for several years. In terms of the number of long range missiles on launch stands in the late fifties, the answer again is yes. The Soviets always had many more medium-range (200-500 mile) and intermediate-range missiles in place in Europe than did the United States. After 1956 the Soviet Union's nuclear-tipped MRBMS and IRBMS trained on western Europe effectively made the United States' NATO allies hostages to Soviet security from an American nuclear attack. The relatively few American MRBMS and IRBMS stationed overseas were never meant to serve more than a stopgap purpose until the ICBMS were ready. As for operationally deployed ICBMS, there apparently was an interval—sometime between late 1959 and the early part of 1961—when the Soviets had a small edge. According to one estimate, by the spring of 1961, fifty Russian ICBMS stood ready to fire as opposed to twenty-seven American.

Clearly, neither the Soviet Union nor the United States manufactured great numbers of the first-generation, liquid-fueled ICBMS they designed and developed in the fifties. The explanation for this on the American side was the decision to rely on a few dozen liquid-fueled missiles and SAC's enormous nuclear might for the short run and on solid-fueled missiles, both sea-going and land-based, over the long run. On the Soviet side, the explanation seems to be partly technical—the Russians evidently had trouble developing ICBMS that were reliable enough for deployment in large numbers—but mostly economic. Throughout the late fifties the USSR's military spending continued to rise dramatically while its economy began to sag. The effort to translate ICBM prototype development into serial production apparently proved more costly than the Soviets had anticipated. Although they did succeed in manufacturing enough shorter-range missiles to cover western European targets, their ICBM capability grew more slowly than both they had hoped and the West had feared.

Meanwhile the American leadership was able to keep fairly close watch on Soviet ICBM deployment through a series of photographic missions carried out by the CIA with a specially designed reconnaissance aircraft, the U-2. Beginning in the fall of 1956, U-2s periodically flew from bases in Turkey and Pakistan across the central and western USSR, photographing the Russian landscape with amazing detail at altitudes beyond the range of anti-aircraft rockets. Data collected from these U-2 missions provided the most solid evidence the United States could gather that the Russian ICBM program was progressing much less rapidly than American prophets of doom had predicted. The USSR's minimum deterrent was stronger and more credible than ever, but the total American nuclear delivery capability still far outweighed the Soviet capability to attack North America.

The administration was never able to convince its critics of this basic reality. Of course numerical superiority, as Eisenhower fully realized, did not measure out to security, a commodity that could no longer be purchased with weapons in the thermonuclear age. It made no sense, the President thought, for the country to spend huge new sums in pursuit of the mirage of absolute security. By the mid-fifties the administration had essentially given up the notion of long term nuclear superiority in favor of the concept of sufficiency. It was enough, in Eisenhower's view, for America to be able to survive a Soviet nuclear strike and then return a devastating retaliatory blow. American strategic forces should remain powerful enough to destroy the Soviet Union once—not a dozen times over.

If sufficiency had become the basic goal of the administration's strategic thinking, it also strongly influenced planning for limited warfare. Massive retaliation, insofar as it had ever been a viable concept, was pretty moribund by 1957. In mid-decade the administration had begun moving toward what some called the "New New Look," of which one of the main features was a gradual expansion of America's capability to fight relatively small-scale conflicts. As early as October 1956 John Foster Dulles had stated publicly that "it would be reckless to risk everything on one form of armament. . . ." The United States, said Dulles, should be able to counter localized Communist aggression "without our action producing a general nuclear war." In effect, the man most closely identified with the doctrine of massive retaliation had acknowledged that because the Soviet Union was now able to inflict terrible damage on the United States, American military power must become more diversified to protect interests that were more far-flung than ever.

Yet the administration still sought to stabilize military costs. Rather than a big expansion of the Army, which would have been both enormously expensive and politically unpopular, Eisenhower and his military planners chose to equip American conventional forces with "tactical" nuclear-tipped missiles. Much of the nuclear testing carried on by the United States in 1956–1958 aimed at improving existing low-yield nuclear weapons for use in battlefield situations. Nothing better exemplifies the remarkable escalation of military thinking in the fifties than the conclusion that the use of such weapons—which during the Indochina and Formosa Strait crises of 1954 had seemed a way to avoid stalemated limited war—had now come to look like a reasonable alternative to an all-out nuclear exchange.

Despite the fact that by 1957 the administration had already gone a considerable way toward rebuilding a limited-war capability, charges persisted—indeed intensified—that its military policy was still a matter of all or nothing. Such charges figured prominently in two well-publicized critiques of the status of the nation's defenses—one governmental, the other done outside government —which received much publicity in the aftermath of the sputniks.

The first was the report of a panel Eisenhower had originally set up in the spring of 1957 to study the nation's civil defense system, especially the problem of fallout shelters. Bearing the official title Security Resources Panel of the Office of Defense Mobilization Science Advisory Committee, and headed by H.

Rowan Gaither, chairman of the board of the Ford Foundation, the group began with the assumption that it could not properly evaluate the fallout shelter question without studying the whole issue of national defense. Made up mostly of corporate executives —"managers and advisers to the new, mushrooming high-technology industries," as Richard Barnet has described them—the panel became increasingly alarmed by its findings.[4] "I felt as though I was spending ten hours a day staring straight into hell," one member later remarked.

The Gaither Report, as the panel's conclusions were called, went before the National Security Council on November 7. The President heartily agreed with some points in the report, such as the need for reorganizing the Defense Department, for dispersing SAC's North American bases and keeping more bombers on in-flight alert, and for placing ICBMs in hardened underground silos as soon as possible. Others he found farfetched, such as a proposal for tunneling SAC runways into mountainsides. Two recommendations—for an elaborate nationwide fallout shelter program and for a rapid expansion of conventional forces—he rejected entirely.

When NSC and the President failed to share their sense of crisis and danger, the members of the Security Resources Panel sought to win support within the State, Defense, and Treasury departments and the Bureau of the Budget. They made little headway. Secretary of State Dulles, Secretary of the Treasury Anderson, and Budget Director Percival Brundage all refused to countenance the kind of drastic jumps in military spending that would be necessary to finance big increases in conventional force levels. Dulles, moreover, cautioned that an extensive shelter program might frighten the NATO countries into thinking the

4. Besides Chairman Gaither, the Security Resources Panel included Robert C. Sprague, chairman of the Sprague Electric Company; William C. Foster, a top executive with the Olin Mathieson Chemical Corporation; Robert A. Lovett, Truman's Secretary of Defense and now an officer in various defense-related corporations; Frank Stanton, president of the Columbia Broadcasting System; John J. McCloy, who had held several high positions in the Truman administration and was now president of the Chase Manhattan Bank; and Jerome B. Wiesner, a physicist at the Massachusetts Institute of Technology. After Gaither became ill the panel reorganized with Sprague as director and Foster as codirector.

United States was preparing for nuclear war. In his State of the Union message the President ignored the Gaither Report and even proposed some reductions in conventional forces and the civil defense program to pay for greater missile costs. Senator Johnson, other leading Democrats, and some Republicans called on the administration to publish the document, but Eisenhower adamantly kept it classified, even after members of the Security Resources Panel leaked its essential contents to friendly congressmen and the news media.

At the same time that the nominally secret Gaither Report hit the headlines, the Rockefeller Brothers Fund published the national defense portion of a general inquiry into American governmental, economic, and educational resources being conducted by its Special Studies Project. The director of the project was Henry A. Kissinger, a Harvard University political scientist. Though only thirty-four years old, Kissinger had an extensive background as a Defense Department consultant in both the Truman and Eisenhower administrations. The previous summer he had published a much-praised study of contemporary military strategy called *Nuclear Weapons and Foreign Policy.* Kissinger's main premise was that since the United States and the Soviet Union had arrived at a nuclear stalemate, all-out war was "no longer a conceivable instrument of policy. . . ." Even so, Communist moves in various parts of the world would continue. The United States must therefore be prepared to contain localized Communist aggression by the use of modern, highly mobile conventional forces. In such small-scale conflicts "tactical" nuclear weapons, employed for limited battlefield purposes, provided a rational option to a strategic nuclear exchange.

Kissinger himself wrote most of the Rockefeller Brothers Fund study of military policy. Not surprisingly, it followed rather closely his reasoning in *Nuclear Weapons and Foreign Policy.* Like the Gaither Report, the Rockefeller Fund document advocated the centralization of authority in the Secretary of Defense, elimination of interservice rivalry by assigning specialized functions to the individual services, faster missile development, dispersal of sac bases, and the construction of a nationwide system of fallout shelters. Even more strongly than the Gaither panel, Kissinger and his associates urged a "flexible" military establishment, one that could deter an all-out nuclear strike, fight limited nuclear wars, or counter internal Communist subversion, which Kissinger, in a unique semantic construction, termed "non-overt aggression."

The Gaither and Rockefeller Brothers Fund studies, along with Johnson's subcommittee hearings, seemingly documented the shortcomings of administration planning and served to fuel the raging controversy over military policy in the first half of 1958. Eisenhower refused to release intelligence data on the Russian missile program, especially that gained from the U-2 missions, which would at least partially have undercut the allegations of strategic vulnerability. The specter of the missile gap persisted for the remainder of his term. So did arguments over limited-warfare capabilities. Although the buildup in "tactical" nuclear weaponry under the New New Look proceeded, Eisenhower steadfastly resisted the mounting pressure for big manpower increases in the Army and Navy. The Democrats—led by Johnson and increasingly by John F. Kennedy—together with Army spokesmen like Generals Gavin and Maxwell Taylor (who angrily resigned as Army Chief of Staff in mid-1959), continued to argue that America's conventional forces were woefully weak and poorly equipped. Thus "flexible deterrence," like the missile gap, would be a potent issue for the Democrats in the 1960 presidential campaign.

VI

A rush of new international crises in the second half of 1958 made the controversy over military capabilities still more acrimonious. In mid-July the Middle East flared up again. In oil-rich Iraq, hitherto friendly to the West, ultranationalist army officers overthrew the government and killed young King Faisal, the crown prince, and the prime minister. The new Republic of Iraq quickly broke off the Arab Union with Jordan and announced a policy of friendship toward the United Arab Republic. Washington received news of the Iraqi coup with shock and alarm. Not only had anti-Western elements gained power in the only Arab state that was a member of the Baghdad Pact, but it seemed that the revolutionary spirit in Iraq was about to spill over into neighboring Jordan and tiny Lebanon on the Mediterranean coast.

The disorders in Iraq, Jordan, and Lebanon arose from widely varying internal circumstances. The common ingredient in each situation, however, was passionate Arab nationalism and admiration for President Nasser of the UAR. In Iraq there had long been widespread dissatisfaction with the strong pro-Western sympathies of the king and premier. King Hussein of Jordan had the same kind of trouble, aggravated by the presence within his country of large numbers of Moslem refugees driven out of Palestine during the first Arab-Israeli war in 1948–1949. Since May sporadic civil war had raged in Lebanon between Moslems and Christians, who made up nearly equal portions of the population. The major precipitant of the strife in Lebanon was the refusal of Camille Chamoun, the country's Christian, pro-Western president, to give assurances that he would not seek another term. Chamoun charged that the UAR was sending massive quantities of arms and men from Syria to the Moslem rebels. In June a team of United Nations observers could find no evidence of Syrian military personnel inside Lebanon and could turn up only a few Syrian arms.

Within the Eisenhower administration, however, there was a strong consensus that the UAR was the main culprit in the Lebanese civil conflict, and a strong suspicion that Communist or pro-Communist elements were effectively exploiting the situation. It seemed that, in the Manichean phraseology of the period, Lebanon and perhaps Jordan were about to "go down the drain" and thus be "lost" to the West. When President Chamoun on July 15, the day after the Iraqi coup, urgently asked for American help to stop the "indirect aggression" against his country, Eisenhower and Secretary Dulles were ready to act. Even though he had earlier acknowledged in a National Security Council session that there was no hard evidence of either Soviet or UAR involvement in Iraq, Jordan, or Lebanon, Dulles now declared to congressional leaders that "recent Soviet political activities" in the Middle East made it imperative to "bring a halt to the deterioration in our position. . . ." Only a few congressmen were outright enthusiastic about American intervention; some, like Senator J.

William Fulbright, expressed doubts about both the legitimacy and the necessity of such a step. Affairs in the Middle East were too confused and cloudy for the President specifically to invoke the Eisenhower Doctrine, which had referred only to "overt armed aggression." Yet as Eisenhower later wrote, "the issue was clear to me—we had to go in."

Late in the morning of the fifteenth, Ambassador Henry Cabot Lodge announced in the UN Security Council that the United States was dispatching troops to Lebanon. While Lodge was speaking an initial detachment of 5,000 Marines from the Sixth Fleet splashed ashore at Beirut, the capital of Lebanon, as swimsuit-clad tourists watched curiously from the nearby beaches. The Marines quickly secured their beachhead and other positions on the outskirts of the city and at the Beirut airport. The next day they moved into Beirut itself, but they had orders to stay out of the rebel-held Moslem sections and not to fire at anyone unless fired upon first. Eisenhower's reasoning was that the occupation of a few strategic points and, beyond that, simply the show of American force should be sufficient to tip the balance in favor of Chamoun's government. If the Lebanese army could not quell the rebels with this limited American aid, then, as Eisenhower said in his memoirs, "we were backing up a government with so little popular support that we probably should not be there."

That night, in a national radio-television talk, the President justified himself largely by way of historical analogy. He pointed out the dire consequences that had followed the failure to resist aggression in Czechoslovakia in 1938 and China in 1949. His present decision, he contended, was analogous to President Truman's determination to intervene in Greece in 1947 and Korea in 1950 and the West's resistance to Communism in Indochina.

Eisenhower's reading of recent history may have been grandiosely self-serving, but his action, once taken, met no open opposition in Congress. While there was considerable popular protest in Britain against the American intervention, Harold Macmillan's Conservative government was willing, on July 17, to land paratroops in Jordan under American air cover. In the Security Council the Soviet delegate branded the American military move "an open act of aggression," while the UAR spokesman called it "another Suez." After announcing new military exercises near the USSR's Turkish and Iranian borders, the Soviets vetoed Lodge's Security Council resolution for an international military force to keep order in Lebanon. Khrushchev countered with a call for a major-power summit conference on the Middle East, at the same time that he talked ominously about sending Russian "volunteers" to the area.

Yet short of war, which nobody wanted, there was not much either Khrushchev or Nasser could do about the American presence in Lebanon. By August 8 American troop strength had built up to nearly 14,500 men, including a tank battalion and an artillery battery equipped with short-range atomic rockets. In the meantime Deputy Undersecretary of State Robert Murphy negotiated a settlement almost identical to one Nasser had proposed in June: Chamoun agreed to resign, after which the Lebanese parliament would elect General Fuad Chebab, commander of the army and a moderate nationalist acceptable to both Moslem rebels and pro-government Christians. The rebels were to receive full amnesty. By the time the terms of the settlement were fulfilled and Chebab assumed the presidency in September, American troop withdrawals were already well under way. Within a month the Americans were gone, as were all the British troops sent to Jordan. In the UN, meanwhile, the Arab states presented a plan, unanimously adopted by the General Assembly, whereby in exchange for American and British evacuations they pledged not to interfere in each other's internal affairs.

The Anglo-American Middle East operation seemed to have been almost wholly successful. Civil order had returned to Lebanon, Jordan was relatively quiet, and the Allies had deterred "aggression" without having to kill anybody. Over the long run, however, Eisenhower's decision to send in the troops probably damaged the efforts of the United States to build a good image in the Middle East, and in Asia and Africa as well. For many people throughout the "underdeveloped areas," Lebanon was but another example of Western imperialist intrusion into the affairs of smaller states.

The immediate aftermath of Lebanon, moreover, was hardly

encouraging to American policy makers. Even though Iraq broke off relations with the UAR after an abortive uprising of pro-Nasser insurgents, the government in Baghdad accepted a steady stream of arms from the Soviet Union. And in March 1959 Iraq formally withdrew from the Baghdad Pact. The four remaining Pact countries reorganized as the Central Treaty Organization (CENTO), the name signifying the coalition's central geographical position between NATO and the Southeast Asia Treaty Organization in the global system of alliances the Truman and Eisenhower administrations had built over the past decade. Although the United States was not a formal member of CENTO, it did sign strong bilateral military agreements with Turkey, Pakistan, and Iran.

As the decade of the 1950s neared an end, the United States was more heavily committed in the Middle East than ever, but its position was weaker than at any time since it began to supplant the British and French after World War II. The American government was still on good terms with several Arab countries, and Middle Eastern oil continued to flow freely into the West. But Nasser-style Arab nationalism remained the most potent factor at work in the area. Soviet influence had never been stronger. The armed forces of Egypt, Syria, and Iraq were equipped with Russian-made aircraft, tanks, and artillery, and Egypt was pushing forward work on its Aswan Dam with a huge low-interest Russian loan secured late in 1958. Arab hatred of Israel, and the informal but apparently irrevocable American commitment to preserve the Jewish state, made for circumstances in which the Soviets could continue to pose quite effectively as the champion of pan-Arabism. The delicate balancing act the Eisenhower administration had tried to carry off in the Middle East had not worked. Realistically, the prospects for American policy there were not bright.

VII

The Lebanon imbroglio had just begun to clear up when the Formosa Strait again became the focal point of the undiminished enmity between the United States and the People's Republic of

China. On August 22, 1958, after three and a half years of relative quiet, Communist shore batteries suddenly resumed around-the-clock shelling of the Quemoy islands in Amoy harbor. In the interval since the 1954–1955 Strait confrontation, Chiang Kai-shek had stationed some 100,000 men, a third of his total ground forces, on Quemoy and the Matsu group to the north. Chiang's efforts thereby to force the United States into an express commitment to defend the vulnerable offshore islands seemed to be paying off when, on September 4, Dulles announced "we have recognized that the securing and protecting of Quemoy and Matsu have increasingly become related to the defense of Taiwan [Formosa] . . . ." Eisenhower ordered warships of the Seventh Fleet to escort Nationalist supply ships from Formosa to within three miles of the Quemoys. Although mainland batteries drove off several resupply efforts, the Communists were careful not to fire on American vessels. Meanwhile United States aircraft kept the Nationalist forces fairly well supplied by airdrop.

One September 11 the President once more went before the television cameras for a crisis speech. Disregarding the judgment of the Joint Chiefs of Staff, who advised that the offshore islands should be evacuated or at least reduced to small garrisons, and of Secretary of Defense McElroy, who thought Chiang wanted to provoke a war between the United States and mainland China, Eisenhower pledged American forces to defend Quemoy and Matsu. Again he felt called on to give a short history lesson. Abandoning the offshore islands, the President warned, would constitute a "Western Pacific 'Munich' " and only encourage further aggressive Communist actions. Then came a restatement of one of the major tenets of the cold war creed: "If history teaches us anything, appeasement would make it more likely that we would have to fight a major war." "There is not going to be any appeasement," Eisenhower concluded, "and I believe there is not going to be any war."

Khrushchev personally cautioned Eisenhower that any American attack on the Chinese mainland would bring the Soviet Union to the aid of its Communist ally and "doom to certain death sons of the American people." Yet the Soviet leader carefully skirted the question of the offshore islands. Moreover, the

Soviets did not send air-to-air missiles to the People's Republic air force, whereas Nationalist interceptors equipped with such American-made weapons were able to achieve air superiority over Quemoy.

At home, however, the administration ran into more opposition than it had on any single foreign policy issue to that time. Vast numbers of Americans simply would not be convinced that keeping Chiang's troops on a group of barren little islands off the Chinese coast was worth the risk of possible nuclear devastation. Most Democratic congressional leaders were either lukewarm or openly unhappy with the Quemoy-Matsu commitment. The State Department confirmed that 80 percent of the letters it had received on the issue either criticized or expressed fright regarding the course the administration was following. Even Dean Acheson protested that the offshore islands "are not worth a single American life." Added to the widespread domestic criticism was a torrent of complaints from the United States' European allies. British Prime Minister Macmillan could not bring himself to repudiate the American position, although he was convinced that, as he said in his memoirs, the People's Republic had "an unanswerable case to the possession of the islands."

Unable to rally either the nation or America's allies behind its policy, the administration began to back down, at least a little. On September 30 Dulles acknowledged in a press conference that the United States was under no legal obligation to defend Quemoy and Matsu. In fact, Chiang's concentration of so many troops on the islands had been "rather foolish." If the Communists agreed to a de facto cease-fire, then Nationalist forces on Quemoy and Matsu should be reduced.

The Peking government, anxious to avoid war with the United States and unable to starve the offshore garrisons into submission, quickly picked up Dulles's signal. On October 6 Peking announced a one-week suspension of the bombardment on the condition that the United States stop escorting Nationalist ships across the strait. After Washington agreed to this arrangement, the Communists extended the cease-fire by two weeks. Later that month Dulles flew to Formosa and persuaded Chiang to pull back some of his troops from the offshore islands and to renounce the use of force to regain control of the mainland. Meanwhile, in Geneva, American and Chinese representatives, who had been meeting since early September on the question of American prisoners still held in China, began to exchange proposals for a peaceful settlement in the strait. Nothing came of these talks, but at least they were symptomatic of a considerable cooling of tensions. With the expiration of the two-week cease-fire, the mainland government said that henceforth it would shell Quemoy only on alternate days of the month. This strange pronouncement marked the passing of the second Formosa Strait crisis.

Yet little had really changed in the United States' relations with the People's Republic of China. The Communist regime remained as determined as ever to gain (or regain) Quemoy, Matsu, and all the other Nationalist-held islands, including Formosa itself. The United States was still determined to maintain the status quo in the Formosa Strait region and, as far as possible, to isolate mainland China from what administration spokesmen sometimes referred to as "the civilized community." Early in December 1958, in one of his last major speeches, Dulles reiterated the administration's unflagging refusal to extend diplomatic recognition to the Peking government. Recognition, Dulles proclaimed in his best apocalyptic manner, would mean that the Pacific, now "a friendly body of water," would "in great part be dominated by hostile forces and our own defenses [would be] driven back to or about our continental frontiers." Dulles's death five months later brought some moderation in the administration's rhetoric, but American policy toward China softened not at all.

VIII

For those people—probably a majority in the Eisenhower administration, in Congress, and in the country as a whole—who still thought in terms of the monolith of international Communism, there seemed to be a stepped-up Communist offensive around the globe during the last half of 1958. In actuality, the Soviet Union was far from the controlling agent in the Middle East, although militant Arab nationalism did further Russian ambitions in the area to some extent. Nor had Moscow been behind mainland China's latest efforts to seize the offshore islands. Despite the appearances of amicability and unity, Mao Tse-tung, Chou En-lai, and their associates in Peking were becoming increasingly unhappy with Russian leadership of the Communist countries. Below the surface of Sino-Soviet relations, tensions were growing which would erupt in an irreconcilably bitter quarrel in the early sixties. In the fall of 1958, however, it appeared that almost everywhere, as *Newsweek* magazine characterized it, "the Reds" were "turning the screws." Coming on the heels of the Formosa Strait crisis was the scariest East-West clash over Germany since the Russian blockade of the city of Berlin in 1948–1949.

In March 1958 Nikita Khrushchev had gained supreme power in the Soviet government, succeeding Bulganin as premier while retaining the chairmanship of the Communist party. Now, on November 10, he told a Soviet-Polish friendship rally in Moscow that it was time to terminate the occupation arrangement for Berlin established in 1945, whereby the city had been divided into four zones administered by the USSR, the United States, Great Britain, and France. The Soviets, he said, were prepared to relinquish their responsibilities in Berlin to the government of the Democratic Republic in East Germany. Seventeen days later Russian officials informed the other three occupying powers that within six months there must be a solution to the problem of Berlin based on the conversion of West Berlin into an autonomous free city. If no settlement were reached by May 27, 1959, the USSR would proceed on its own, transferring to the East Germans control over air, highway, rail, and water routes into West Berlin. Shortly thereafter Khrushchev explained that because the Western countries had refused to conclude a German peace treaty recognizing the "reality" of two Germanys, the Soviet Union was acting to end the "abnormality" of the Berlin situation.

What made the Russian pronouncement so critical was the threat to give the East Germans control of access to the city. If that happened, the Western allies would presumably have to deal directly with the German Democratic Republic in order to supply the 10,000 Western troops in Berlin across the 110 miles of East German territory. In effect, therefore, the West would have to acknowledge the legitimacy of the East German regime and accept the permanent division of Germany, both of which the United States and its allies had steadfastly refused to do. The Western policy position on Germany remained what it had been since the late forties: Germany should be reunified on the basis of free elections in both parts of the country. No peace treaty was possible before reunification. Once unified, Germany should have the option of joining the North Atlantic Treaty Organization. As for Berlin, no alteration of the status quo was acceptable until the larger question of Germany had been settled.

While that was official NATO policy, sentiment in the Western capitals was hardly uniform. The French had never been enthusiastic about German reunification. At the same time, the French government under Charles de Gaulle, who had come out of retirement earlier in the year to assume the presidency, took a hard line on preserving the Allied position in West Berlin. West Germany's Chancellor Konrad Adenauer, a warm friend of Secretary of State Dulles, was even more of a hard-liner. The British were much less adamant. Feeling intense pressure from the opposition Labour party not to let the United States drag Britain into war, Conservative Prime Minister Macmillan was willing to consider the free-city concept and otherwise to seek some sort of compromise with the Russians. For Eisenhower and Dulles there was nothing to negotiate about as far as Berlin was concerned. Again Dulles saw the task of diplomacy as a matter of bolstering the Western resolve to stand firm. "We are most solemnly committed to West Berlin, if need be by military force," was his reply to the Russian ultimatum.

Soviet motives in bringing on a new Berlin crisis in 1958 were complex. It appears that Khrushchev viewed West Berlin as an instrument for gaining what had been the foremost goal of Soviet European policy since World War II: to minimize German power in central Europe and especially to keep the Germans from ever again threatening Russia militarily. Thus the Russians were not only determined to keep Germany partitioned, but they wanted absolute guarantees from the Allies that West Germany would never be allowed to have nuclear weapons. West Germany had been a member of NATO since 1955, and now it appeared to the Russians that the United States was moving toward the nuclearization of the Federal Republic's armed forces.

The Bonn government already had American-made cannon which could fire atomic shells and aircraft capable of delivering so-called tactical atomic bombs. The United States kept tight control over the actual nuclear explosives, and at the December 1957 NATO Council meeting Adenauer had turned down the American proposal for stationing IRBMs in West Germany. Nevertheless, Khrushchev feared that the construction of IRBM sites in Italy and Great Britain was a prelude to giving atomic weapons to the Federal Republic. The Soviets knew full well that it would take no more than one relatively small West German atomic bomb to destroy the whole Communist leadership in Moscow. And what if Adenauer's government were able to threaten East Germany with nuclear arms? While such fears may have seemed farfetched, even paranoid, to Western leaders, for the Russians they were quite real. Soviet anxieties about a rearmed Germany, Adam Ulam has observed, "have never been properly understood in the West . . . ."

Yet if limiting German power was the Soviets' overriding concern, the Berlin question itself was also vitally important to them. Khrushchev described Berlin as a bone in his throat, and with good reason. Since 1949, when the Allies had begun keeping statistics, nearly three million people had fled to the West through West Berlin. By 1958 the annual rate of departure from East Germany was about 300,000 persons, most of whom were young and professionally trained. Moreover, the Allies had created a vast espionage establishment in West Berlin, where they also operated powerful radio transmitters which continuously broadcast the Western propaganda line into East Germany. By 1958 the United States government had put some $600 million into West Berlin's economic development to make it the leading manufacturing city in Germany. For the Allies, in short, West Berlin had become a glittering showcase of capitalism, while for the Soviets the city was a constant aggravation and embarrassment.

A year earlier there had been a promising opportunity for negotiating a pullback of NATO and Warsaw Pact forces and perhaps laying the basis for an equitable resolution of the whole

German question. In October and November 1957 Polish Foreign Minister Adam Rapacki, obviously with Moscow's approval, had presented two proposals for the denuclearization and ultimate demilitarization of central Europe. The "Rapacki Plan," as the combined proposals were called, would have established a nuclear-free zone consisting of Poland, Czechoslovakia, and East and West Germany, with provision for both ground and aerial inspection procedures to prevent either the manufacture or stockpiling of nuclear weapons within the zone. After denuclearization, conventional forces would be reduced by phases and eventually eliminated. Nikolai Bulganin, then still Soviet premier, formally endorsed the Rapacki Plan in December, warning the Western countries at the same time that stationing IRBMs in West Germany "may set in motion forces in Europe and entail such consequences as even the NATO members may not contemplate."

That same month George Kennan, who had been dismissed by Dulles in 1953 but was still widely regarded as the leading American Sovietologist, completed a series of three lectures aired by the British Broadcasting Corporation. Published at the beginning of 1958 as *Russia, the Atom, and the West,* Kennan's lectures contained cogent arguments for what he called "disengagement" in central Europe. Though severely criticized by Dean Acheson, the influential French historian Raymond Aron, and other Western "realists," Kennan greatly stimulated public discussion of the German situation in the NATO countries at a time when the Soviet bloc was making a strong overture for negotiations.

Yet because the Eisenhower administration would not budge from the longstanding American position on German reunification, there was no real chance of progress toward arms reductions in central Europe. Dulles, spurred on especially by Adenauer, would not hear of a German settlement without free elections and the NATO option, although there is considerable evidence that during the last year of his life he came to feel there might be some good in mutual troop pullbacks. At any rate, formal Western policy remained the same after the Rapacki proposals as before. This stubbornness, according to Ulam, constituted "one of the most fundamental errors of Western policy in the postwar period."

Thus by the end of 1958 Nikita Khrushchev had adroitly caught the West in the trap of its own inflexibility. In mid-December Dulles left Walter Reed Hospital, where he had undergone treatment for his spreading abdominal cancer, and flew to Paris for the NATO Council meeting. There he admonished his colleagues not to give in to Russian blackmail. The West must be ready, if it came to that, to fight a nuclear war in defense of its rights in West Berlin. In their formal answer to the Soviet demands, the NATO Council members tried to steer the Russians away from the narrow issue of a free city in West Berlin by contending that "the Berlin question can only be settled in the framework of an agreement with the USSR on Germany as a whole." Yet the Soviets, while they kept their sights on the larger goal of German demilitarization, refused to relent on the six-month deadline for a settlement on Berlin. As the year ended the date May 27, 1959, loomed ever more ominously over the whole world.

The two years since his reelection had been rough ones for Dwight Eisenhower. Besides the turbulent course of events in the Middle East; the trials of dealing with an increasingly cranky Democratic Congress; the Little Rock disturbances; the national clamor over the sputniks, the missile gap, and overall defense policy; another war scare in the Formosa Strait; and now the Berlin crunch, the President had had to worry about an economic recession in which industrial production dropped 14 percent and unemployment climbed to 7 percent, the peak for the decade. Feeling the heat of widespread personal criticism for the first time, Eisenhower had watched his national approval score as measured by the opinion polls drop from 79 percent at the beginning of his second term to 49 percent in April 1958, one of the sharpest declines the pollsters had ever recorded. The President's standing in the polls had improved a few points after that, but at the end of the year it was still lower than the lowest point of his first term. On top of everything else, in June 1958 a House investigating committee had heard testimony that Sherman Adams, the President's most trusted subordinate, had interceded with federal regulatory commissions to get preferred treatment for New England textile manufacturer Bernard Goldfine. Even though the House committee subsequently exonerated the Assistant to the President and Eisenhower affirmed his confidence in Adams, the Adams-Goldfine affair had become too much of a political liability for the GOP in an election year. Pressured especially by right-wing Republicans, who had never liked Adams anyway, the President in September had finally and "sadly" accepted Adams's resignation.

The charges against Adams, when added to the country's economic troubles and slackening public confidence in the administration's foreign and military policies, gave the Democrats a potent case in the congressional campaigns that fall. The result was a near disaster for the Republicans, the most massive defeat the GOP had suffered since the Democratic avalanche of 1936. Not only did the Democrats gain majorities of 64–34 in the Senate and 282–154 in the House of Representatives but they also won twenty-six gubernatorial races, leaving in office only fourteen Republican governors. Among the beaten Republican gubernatorial hopefuls was William Knowland, who had resigned as Senate minority leader to try for the California statehouse. About the only bright spot for the GOP was New York, where Nelson Rockefeller, showing remarkable popular appeal, bucked the Democratic tide and beat Averell Harriman for the governorship.

Eisenhower thus became the first President to have to deal with three successive Congresses controlled by the opposition party. Now sixty-eight, he would also be the oldest President by the time he left office. Deprived of the managerial abilities of Sherman Adams, soon to lose the towering presence of John Foster Dulles, confronting a Congress that seemed to be dominated by the "spenders," Eisenhower looked like a much-weakened chief executive. Yet the last two years of his Presidency would prove him to be a lot tougher than many had supposed. At home Eisenhower would stubbornly and vigorously defend "fiscal integrity" against congressional efforts to exceed his budget requests. And with Dulles gone he would draw on amazing reserves of energy in an almost obsessive quest for global peace. The President's performance in 1959–1960 can be characterized, without exaggeration, as the "Eisenhower resurgence."

VII

The Eisenhower
Resurgence

THE November 1958 issue of the monthly magazine *Commentary* carried an analysis of Eisenhower's Presidency by the journalist William V. Shannon. Published on the eve of the big Democratic victory in the congressional and state elections, Shannon's article set forth what was rapidly becoming the most common interpretation of the thirty-fourth President among political liberals. At the beginning, Shannon acknowledged, the country had needed Eisenhower, mainly to end the Korean war and cool the passions aroused by McCarthyism. But Eisenhower's usefulness had soon passed. Because he had "lived off the accumulated wisdom, the accumulated prestige, and the accumulated military strength of his predecessors," he would leave office with the country's domestic and foreign policies "about where he found them in 1953. No national problem . . . will have been advanced importantly toward solution." The Eisenhower years had therefore been "the time of the great postponement."

Eisenhower probably never read Shannon's article, but he doubtless felt the sting of the growing number of similar complaints as he began the last two years of his term. In need of frequent respites from the day-to-day grind of the Presidency, no longer able to rely on Sherman Adams to keep the White House staff functioning smoothly, and aware that John Foster Dulles would not be able to carry on much longer, Eisenhower faced an uncertain time within his own administration. The prospect of dealing with the overwhelmingly Democratic Eighty-sixth

Congress, the most liberal since the 1930s, was hardly pleasing to a President whose determination to hold down spending was stronger than ever. On the morning after the 1958 elections he told newsmen that the people had mostly chosen candidates whom "I would class among the spenders . . . . And I promise this: for the next two years, the Lord sparing me, I am going to fight this as hard as I know how." Although the economy had partially recovered from the 1957–1958 recession, it was still sluggish and the unemployment rate still hovered around 6 percent. Congressional pressure to expand existing social welfare programs and undertake new ones could be expected, as well as demands for bigger and more lavishly financed military and space programs.

Nor was the outlook any brighter for the administration's foreign policy at the beginning of 1959. The United States had failed to block the spread of Soviet influence and stabilize political conditions in the Middle East. Leftist-led insurgent forces were struggling to overthrow American-backed regimes in Southeast Asia. Anti-American feelings were surfacing throughout much of Latin America, and in Cuba a revolutionary government about which the Central Intelligence Agency had strong apprehensions had just come to power. In sub-Saharan Africa, which had not greatly concerned American policy makers up to now, unstable new national governments were forming in rapid succession out of former European colonies. And overshadowing everything else at home and abroad was the Soviet Union's ultimatum on Berlin, which had brought on the most direct and dangerous clash of Russian and American wills in a decade. The United States and the USSR seemed to be, as the news media repeatedly phrased it, "on a collision course."

I

After threatening to give the East Germans control of access routes from West Germany into West Berlin and then setting a six-month deadline for making West Berlin a free city, the Soviets on January 10, 1959, sent the Western governments the draft of a German peace treaty to be signed by the major powers and by both East and West Germany as separate states. A conference for the signing of the treaty should be held before the end of March; otherwise the USSR would go ahead and arrange its own treaty with the East German government and declare West Berlin a free city. That would mean the Western powers would have to deal with the East Germans in order to supply their forces in a city where, according to the Soviets, they would no longer have any legal standing.

For the next two months the tension continued to build. While Dulles flew to London, Paris, and Bonn for another round of talks with the Allied leaders, the Pentagon studied various military alternatives, finally proposing a division-sized "probe" of Soviet "intentions" in the event the East Germans took over the border checkpoints. The Western position was a difficult one. Both Eisenhower and Dulles doubted that American public sentiment could be brought to support military action before the May 27 deadline. As Eisenhower observed in his memoirs, it would be hard to convince Americans "why a nation would risk war over an issue so seemingly slight as the nationality of the man who stamps the papers as a convoy proceeds through a checkpoint." Moreover, the West's military capability—short of all-out nuclear war—was quite weak in central Europe. Eisenhower turned down the Pentagon's probe option because it might lead to a ground conflict in which the numerically inferior Western forces would have to take a localized defeat or resort to nuclear weapons. While he remained deliberately vague about possible military responses to Soviet moves, he did tell newsmen on March 11, "We are certainly not going to fight a ground war in Europe. . . . With something like . . . 175 Soviet divisions in that neighborhood, why in the world would we dream of fighting a ground war?" A reporter then asked if the United States would use nuclear weapons "to defend free Berlin." "Well, I don't see how you could free anything with nuclear weapons," the President replied.

Late in February British Prime Minister Harold Macmillan, under fire from both the Labour party and some of his fellow Conservatives for following the American lead on Berlin, accepted a three-year-old invitation from the Soviet government and flew to Moscow for extensive talks with Nikita Khrushchev. The rotund Russian leader—whom Macmillan characterized as an "irrepressible . . . petulant, occasionally impossible, but not unlovable extrovert"—made clear that what he mainly wanted was de facto, not necessarily de jure, Western acceptance of East Germany's separate existence. Khrushchev brushed aside questions about the May 27 deadline, saying that the important thing was progress toward some kind of settlement on Berlin. And while he wanted a summit conference on the issue of European disengagement and disarmament, he was willing for preliminary foreign ministers' talks to precede the summit.

Macmillan came to Washington on March 20. During his and Eisenhower's visit with Dulles, who was again undergoing radium treatments at Walter Reed Army Hospital, the Secretary of State sounded more militant than ever. At one point, according to Eisenhower's recollection, Dulles "asked wryly why we spent $40 billion a year or more to create deterrent and defensive power if, whenever the Soviets threatened us, our only answer would be to buy peace by compromise. 'If appeasement and partial surrender are to be our attitude,' Foster said, 'we had better save our money.'"

At Camp David, however, Macmillan found the President more open-minded. Pleading with Eisenhower to agree to a summit meeting, Macmillan pointed out that it would take only eight hydrogen bombs to destroy Great Britain. Eisenhower finally approved Macmillan's draft proposal for a meeting of the Big Four foreign ministers, with a summit conference to follow if the lower-level discussions showed sufficient progress. Khrushchev quickly agreed to the Western offer. The foreign ministers were to convene on May 11 in Geneva, Switzerland.

On April 15, having received word from the Walter Reed specialists that his cancer was incurable, Dulles submitted his resignation to the President. Struggling to keep his emotions under control, Eisenhower himself made the announcement to the White House press corps. Three days later he named Undersecretary of State Christian A. Herter, Dulles's personal choice, to head the State Department. Sixty-four years old and hampered by an arthritic condition which forced him to walk with crutches, Herter had neither Dulles's boundless energy, powerful intellect, nor commanding personality. Yet he did have extensive experience in foreign affairs dating back to 1916, and he had long been a supporter of a bipartisan foreign policy and collective security arrangements. He was, moreover, far more politically experienced than Dulles, having represented Massachusetts in the House of Representatives for ten years before serving as governor of the state from 1953 to 1957.

By the time Herter went to Geneva for the Big Four foreign ministers' conference, the Western powers had finally reached agreement on their negotiating package. They were now willing to defer free elections until after German reunification, which should be coupled with an agreement to limit armaments in an area of central Europe to be gradually expanded. The Soviets must guarantee Western access to West Berlin until the city as a whole became the capital of reunited Germany. The Russians, however, insisted that the conference first focus on the status of Berlin and on a peace treaty at least temporarily recognizing two Germanys. After agreement had been reached on these matters, the powers would then go on to discuss reunification and arms limitations.

There was never much chance of reconciling these fundamentally divergent approaches to a German settlement, but the talks at least served to distract attention from the looming May 27 deadline. That day came and went, its significance in terms of the Soviet ultimatum obscured by the ironic fact that the diplomats were all in Washington to attend the funeral of John Foster Dulles.

When the foreign ministers returned to Geneva, they could do little more than reiterate their conflicting proposals. The talks adjourned on June 30, reconvened the next month, and then adjourned for the last time early in August. The Western powers could stay in West Berlin for another eighteen months, announced Soviet Foreign Minister Andrei Gromyko, but in the meantime there must be progress toward a final resolution of the Berlin problem.

That final resolution never came, but for a time after the summer of 1959 the Berlin crunch eased considerably, mostly as a result of a remarkable visit Khrushchev paid to the United States in September. The Soviet leader had long wanted to come to America, partly because of natural curiosity, partly because such a trip would be good for his image as a world statesman seeking peace, and partly because he apparently believed the best way to reach important agreements between governments was for heads of state to meet face to face. For his part, Eisenhower was extremely doubtful that anything positive would come from Khrushchev's visit, and he feared that the whole thing would turn into an international spectacle. Yet at the urging particularly of Herter and Undersecretary of State Robert Murphy, the President agreed to invite Khrushchev provided the foreign ministers at Geneva made some progress toward German reunification. Murphy apparently misunderstood Eisenhower's conditions, for he delivered to Frol R. Kozlov, the Soviet first deputy premier then completing a tour of the United States, a note extending an unqualified invitation to Khrushchev. Upon receiving Khrushchev's acceptance, an irked Eisenhower stiffly lectured Herter, Murphy, and others at State on the need to follow the kind of procedures Dulles had established, especially the submission of memoranda on all conferences with the President for Eisenhower's endorsement. "I was chagrined at the way the whole matter had developed," Eisenhower later wrote; now he would "have to pay the penalty of going through with a meeting which, under the circumstances, would be a most unpleasant experience . . . ."

On August 5, just as the Geneva meetings adjourned without accomplishing anything, Herter announced that Khrushchev would come to the United States in September, and that President Eisenhower would visit the Soviet Union the next year. Meanwhile Vice President Nixon traveled in the USSR, having gone first to Moscow to open an American trade exhibit. Evidently Nixon himself had sold the United States Information Agency on the value of his going to Russia. Eisenhower, it seems, placed little importance on the trip and certainly did not see it as a prelude to Khrushchev's visit. Nixon, however, got a substantial political dividend from his Russian travels, especially from his impromptu "kitchen debate" with Khrushchev during a televised tour of a model home on display at the American exhibit.

Before Khrushchev's arrival Eisenhower flew to Bonn, Paris, and London to reassure America's allies that he and the Russian leader would make no deal behind their backs, that in fact there would be no negotiations of any kind, only informal discussions to "melt a little of the ice," as Eisenhower put it. French President de Gaulle was particularly skeptical; restive under American hegemony, he had already demanded the formation of a NATO directorate which would give France an equal voice in alliance decisions and had refused to allow American missile bases on French territory.

On September 15 Nikita Khrushchev, the first Russian head of state ever to visit the United States, arrived at Andrews Air Force Base outside Washington. In his response to Eisenhower's welcoming remarks, he pointedly referred to the Soviet *Lunik II* rocket, which had hit the moon on target less than two days earlier. Then commenced the spectacle Eisenhower had anticipated. After a round of dinners and meetings in Washington, Khrushchev took off on a dizzying cross-country jaunt which included stops in New York, Los Angeles, San Francisco, Iowa (to visit a huge corn farm), and Pittsburgh. Preceded by phalanxes of security operatives and followed by swarms of reporters and cameramen, the Soviet premier was alternately jocular, philosophical, folksy, and boastful. Without question his most quoted (and misunderstood) statement was that because socialism's productive potential was superior to capitalism's, "we will bury you." Whether exchanging pleasantries with groups of businessmen, verbally sparring with labor leaders, or keeping his composure in the presence of Los Angeles's boorish mayor, Khrushchev demonstrated his talents as a born actor. His trip across the continent and back was a theatrical tour de force.

The last days of Khrushchev's two-week visit were spent in talks with Eisenhower at Camp David. There Khrushchev called for "peaceful coexistence" between East and West—and canceled the time limit for a settlement on West Berlin. Eisenhower admitted that the Berlin situation was "abnormal" and that its solution "should not be prolonged indefinitely." At the same time, the President was happy that "we can now negotiate . . . without an axe hanging over our heads." The preconditions for a summit, he said, had been fulfilled. The two leaders announced that they would meet with Macmillan and de Gaulle at Paris the coming spring, when, as Khrushchev added, "everything is in bloom." Following the summit the President would visit the Soviet Union. Khrushchev then flew home, with the international press already reporting an apparent new mood in Soviet-American relations, a "spirit of Camp David."

Now began in earnest the campaign of "personal diplomacy" which would mark Eisenhower's last year in office. Persuaded by Herter that visits to different countries would promote the cause of peace and by Press Secretary James Hagerty that such travels would be good for domestic politics, the President on December 3 embarked on a nineteen-day "goodwill tour" which took him to eleven different countries in Europe, Asia, and North Africa. Stopping first in Rome, where he met Pope John XXIII, Eisenhower flew on to Turkey and Pakistan before turning north for a stopover in Kabaul, Afghanistan. From there he went to New Delhi, the Indian capital, where his motorcade moved through crowds estimated at a million and under banners reading "Welcome, the Prince of Peace." After discussions with Indian Prime Minister Nehru, the President reversed directions, flying to Tehran in Iran. From there he journeyed to Athens and on to Paris, where he, Macmillan, de Gaulle, and Adenauer agreed that May 16, 1960, would be the opening date for the summit conference with Khrushchev; Eisenhower would go to the USSR in June. After two more stops—in Madrid for a state visit with the dictator Francisco Franco, who allowed the Strategic Air Command to maintain bases in Spain, and in Casablanca for an exchange of amenities with King Mohammed V—the President arrived back at Washington on December 22.

II

Whether Eisenhower's 22,000-mile journey did anything to promote peace is questionable, but the trip was unmistakably good for his personal standing at home. At the beginning of 1960 the Gallup poll showed that his approval rating had soared to 71 percent, close to what it had been three years earlier. Fortified by reviving public confidence in his leadership and urged on by

Secretary of the Treasury Robert Anderson and Maurice H.
Stans, who had become his Budget Director in 1958, the President proved more than ever a resolute champion of fiscal restraint. Much of the story of Eisenhower's resurgence in
1959–1960 has to do with his dogged defense of restrictive
budgets against congressional efforts to add new domestic programs and fund existing ones at levels Eisenhower himself had
proposed early in 1957. And while the President was willing to
see modest growth in military expenditures, he continued adamantly to resist calls for big new allocations for missile and space
projects and conventional forces. Early in the 1959 congressional
session he told Republican leaders on Capitol Hill, "Every sort
of foolish proposal will be advanced in the name of national
security and the 'poor fellow.' We've got to convince Americans
that thrift is not a bad word." "Good budgeting," Stans remarked,
"is the uniform distribution of dissatisfaction."

In 1959 Eisenhower vetoed two public housing bills, two large
public works appropriations, and various other domestic measures he considered extravagant. Relations between the President
and Congress became outright hostile in June, when the Senate,
by a vote of 49–46, refused to confirm Eisenhower's nominee for
Secretary of Commerce, Lewis Strauss. As chairman of the Atomic
Energy Commission from 1952 to 1958, Strauss had made many
enemies on Capitol Hill by his generally high-handed conduct
and especially by his support for the Dixon-Yates contract. His
leading foe in the Senate was Clinton Anderson of New Mexico, a
staunch public-power advocate, whose position as chairman of
the Joint Committee of Congress on Atomic Energy had often
put him at odds with Strauss.[1] Anderson spearheaded the public
fight against Strauss's confirmation, while Democratic Leader
Lyndon Johnson, not wanting to jeopardize his presidential hopes
by going against the majority of Senate Democrats, had no choice
but to join the fight. Strauss thus became the first nominee for a
cabinet-level appointment to be rejected since 1925.

1. Apparently Senator Anderson also felt some anger over Strauss's
role in the harassment and eventual dismissal as AEC consultant of J.
Robert Oppenheimer in 1953–1954, and remorse over his own passivity
during the Oppenheimer episode.

Congress also continued to give Eisenhower a hard time on military policy and military funding. In 1959 Johnson's Preparedness Subcommittee held extensive hearings on the administration's fiscal 1960 military budget, which, at $41 billion, was only $145 million greater than the previous year's. Again Secretary of Defense McElroy proved a poor witness for the administration, acknowledging that the Joint Chiefs of Staff were all doubtful about the budget and that it was not the administration's "intention or policy" to match Russian production of intercontinental ballistic missiles. This disclosure in turn opened the way for the usual special pleading before Johnson's subcommittee and other congressional bodies by each of the Chiefs, by General Bernard M. Schriever, Commander of the Air Force's Ballistic Missile Division, and by Roy M. Johnson, Director of the Advanced Research Projects Agency, which Eisenhower had set up early in 1958. Again Senator Johnson and Democrats in general bemoaned the slow pace of missile development, the failure to beef up conventional forces, and what they regarded as overall short-sightedness in administration military planning. Again there was gloomy talk about the "critical years" of the early sixties, when the Soviets supposedly would have a three-to-one advantage in ICBMs. Yet the military boosters in Congress still were not able to add significantly to the amounts Eisenhower had budgeted.

The story was much the same the next year, when the administration's budget essentially held the line on military outlays to project a $4.2-billion surplus for the end of fiscal 1961. Thomas Gates, Eisenhower's third Secretary of Defense, reported that the United States would have three fireable Atlas ICBMs on their launching stands in 1960, as opposed to about ten for the USSR.[2] He reminded the skeptical congressmen, however, that the Air Force was nearing operational status with its second-generation, liquid-fueled Titan ICBM, and that the combined power of SAC, of the Navy's carrier-based and submarine-based aircraft and missile capabilities, and of the land-based Thor and Jupiter intermediate-range missiles in place overseas was still much greater than that

---

2. Neil McElroy resigned as Secretary of Defense late in 1959 and returned to Procter and Gamble.

of the Soviets. In this election year, however, the Democrats were more insistent than ever that America's retaliatory capacity could be wiped out by a missile-borne nuclear strike, and that the peril would be even greater in the years to come. Senator Stuart Symington, for example, was convinced that predictions of a threefold Soviet missile lead by 1963 were still right. More than ever the Democrats argued with the administration about whether the nation's military establishment had the proper mix of strategic and tactical forces.

Eisenhower was no less resistant to pressures for social welfare legislation in 1960. The threat of his veto, combined with the inability of northern Democrats to unify in order to offset Republican and southern Democratic opposition, limited significant domestic legislation in 1960 to a second and still-inadequate Civil Rights Act. This was the only major legislation on which the administration and the Democratic leadership were able to agree. Efforts to expand federal aid to elementary and secondary education, to increase the federal minimum wage and broaden its coverage, to enlarge public housing programs, and to establish federally financed medical coverage for the elderly (already dubbed "Medicare") all failed to clear Congress in either the regular session or the rump session held after the presidential nominating conventions that summer.

While Eisenhower's determination to hold down domestic and direct military spending toughened in 1959–1960, he was more convinced than ever that mutual assistance expenditures were sound and necessary. In this area, however, his problem remained what it had been since the beginning of his Presidency: to convince Congress and the public that money granted and loaned to foreign governments was not a vast giveaway. In 1959 the administration sponsored the formation of the Committee to Strengthen the Frontiers of Freedom, a nonpartisan organization of nationally known people supporting the foreign aid program. With such notables as James B. Conant, Henry Luce, Averell Harriman, and Leonard K. Firestone lending their names to its work, the committee staged public rallies, organized letter-writing campaigns, and generally tried to influence Congress in behalf of the overseas assistance portions of the administration's budgets. In 1960

Secretary of Defense Gates worked closely with the committee and through the Defense Department's intricate and powerful network of contacts in industry, finance, and labor. Enlisted in the national lobbying effort, besides the Army and Air Force associations and the Navy League, were such organizations as the Chamber of Commerce, the American Legion, and the leadership of the AFL-CIO. The effort paid off when Congress cut the foreign aid allocation by only 9 percent, the smallest reduction of Eisenhower's Presidency, even though he had asked for about a billion dollars more than in 1959.

III

Despite his troubles with Congress, Eisenhower remained popular with the American public, a fact largely attributable to his continuing pursuit of personal diplomacy. Late in February 1960 the President began a two-week tour of Latin America. His itinerary included Puerto Rico, Brazil, Uruguay, Argentina, and Chile. Again there were huge, overwhelmingly friendly crowds, warm greetings from heads of state, and an overall appearance that the President was loved and admired by the people of the world. American policy and American interests, so it seemed, were in good shape. Overlooking the Guatemalan episode of 1954, Eisenhower pledged that the United States would stay out of the internal affairs of the Latin American countries, but that his government would offer more economic assistance and cooperation to raise living standards in America's sister republics.

All the same, the Latin American trip showed Washington's growing anxiety about unstable political conditions in the nations to the south. In May 1958 Vice President Nixon had been spat upon, hit with rotten eggs, and generally roughed up by angry crowds in Lima, Peru, and Caracas, Venezuela. Hearing of the Caracas disturbances, Eisenhower had ordered a thousand marines flown to Puerto Rico and the American naval base at Guantanamo Bay, Cuba, for a possible rescue operation. A shocked American correspondent expressed the common feeling in the United States when he cabled from Caracas: "How in God's name could something like this happen in our own hemisphere backyard?" Nixon's calm courage—"I tend to become analytical and cold in a tough situation," he said in Lima—earned him a hero's reception when he got back to Washington. His ordeal had convinced him that, as he reported to Eisenhower, "the threat of Communism in Latin America is greater than ever before."

The Vice President's statement reflected the common cold war tendency to see almost any kind of political disorder as Communist-inspired, but in fact the politics of the Latin American countries did run to ideological and emotional extremes. The Eisenhower administration, like every administration since Woodrow Wilson's, preferred middle-of-the-road governments chosen in free elections and committed to moderate programs of reform, which would not jeopardize private American industrial, commercial, and financial interests. Yet while Washington officially frowned on rightist military dictatorships, it was willing to live with such regimes rather than see the triumph of left-wing revolutionary movements dedicated to radical alterations of the social and economic status quo. Above all, the American government wanted stability in Latin America.

Nowhere had American economic overlordship been more firmly established than in Cuba, and nowhere were the shortcomings and contradictions of American policy more evident than in the Eisenhower administration's relations with the new revolutionary government of the island republic. Americans might still congratulate themselves on having gone to war with Spain in 1898 to free Cuba, but in fact Cuba had never been truly independent. Besides building and maintaining the sprawling Guantanamo naval base on Cuba's southeastern coast, exercising a virtual veto over the country's foreign policy for more than three decades after 1898, and intervening periodically to put down political unrest and straighten out its finances, Washington had fostered the growing dominance of the Cuban economy by American investors.

By the late fifties American capital controlled nearly all of Cuba's oil production, 90 percent of its mines, 80 percent of its public utilities, half its railways, 40 percent of its sugar production, and a quarter of its bank deposits. In 1957 American firms made profits of $77 million from their Cuban investments while employing only a little more than one percent of the country's population. Cuba had little to sell to other countries besides sugar, for which the United States was the major market. By manipulating the sugar import quota assigned to Cuba, the American government had been able to cause drastic fluctuations in the Cuban economy since the late nineteenth century. At the beginning of 1959 some 600,000 Cubans were unemployed, about the percentage of the work force that had been jobless in the United States during the Great Depression. Some 40 percent of Cuba's population were illiterate, and in the rural areas an estimated 95 percent of the children suffered from parasitic diseases. Forty-six percent of the total land area on the island was controlled by 1.5 percent of the landowners.

Until the end of 1958 Cuba was ruled by the dictatorship of Fulgencio Batista, one of the bloodiest, most repressive regimes in all Latin America. With an army whose officer corps was largely trained in the United States and whose equipment was almost entirely American-made, Batista crushed all political opposition before 1956. Late that year a band of revolutionists led by Fidel Castro, a young lawyer who had spent two years in Batista's prisons and then had lived in exile in New York City and Mexico, landed in Oriente province and went into hiding in the Sierra Maestra Mountains. From this stronghold Castro-led rebels carried on increasingly effective guerilla operations against the government. Many people in the United States sympathized with Castro and his men, whose romantic appeal was enhanced by their youthful, bearded countenances and their rhetoric of democracy and constitutional liberty. A few Americans even went to fight with Castro, while others helped smuggle arms to the rebels from Florida. In December 1958 most of Batista's army abandoned the dictator. With his regime crumbling, Batista fled to the Dominican Republic, and on New Year's Day 1959, Castro rode atop a tank into Havana to take over the government.

Washington kept a watchful eye on what was happening in Cuba. Already CIA Director Allen Dulles had reported to Eisenhower that "Communists and other extreme radicals appear to have penetrated the Castro movement." While promising full civil liberties and representative government, Castro quickly showed that his main concern was breaking up the enormous sugar plantations and cattle ranches and redistributing the land to peasant families. Americans owning more than a third of this property began to protest loudly when Castro offered compensation at the values they had reported for tax purposes rather than at what they now claimed their holdings were worth. Meanwhile Castro's government set up military courts and began to try hundreds of leading "Batistianos," especially officials of the national police. Staged as public exhibitions, often televised, and carried out with little regard for legal procedures, these trials and the speedy executions that followed initially did more than anything else to turn American public sentiment against the Cuban revolutionists.

From Congress came angry protests and warnings. Castro and his associates should "drop down on their knees before their Maker and ask for forgiveness," declared Wayne Morse, chairman of the Senate Subcommittee on Latin American Affairs. Representative Wayne L. Hays, an Ohio Democrat, called for restrictions on American tourist travel to Cuba and a trade embargo if Castro did not stop the trials. Representative Victor L. Anfuso of New York, another Democrat, thought Castro "no better than Batista." As chairman of the House Committee on Agriculture, Anfuso threatened to ask for a reduction in Cuba's sugar quota to teach the Cuban leader "the facts of life, particularly as they affect the economy of his country."

The administration soon extended recognition to the revolutionary government, but as the weeks passed Eisenhower's unhappiness with the continuing executions and his suspicions of Communist influence both grew rapidly. Thousands of Cuban refugees arrived in the United States. Many of them had supported Batista; a few were middle-class liberals already disillusioned with the new regime's strong-arm methods. From the refugees came reports that Communists controlled the labor unions and were infiltrating the armed forces. Late in March Allen Dulles told the President that Castro had become virtually a dictator, that Communists were operating openly and legally in Cuba, and that Castro's brother Raul was "awfully close" to being a Communist.

In April 1959, at the invitation of the American Society of

Newspaper Editors and against the wishes of an irritated Eisenhower, Castro came to the United States. The President refused to see him. Castro's reception from the editors, however, was friendly enough, and in New York City, where he went after a week in Washington, big, enthusiastic crowds greeted him. Castro talked of continued friendship with the United States, defended the trials and executions as just punishment for "war criminals," and offered assurances that all expropriation of foreign-owned property would be legal. Communism was not gaining ground in Cuba, he insisted. Such statements, made publicly in Washington and New York, probably did not differ much from what Castro said in a three-hour conference with Vice President Nixon. Yet Nixon, in his formal report to the State Department and the CIA, concluded that the Cuban leader was "either incredibly naive about Communism or under Communist discipline."

In retrospect, it is apparent that neither was the case in 1959. The tragic reality is that Castro and the American government—under both Eisenhower and his successor, John F. Kennedy—had fundamentally differing conceptions of what kind of revolution Cuba should have. Washington wanted Castro to accept United States leadership in the Western Hemisphere, staff his government with people of moderate views, reinstitute civil liberties, and proceed gradually with land reform, compensating American property interests at the prices they asked. In general, the revolution should not overturn the existing foundations of power and influence.

Yet as Stephen Ambrose has observed, "there was little point to having a revolution if the basic economic structure were not changed, beginning with the expropriation of foreign-owned property." To accomplish the social transformation he envisaged for Cuba, Castro was willing to take the support of Communists or anybody else. Yet he also needed foreign capital for economic development. Early in May he appeared before an economic conference of the Organization of American States in Buenos Aires. After describing conditions in his country, he asked for a ten-year, $30-million loan from the United States. There he got essentially the same answer he had received in talks with officials in Washington and financiers in New York: Economic

assistance would depend on whether Castro's government stabilized Cuba's finances, which would necessitate tight credit
policies and a balanced budget. Such policies would, of course,
severely hamper the broad development program Castro was
planning. Frustrated, he went home to proclaim a sweeping
Agrarian Reform Law aimed at breaking up the large estates,
redistributing land to peasant families, requiring all sugar to be
processed by Cuban-owned firms, and diversifying crops. At
the same time, the Cuban government took the first steps toward
nationalizing other kinds of foreign holdings.

Through the summer and fall United States–Cuban relations
steadily worsened, a process highlighted by the ouster of President Manuel Urrutía, a liberal who had denounced the presence
of Communists within the government. By November all private
businesses in Cuba were under government control. The following February, Soviet Deputy Premier Mikoyan visited Cuba to
sign an economic agreement whereby the USSR would buy Cuban
sugar at a lower price than the United States had been paying, in
exchange for $100 million in low-interest credits.

It was mainly the course of events in Cuba, especially the
trade pact with the Soviets, that prompted Eisenhower's Latin
American trip later that same month. On March 17, 1960, less
than two weeks after his return, the President formally approved
a cɪᴀ plan to train Cuban emigrés for an invasion effort against
the island. Set up mainly in Guatemala, the training operations
proceeded erratically in the midst of bickering between ex-Batistianos and former supporters of the revolution.

By July, with Castro moving to confiscate what was left of the
original billion dollars worth of American investments, official
Washington had run out of patience. Congress empowered the
President to fix the import quota on Cuban sugar at whatever
level he saw fit, and Eisenhower quickly cut Cuba's 1960 quota
by 700,000 tons. Later that year he completely excluded Cuban
sugar from the American market for the first three months of
1961, an action that would be renewed by his successor. Castro's
response was to move even closer to the Soviet bloc. That same
July Cuba concluded economic agreements with various East
European countries, and Nikita Khrushchev announced that Rus-

sian missiles would protect Cuba from attack by the United States. *Life* magazine proclaimed "Communism's take-over in Cuba."

The Eisenhower administration had obviously set itself to bring down Castro, by one means or another. It was difficult, though, to convince the member nations of the OAS that Cuba had in fact become a Communist satellite and a menace to the rest of the hemisphere. Over much of Latin America Castro was a glamorous and heroic figure, the leader of a successful uprising against the agents of "Yankee imperialism." Certainly the United States could make little headway in converting to anti-Castroism the biggest and most nearly democratic countries of Latin America—Mexico, Venezuela, Brazil, Argentina, Chile—as long as it remained on good terms with the dictatorship of Rafael Trujillo in the Dominican Republic.

Besides maintaining a police state that was at least as cruel as Batista's had been in Cuba, Trujillo had also instigated an unsuccessful plot to assassinate Romulo Betancourt, Venezuela's liberal president. With Cuban sugar imports cut, American companies initially began to buy more sugar from the Dominican Republic. On August 20, however, Secretary of State Herter took the lead in getting the OAS foreign ministers, meeting in San Jose, Costa Rica, to adopt unanimously a resolution condemning the Trujillo government and calling on the OAS member states to break off diplomatic relations with the Dominican Republic. The State Department shortly closed its embassy in Santo Domingo, and Eisenhower got congressional authorization to reduce the Dominican Republic's sugar quota. Beyond that, however, the administration could only hope for some kind of non-Communist coup against Trujillo. As Eisenhower observed later, "Manifestly our hands were tied until we knew for certain that a Castro-type would not succeed Trujillo. . . ." Washington still was better able to tolerate repressive stability than revolutionary upheaval.

Even so, the year 1960 brought intensified American efforts to blunt the appeal of radical revolutionary elements by promoting moderate reform programs in the Latin American countries. The realization had finally dawned across official Washington that Latin America, with its poverty-stricken masses and runaway birthrate, was as much a part of the "underdeveloped world" as Asia and Africa. The President began to listen more to people like his brother Milton Eisenhower, Nelson Rockefeller, and Undersecretary of State Douglas Dillon, who argued that the United States had to stop supporting rightist dictatorships and bolster the forces of liberal social change in the hemisphere. Administration spokesmen began to speak of the necessity for "orderly reform" to improve living conditions throughout Latin America. President Eisenhower declared that the choice was "social evolution or revolution."

In September, at Bogotá, Colombia, Dillon told the OAS's Special Committee for Economic Cooperation that the task was "nothing less than to lift whole segments of the population into the twentieth century." With Cuba dissenting, the Special Committee adopted the Act of Bogotá, whereby the United States and the other American republics agreed to join in a broad program of financial assistance which would be channeled through the Inter-American Development Bank, set up by the Eisenhower administration two years earlier. The particular goals of the Bogotá agreement were to improve public health efforts, to reform tax structures, to expand public housing and educational facilities, and to help peasants acquire land and increase its productivity. Congress subsequently appropriated an initial $500 million for the new program.

All this activity in the last months of Eisenhower's Presidency looked most impressive on paper, so much so that early in 1961 President Kennedy would be able to add little except an appealing title—Alliance for Progress—to the efforts begun under the previous administration. Yet the new economic program for Latin America—administered by slow-moving, often corrupt bureaucracies, opposed at every turn by landowning elites, and never able to keep pace with surging population growth—was much too little, much too late, and much too oriented toward existing power structures. The next decade would bring a succession of military coups in Latin America, deepening poverty and despair over much of the region, and eventually a drift back into the apathy and neglect that had characterized United States policy toward the countries to the south at the beginning of the Eisenhower period.

IV

If, in the first months of 1960, the Eisenhower administration was increasingly alarmed over the appearance of a new Communist threat to United States hegemony in the Western Hemisphere, its relations with the old Communists in the Soviet Union seemed to be less hostile than at any time since 1956. Just recently the two superpowers had reached their first substantive agreement in the field of disarmament and arms control. The Antarctic Treaty—signed by the United States, the USSR, and ten other countries on December 1, 1959—established a nuclear-free zone around the Antarctic ice mass and set up inspection and enforcement procedures.

No further progress on disarmament was forthcoming at the sessions of a new ten-nation Commission on Disarmament, held during March and April 1960 at Geneva. There the Soviets restated a plan for complete disarmament within four years which Khrushchev had dramatically presented to the United Nations General Assembly the previous September. The Western powers countered with a slower-paced, more limited plan, including the creation of a study group on inspection procedures. The two proposals, embodying the same basic approaches the opposing power blocs had taken during their last disarmament exchanges in 1957, were still mutually unacceptable. The commission adjourned until June.

In the interim the long-awaited Big Four summit conference was to take place in Paris. Eisenhower actually expected little to come of the meeting with Khrushchev. He and the other Western leaders had not yielded an inch on the issues of Germany and Berlin since the previous summer, although Prime Minister Macmillan doubtless would have liked to make some further effort at compromise. And Khrushchev, since his American trip, had several times publicly reaffirmed his intention to sign a separate treaty with the East German government. Yet even if the Paris conference did not reconcile the conflicting stands of East and West on Germany and Berlin, there was widespread hope that the gathering would further ease cold war tensions. It might even improve the climate for the work of the Disarmament Commission and also for the negotiations on a nuclear test ban still proceeding sporadically at Geneva.

Then, at the beginning of May, came one of the biggest diplomatic explosions of the cold war period, one that wrecked the summit and produced a new time of abrasiveness and rancor in Soviet-American relations. On May 1 an American U-2 reconnaissance plane, the kind the CIA had been using in aerial surveillance over the USSR for the past three and a half years, took off from Adana, Turkey, to photograph suspected missile bases in central Russia. Over the eastern Ural mountain range near Sverdlovsk, pilot Francis Gary Powers evidently had some problem with his aircraft and had to drop down a few thousand feet, low enough to put him within reach of Soviet surface-to-air rockets. Suddenly his plane was hit. At 15,000 feet Powers bailed out. Upon hitting the ground he was quickly captured.

Initially the Soviet government said nothing about downing the U-2. An intense debate over what should be done in view of the upcoming summit conference apparently took place within the Kremlin. The Soviets had long known about the U-2 flights, but up to now they had been unable to do anything about them. While Khrushchev probably still wanted the summit, he also had to contend with his own militant cold warriors, who had never liked the more conciliatory policies the leadership had pursued since Stalin's death, and who now demanded that Khrushchev take a tough line on the overflights and on the whole range of issues in East-West relations. Khrushchev was also having trouble with the Chinese, already resentful because the Russians would not help them develop a nuclear capability and disdainful of Khrushchev's calls for peaceful coexistence with the capitalist West. In possession of proof that the United States had deliberately and systematically violated its air space for years, Khrushchev would have run grave political risks both at home and abroad if, for the sake of the summit, he had gone ahead as if nothing had happened.

On May 3, with rumors already circulating in various capitals about a missing American aircraft in the Middle East, a spokesman for the National Aeronautics and Space Administration announced that a U-2 "research airplane," gathering weather data for NASA and the Air Force Weather Service, had apparently crashed in Turkey. The NASA spokesman was telling the truth as much as he knew it; U-2s had flown weather missions in the Middle East for NASA, but its officials were ignorant of the spy flights. Two days later Khrushchev revealed a part of the real story, reporting only that an American aircraft had violated Soviet air space and been shot down. He added that if a Russian plane had similarly intruded over the United States, SAC's bombers would have headed for their designated targets, and "That would mean the outbreak of war."

On the seventh, after the State Department had insisted that there "never has been" any "deliberate attempt to violate Soviet air space," Khrushchev told the Supreme Soviet that the wrecked U-2 and its pilot, "quite alive and kicking," were in Moscow. The pilot had confessed to espionage; the cameras aboard his plane contained film of Russian military installations. Trapped in its own lies, the Eisenhower administration first weakly acknowledged that an American aircraft had "probably" flown over Soviet territory on an intelligence mission. Secretary of State Herter then openly justified the U-2 flights on the grounds that the USSR's refusal to agree to mutual air surveillance had made them necessary. Although Khrushchev suggested that Eisenhower had not been aware of the spy missions, the President, sensitive to long-standing Democratic complaints that he did not really run his administration, decided on May 11 to take full personal responsibility for the whole U-2 intelligence program dating back to 1956. "No one wants another Pearl Harbor," he told newsmen. Therefore the United States had to have "knowledge of military forces and preparations around the world. . . ." His statement was an unprecedented act in the history of espionage, the first time a head of state had openly admitted that his country was spying on others. It was all right to lie "when there is even a 1 per cent chance of being believed," Eisenhower wrote in his memoirs, "but when the world can entertain not the slightest doubt of the facts there is no point in trying to evade the issue."

While there was some criticism of the timing of Powers's mission and of the phony NASA cover story, most of Congress and

Americans in general did not question the national security rationale behind the spy flights. Eisenhower was still willing to go to Paris and even to Moscow afterward. Khrushchev furiously denounced the United States' "aggressive acts," demanded an apology from Eisenhower, and threatened Turkey and other "accomplices"; yet he arrived in Paris on May 14 saying that he would do everything he could to make the conference a success. But the next day he laid down his conditions for proceeding with the meetings in a letter to Macmillan, and on the sixteenth, as soon as the first summit session opened, he was on his feet loudly repeating them to the assembled dignitaries. Under the circumstances, he said, the invitation to Eisenhower to visit the USSR must be withdrawn. Now Eisenhower must repudiate the U-2 flights, promise that there would be no more, and "pass severe judgment" on those responsible. Again the Russian leader had given the President an opportunity to dissociate himself from the CIA's aerial spy program, but by this time it was much too late for anything like that.

Eisenhower replied that since the flights had ended and were not to be resumed, there was no reason why the conference should not go on. Khrushchev and his delegation then walked out. Later, before the crowd of international newsmen, he fulminated at even greater length. The next day, after refusing to meet again with the Western leaders, he and his entourage flew home. There he said that there was no chance for another summit conference for six or eight months, and that he would be willing to discuss the Berlin question only with Eisenhower's successor.

In the United States there continued to be substantial criticism of the administration's handling of the U-2 affair, but the overwhelming reaction to the events in Paris was sympathy and support for the President. Outside the United States, however, Khrushchev had apparently scored a success in the incessant cold war propaganda game. Around the world leftists and ultranationalists chortled over the discomfiture of the American government and cheered Khrushchev's Paris performance.

The summit blowup destroyed whatever slim chance there might have been for constructive work by the UN Commission on Disarmament, which reconvened in Geneva early in June, or for the stalled test-ban negotiations. Again the Western and Eastern blocs talked past each other in presenting their proposals. After another round of rhetorical thrusts with the Western delegates, the Soviet and East European representatives walked out of the Disarmament Commission near the end of the month, thus bringing to a dismal end the formal disarmament negotiations of the Eisenhower period. The test-ban talks broke up about the same time.

That same month, in an effort to recoup some of the ground the United States had supposedly lost as a consequence of the U-2 fiasco and the summit collapse, Eisenhower left on still another good will tour, this one with stops scheduled at Formosa, the Philippines, and Japan. It was a most inopportune time for a visit to Japan. At the beginning of the year Eisenhower and Japanese Premier Nobusuke Kishi had signed a new military treaty which bound Japan even more closely to the United States and approved the stationing of American forces in Japan for another ten years. In reply to Kishi's argument that Japan now had more control over the forces stationed on its territory, neutralists and pacifists, organized in the powerful Socialist party and the much smaller Communist party, charged that the treaty would ensnare their country in the cold war. Moreover, Japanese nationalists were unhappy because the treaty said nothing about the return of the Ryukyu and Bonin islands, occupied by the United States since 1945.

The Japanese Diet ratified the treaty in May. Nevertheless, leftist demonstrations against the pact intensified as the date for Eisenhower's visit approached. The worst outbreak came on June 16, only three days before the President was to arrive in Tokyo, when thousands of students broke into the Diet compound itself to denounce Kishi and the United States and wave "We Dislike Ike" signs. Secretary Herter first said that Eisenhower would go ahead with his planned itinerary, but on the seventeenth Kishi had to radio the President in Manila that the Japanese government could not guarantee his safety. Eisenhower had no choice but to call off the rest of his trip and fly home from the Philippines.

The experience was a humiliating one for the President, who

had now seen two invitations for state visits withdrawn within two months. Although the reasons for the turbulence in Japan were generally misunderstood in the United States, where the tendency was still to blame Communists for whatever troubles American policy encountered, the cancellation of the trip to Japan lent added weight to election-year charges that the United States suffered from declining prestige throughout the world.

V

"National prestige" may be a fuzzy abstraction, but for great numbers of Americans in 1960 it had become a real, measurable quantity. Moreover, the United States seemed to be rapidly losing it. In part the notion of declining American prestige was a creation of the news media and the publicists of the Democratic party. Yet in part it was also a logical consequence of the stress the Eisenhower administration had placed on psychological warfare, of which the President's world travels in the past two years had been the most dramatic manifestation. Since the mid-fifties both the administration and the Democratic opposition had embraced the premise that the nation's vital interests—indeed its very survival—depended to a great degree on winning over the "uncommitted" nations of Asia and Africa. The Soviets had vigorously joined with the United States in this global contest to build the most favorable national and ideological image. Thus, whether or not it had any relation to reality, the strategy of image-building and prestige-seeking had become a crucial element in the cold war.

However abstract the notion of national prestige may have been, the allegation that it had steadily eroded under Republican leadership would play a major role in the 1960 presidential campaign. The GOP, recalling the outpourings of apparently genuine affection from the swarming crowds which had greeted the President in Europe, the Middle East, southern Asia, and Latin America, insisted that the United States was more highly regarded around the world than ever before. The Democrats, pointing to the rough treatment Nixon had encountered on his 1958 South American trip, to the anti-American riots which had made it unsafe for Eisenhower to go to Japan, and to the globally embarrassing U-2 affair, warned that America was in trouble almost everywhere. Only vigorous new Democratic leadership, they argued, could restore the nation's deteriorating position abroad.

Closely related to the issue (or pseudoissue) of national prestige was the debate over national purpose and direction, which reached its high point in the 1960 campaign. Ever since the Soviet space triumphs in the fall of 1957, many articulate Americans had questioned whether the American people still had the drive, vigor, ingenuity, and commitment to greatness they had supposedly demonstrated earlier in their history. It was not enough, such concerned citizens asserted, for America to lead the world in gadgetry and gimmickery; the nation must also be willing to make sacrifices, to stiffen for the cold war challenges ahead. Americans seemed apathetic, confused, adrift. The nation suffered from a "paralysis of will," Adlai Stevenson declared early in 1959. Committed only to "pleasure and profit" and "the pursuit of ease," the people had no understanding of "the rigors and rewards of creative activity."

In the spring of the next year *Life* magazine and the *New York Times,* perhaps the two most influential publications in the country, began jointly to publish a series of commentaries on "the national purpose" by such diverse figures as Stevenson, the evangelist Billy Graham, Walter Lippmann, President John Gardner of the Carnegie Corporation, and the poet Archibald MacLeish. The contributors were almost unanimous in the view that something was lacking in the national spirit. Lippmann, for example, thought Americans had succumbed to a suffusive complacency. "We talk about ourselves today," he observed, "as if we were a completed society, one which has achieved its purposes, and had no further business to transact." "Why," Stevenson wanted to know, "is there a slackness about public problems and a wholesale retreat to the joys of private life?"

Such post-sputnik jeremiads may even have begun to get to Eisenhower. His 1959 State of the Union message had mentioned the need for a formal study of national purposes and priorities, and in February of the next year he set up a President's Commission on National Goals "to develop a broad outline of national objectives and programs for the next decade and longer."

Chaired by Henry M. Wriston, president of Brown University, and consisting of notables from government, industry, education, and labor, the ten-member commission published its findings late in November 1960 in a volume entitled *Goals for Americans.*[3] The report inquired into both international and domestic prospects. Assuming continued conflict and confrontation between the United States and the Communist countries, the commission advocated bigger military outlays for the decade ahead. The American government should act both to stimulate a faster rate of economic growth at home and to help boost the economies of the "underdeveloped nations," which would become the principal battleground of the cold war. Besides a continuously expanding economy, the major domestic goals should be to improve the nation's public educational system, to make college and university training available to all, to do more to promote basic research in the natural sciences, to uplift the arts and make them universally enjoyed and appreciated, to reform the operations of the federal government, and, above all, to insure every citizen the basic right to vote.

The Commission on National Goals is significant in several ways. It was, first of all, one more example of the historic American penchant for self-examination, and it was the principal manifestation of the conviction, widespread in the late fifties, that the American people needed a clear reaffirmation of what their national existence was all about and where their society was supposed to be heading. Moreover, the Commission on National Goals, like the Gaither panel three years earlier, demonstrated that special presidentially appointed study groups often reach

3. The other members of the National Goals Commission were George Meany, president of the AFL-CIO; President Clark Kerr of the University of California; James Bryant Conant, still directing a study of the American high school for the Carnegie Corporation; Crawford H. Greenwalt, president of E. I. du Pont de Nemours and Company; General Albert Gruenther, head of the American Red Cross; Edwin Canham, editor of the *Christian Science Monitor;* former Governor Colgate W. Darden of Virginia; Frank Pace, Jr., chairman of the board of the General Dynamics Corporation; and James R. Killian, who had stepped down from the chairmanship of the President's Science Advisory Committee to return to the Massachusetts Institute of Technology, but who was still a member of PSAC.

conclusions which exceed and even conflict with the views of the Presidents who establish them. Finally, although the commission deliberately withheld its report until after the presidential election, the goals it outlined were strikingly similar to the New Frontier program John F. Kennedy sketched in his successful campaign. In hearty agreement with the conclusions of the commission, Kennedy named William P. Bundy, its staff director, to the key post of Deputy Assistant Secretary of Defense for National Security Affairs in his new administration.

VI

Kennedy won the Presidency in 1960 after what was probably the most grueling national election campaign in the country's history. Kennedy's drive for the Democratic presidential nomination had actually begun as far back as 1956, when he narrowly missed being the party's vice presidential choice. Determined to head the national ticket in 1960, he spent much less time representing Massachusetts in the Senate than he did touring the country to win over party workers and make himself better known nationally.

Able to draw on the eager talents of a large, gregarious family and a sizable family fortune, Kennedy built up a remarkably efficient political organization. Photogenic, looking considerably younger than he actually was (he turned forty-three in May 1960), Kennedy had the further advantages of a record of heroism in the Second World War and a young, attractive wife. Helping him win the respect of intellectuals was his Pulitzer Prize–winning volume of biographical sketches, *Profiles in Courage* (1956). His campaign speeches—terse yet eloquent, punctuated by apt quotations from a wide range of literary and historical sources —added to the impression that here was a politician of exceptional intelligence and learning. Kennedy also benefited from a lack of clear political identification. Although his record in the House of Representatives from 1947 to 1952 and in the Senate since 1953 had been vaguely liberal, he had usually steered away from controversy and had often missed critical votes, such as that on the Senate resolution censuring Joe McCarthy in 1954.

Kennedy's major political handicap was his Roman Catholicism. Yet by confronting the issue forthrightly in the primary campaign, especially in mainly Protestant West Virginia, he effectively neutralized it. The Kennedy "charisma," as some journalists were already characterizing his appeal, drew and excited huge crowds, which included unusually high proportions of young people. Beginning in New Hampshire in March, Kennedy swept through primary after primary. After he won more than 60 percent of the vote in West Virginia, Senator Hubert Humphrey, his foremost rival in the primaries, withdrew from the presidential race. Kennedy was far ahead in delegate votes by the time the Democratic convention opened in Los Angeles on July 11.

Lyndon Johnson, kept in Washington most of the past four years by his duties as Senate majority leader, had sought delegate support outside the primaries on the basis of his reputation as the country's most effective legislator since Henry Clay. Even though he got most of the credit for the Civil Rights Acts of 1957 and 1960, as a Texan and quasisoutherner Johnson was preferable in the southern delegations to Kennedy, who had strongly endorsed school integration and additional civil rights legislation during the primary campaign. Aside from this difference, which was much more a matter of contrasting backgrounds and styles than substantive belief, the views of Johnson and Kennedy varied little. Both talked about more dynamic, imaginative efforts to resist Communist expansion and "restore" American world leadership, about beefing up the armed forces, about a bigger and more ambitious space program, about stimulating the sluggish economy and reaching higher growth rates, about a stronger federal commitment to uplift the nation's poor.

Adlai Stevenson may have entertained some hope of a third try at the Presidency, although he had reverted to his enigmatic 1952 manner. A noisy pro-Stevenson demonstration at the Democratic convention, prompted by his entry into the convention arena, was more a spontaneous show of affection and gratitude than a sign of support for his nomination. Mrs. Eleanor Roosevelt, the Democrats' matriarch, backed Stevenson as she had in 1956, but she had scant influence among the delegates. Senator Stuart Symington, with Harry Truman's endorsement, would have liked to be a presidential candidate. Symington, though, had decided against making an active try for the nomination, choosing instead to wait for some kind of stop-Kennedy movement.

Such a movement never got off the ground. Despite misgivings among many Democrats about Kennedy's youth and alleged inexperience and fears that as a Catholic he would suffer the same fate as Alfred E. Smith in 1928, his well-financed and brilliantly managed organization rolled on. Kennedy's nomination came easily on the first ballot. He then surprised everyone by offering the vice presidential spot to Johnson. What was even more surprising was that Johnson was willing to give up his powerful post as Senate majority leader to accept nomination for an office which former Vice President John Nance Garner, his old friend and fellow Texan, had described as "not worth a bucket of warm spit." Johnson, however, knew that he would not enjoy the kind of towering presence in the Senate under a Democratic President he had gained under Eisenhower. Still keeping his eye on the top job, he was willing to get as close as possible to the seat of power, and bide his time.

The 1960 Democratic platform closely reflected the views of both Kennedy and Johnson. More must be done for the "developing nations," with the emphasis shifted to economic and technical rather than military aid. The annual growth rate of the nation's economy must be boosted to 5 percent, twice as high as under Eisenhower. The platform accused the Eisenhower administration of shortsightedness and confusion in military planning and weapons development, as a result of which "our military power has steadily declined relative to that of the Russians and Chinese." Pledging to oppose admission of the People's Republic of China to the UN, to prevent the establishment of any Communist-dominated government in the Western Hemisphere, and to defend West Berlin and Formosa, the Democrats showed that their quarrel was not with the premises of Republican foreign policy, only with its conduct. "The issue is not the desire to be firm," the platform announced, "but the capability to be firm." The Democratic civil rights plank, the strongest adopted by either major party to that time, promised enforcement of school desegregation rulings, the creation of a federal Fair Employment Practices

Commission, initiatory action by the Justice Department in civil rights cases, and presidential orders forbidding discrimination in publicly financed housing and on work done under federal contract.

Kennedy's televised acceptance speech, which reached the largest audience ever to witness a political address up to then, projected the image of a confident, tough-minded, vigorous young leader. "It is time for a new generation of leadership," Kennedy proclaimed. Ahead was "a New Frontier—the frontier of the 1960s—the frontier of unknown opportunities and perils. . . ." Kennedy offered the American people not promises but challenges, "more sacrifice instead of more security." The choice facing the country, he said, was "between the public interest and private comfort—between national greatness and national decline. . . ."

When the Republicans met in Chicago the next week, Richard Nixon had an even safer lock on the presidential nomination than Kennedy's before the Democrats met. Anticipating Nixon's nomination, Kennedy had gone out of his way to attack the Vice President as a young man whose ideas nevertheless belonged to the days of William McKinley, and as one who, unlike Lincoln, had shown "charity toward none and malice toward all." The closest thing to a serious challenge to Nixon's claims on the nomination had come from Governor Nelson Rockefeller of New York, who did nothing to discourage efforts to boom him for the Presidency in 1959. Visits with Republican leaders around the country, however, convinced him that he had no chance against Nixon, and at the end of the year he withdrew from the race. Shortly thereafter Nixon announced his candidacy.

Rockefeller, though no longer seeking the nomination, was determined to influence the cop platform. As critical as any Democrat of administration military policy, the New York governor strongly echoed the 1958 Rockefeller Brothers Fund report on national security, especially the recommendations for a mandatory national fallout shelter program, for accelerated icbm development, and for bigger conventional forces. Early in June he angered Eisenhower when, right after breakfasting with the President at the White House, he told newsmen that "our position

in the world is dramatically weaker today than fifteen years ago
. . . . our national defense needs great strengthening." He also
urged Nixon to make known his views on all issues before, not
after the convention.

Rockefeller was obviously in a position to make things difficult
for Nixon if he wanted to. Two days before the Chicago convention was to open, the Vice President and the Governor had a
dramatic secret conference at Rockefeller's personal residence in
Manhattan. As a result of what the press dubbed the "treaty of
Fifth Avenue," Nixon agreed that the party platform then being
drafted in Chicago should have stronger sections on both defense
and civil rights. Thus the platform, while mostly praising the
policies of the Eisenhower administration, did call for faster development and deployment of missiles, and committed the GOP
to a program of action in the field of civil rights which was fully
as far-reaching as what the Democrats had promised. In exchange
for these platform concessions, Rockefeller announced his firm
support for Nixon and even placed the Vice President's name in
nomination at Chicago.

Only the insistence of ten Louisiana delegates on casting their
votes for Senator Barry M. Goldwater of Arizona marred Nixon's
first-ballot victory. Earlier in the evening Goldwater, while readily
acknowledging his unhappiness with the party's platform and
leadership, had withdrawn his name from nomination and
pledged to work for Nixon's election. The new darling of the
Republican right, admired by William F. Buckley and other New
Conservative writers, heir to the old Taftite, unilateralist following in the GOP, Goldwater had presidential ambitions which
would blossom over the next four years. By 1964 his exhortations
for Republican conservatives to take over the party would have
become a reality, and the presidential nomination would be his.

The 1960 presidential campaign broke all records for money
spent, for miles traveled, for television exposure, and perhaps for
physical endurance on the part of the candidates. Both Nixon and
Kennedy had virtually exhausted themselves by election day.
Nixon refused to make an issue of Kennedy's religious affiliation,
but otherwise the two men flailed away at each other in a fashion
rarely seen in presidential races. Yet despite their radically con-

trasting backgrounds, personalities, and political styles, in assumptions and outlook Kennedy and Nixon were not far apart.

Both men were fundamentally cold warriors, dedicated to protecting national interests which they believed to be worldwide and almost everywhere threatened by aggressive, expansionist, nuclear-armed Communism. Both were "internationalists," strong advocates of the collective security orientation of American foreign policy since 1939. Both wished to couple the continuing buildup of American armaments with a more ambitious program of nonmilitary aid in response to what Nixon termed "the revolution of peaceful people's aspirations" in Asia, Africa, and South America. In his acceptance speech Nixon had said that now the greatest danger in the struggle against Communism was "the propaganda that warps the mind, . . . the subversion that destroys the will of a people to resist tyranny." Both Nixon and Kennedy accepted the basic premises of the welfare state, although Kennedy favored a greater degree of federal intervention to foster economic growth and expand economic opportunity. Finally, both believed in a powerful Presidency, dominant in domestic affairs and unchallenged in the making and execution of foreign policy.

The campaign thus featured much haggling over means but little substantive discussion of basic issues. Kennedy, for example, favored financing a national program of medical insurance for the elderly through Social Security taxes, and he futilely tried to get legislation to establish such a program through the Senate during the short congressional session after the Republican convention. Nixon wanted health care for the aged financed by the federal government but outside Social Security, and he also thought assistance should be provided only to needy older persons.

In foreign policy, Kennedy cautiously suggested that the Quemoy and Matsu islands were indefensible, while Nixon vigorously praised the administration's refusal to surrender any more ground to the Communists. Kennedy scored the administration for allowing Communism to gain a foothold in Cuba and called for the use of Cuban exiles in military operations against the Castro regime. Nixon, though fully aware that the CIA was already training Cuban dissidents for an invasion of their homeland, denounced Kennedy's proposal as reckless, on the mistaken assumption that the Democratic candidate knew about the Guatemalan enterprise and was about to give away a military secret.[4] To Kennedy's assertion that the missile gap was wider than ever and that American conventional forces were too weak to fight nonnuclear wars, Nixon replied that the nation's military might had never been greater. There was also much talk about the recent U-2 episode, with Nixon charging that his opponent had wanted Eisenhower to apologize to Khrushchev and Kennedy insisting that he had only questioned the wisdom of the President's assuming personal responsibility for the spy flights.

Because of the essential similarity of the candidates' views, the outcome of the race depended—perhaps more than in other recent presidential contests—on personal images and the voters' "feel" for the two men. Nixon and the Republicans portrayed Kennedy as dangerously immature and irresponsible, and as a tool of the "radical" Americans for Democratic Action. Nixon was supposed to be well equipped for the Presidency by his experience in the Eisenhower administration and his world travels. Mature, sober, realistic, he would, the Republicans advertised, be able to "stand up to the Russians." In the Democratic scenario, Nixon was not only the captive of the decrepit Eisenhower policies but was still, despite his pretensions to statesmanship, the same mud-slinging "tricky Dicky" of the early fifties. Kennedy, on the other hand, would bring fresh, dynamic leadership to "get the country moving again" and shore up America's crumbling prestige around the world.

The high points of the campaign were four nationally televised debates—in fact mostly question-and-answer sessions between the candidates and panels of newsmen—held during September and October. Never had television's image-making power been more evident than in these unique encounters. Nixon, weakened by a knee infection which had necessitated a hospital

4. As instructed by Eisenhower, CIA Director Dulles had given Kennedy national security briefings, including a summary of the situation in Cuba. Dulles had not, however, told Kennedy about the exile training going on in Guatemala. Nixon's assumption that he had apparently was the result of an erroneous report from Secretary of the Interior Fred Seaton.

stay and also victimized by a bad makeup job, seemed haggard and unsure of himself in the first debate, whereas Kennedy exuded confidence and impressed viewers with his quick grasp of facts. Nixon did much better in the other three meetings with Kennedy, but many analysts felt that he never overcame the advantage the Democratic candidate had won at the beginning.

Eisenhower was again a problem for Nixon. The President had waited until March before coming across with a fairly clear, if considerably less than passionate, endorsement of Nixon. When he visited the Republican convention in Chicago, Eisenhower had nothing but nice things to say about his Vice President. But in August, when a newsman asked for an example of a major idea Nixon had contributed to administration planning, the President replied, "If you give me a week, I might think of one. I don't remember." Once more Eisenhower, whose capricious streak seemed most evident when the subject of Nixon came up, had left the impression that he did not really respect the man. For his part, Nixon was in the rather difficult position of having to establish his own identity apart from the administration, while at the same time not seeming to contradict Eisenhower's policies.

Whatever his true feelings about Nixon may have been, the President had little use for Kennedy, and he became increasingly impatient with Nixon's delay in asking for his full participation in the campaign. Finally, only eight days before the election, Eisenhower and Nixon met to plan a series of speeches for the President. From then until election day Eisenhower campaigned energetically for the Republican ticket, including a nationally televised speech on election eve.

Eisenhower's late entrance into the fray was one of the imponderables political scientists would have to deal with in analyzing the outcome of the closest presidential race of the century. Others included Kennedy's religion, which unquestionably lost him Protestant votes but may have gained him even more among Catholics, and Lyndon Johnson's presence on the ticket, which was supposed to win over white southerners. The impact of the four televised encounters with Nixon was still another imponderable, along with the question of whether voters were really as anxious about the missile gap and other supposed shortcomings of administration policy as Kennedy claimed they were.

The election was so close that, according to some estimates, a shift of no more than 12,000 votes in five states would have produced a different result. The early returns on election night had Kennedy way ahead; the television networks' computerized projections forecast a substantial victory for the Democratic ticket. By the early morning hours, however, Nixon was closing the gap rapidly. In some states the outcome was in doubt for days. Nixon carried every western state except New Mexico and Nevada, and he also won Florida, Tennessee, Kentucky, and Virginia in the South. But Kennedy, by narrowly winning such populous states as New York, Pennsylvania, Michigan, Illinois, and Texas, managed to squeeze through. In a record popular vote of nearly 69 million, Kennedy's margin of victory was less than 118,000, or about a quarter of a percentage point. The minor party vote, about half a million, was large enough to keep the victor from gaining a popular majority, although Kennedy's electoral vote margin was a reasonably comfortable 303–219. Fifteen southern electors cast their ballots for Senator Harry F. Byrd of Virginia.

Kennedy's big majorities in the largest northern cities, with their great numbers of Catholics and blacks, won him the Presidency. He had obviously been successful in neutralizing the anti-Communist appeal which had served the GOP so well among Catholic voters in 1952 and 1956, and he had more than restored the level of support blacks had given Franklin Roosevelt and Harry Truman. Apparently the Catholic issue had lost most of its force in American national politics. The election of Kennedy might well be offered as supporting evidence for Will Herberg's thesis that American religious exclusiveness had declined in favor of an encompassing "religion of religion."

The congressional elections reflected the closeness of the presidential race, with the Republicans gaining twenty-four seats in the House of Representatives and reducing the Democratic margin by two in the Senate. The new Congress, more conservative than the previous one, would prove generally unresponsive to the new President's efforts to extend the welfare state.

VII

In contrast to the single perfunctory and chilly meeting Eisenhower had had with Truman after the election of 1952, the President gave the President-elect two rather extensive briefings on December 6, 1960, and January 19, 1961, and CIA Director Dulles briefed Kennedy and his associates on several other occasions. It was in these meetings that Kennedy learned for the first time that since the previous spring the CIA had been preparing anti-Castro refugees for an invasion of Cuba.

Such sessions between those about to give up power and those about to assume it seemed vitally necessary. The two-and-a-half-month interval between the presidential election and Kennedy's inauguration proved an unusually eventful and stressful time for the outgoing administration. A succession of international crises had competed for headlines with presidential politics throughout the summer and fall of 1960, and the atmosphere of crisis persisted after the election and into the first weeks of the new year.

In July, while public attention focused on the Democratic and Republican conventions, sub-Saharan Africa had become an arena of cold war rivalry for the first time. No fewer than seventeen African countries gained their independence during 1960. Most were politically unstable, but the least prepared for independence was the new Republic of the Congo. Deliberately kept in a condition of political backwardness by the Belgians until bloody riots forced the Europeans to withdraw, the Congo began to disintegrate within forty-eight hours after independence ceremonies on June 30. Tribal conflicts, entangled with the machinations of European and American holders of cobalt and copper investments, produced civil war between Katanga province, which declared its secession from the Republic, and the central government at Leopoldville. The Belgian government sent troops into Katanga on the pretext of restoring order and protecting white inhabitants, but actually to safeguard Belgian investments and aid the forces of Moise Tshombe, leader of the secessionists. Patrice Lumumba, the Republic's leftist premier, appealed to the

United Nations for help. Acting on the recommendation of Secretary General Dag Hammarskjold, the Security Council voted to dispatch troops and demand the Belgians' withdrawal.

The American government provided transport aircraft, military equipment, and an initial $5 million for the UN peace-keeping operation. Although the United States and the Soviet Union both voted for the Security Council resolution, they split over what the UN force was supposed to do. The Eisenhower administration backed Secretary General Hammarskjold, who maintained that the UN should only work to restore order, not favor one side over another. The Soviets backed Lumumba's insistence that the international force suppress the secessionist elements and solidify the position of the Leopoldville government. Lumumba sought the same kind of support in Washington on visits there in July and August, but Eisenhower and Herter refused to abandon their increasingly uncomfortable position of neutrality. Meanwhile Khrushchev accused the NATO countries of operating through Belgium to commit armed aggression in the Congo. Hammarskjold, Khrushchev snarled, was a tool of the Western imperialists. Khrushchev's threat to send in troops unless the Belgians withdrew prompted an American counterthreat to "do whatever may be necessary" to keep out non-UN forces.

In September Congolese President Joseph Kasavubu ousted Lumumba. Shortly thereafter Colonel Joseph Mobutu, the army's chief of staff, removed Kasavubu and expelled all the Soviet-bloc technicians, military advisers, and diplomats who had entered the country with Lumumba's approval. Lumumba set up a rival government at Stanleyville, so that there were now four groups contending for power: the followers of Lumumba, those allied with Kasavubu, Mobutu's military government, and Tshombe's regime in Katanga. Subsequently Mobutu and Kasavubu resolved their differences. After Mobutu's troops captured Lumumba toward the end of the year, the central government was somewhat at a loss as to what to do with the ex-premier. Finally, in February 1961, the Leopoldville leadership turned him over to Tshombe, who speedily had him shot.

The Eisenhower administration came to an end with the political situation in the Congo still an incredible mess, and with the Republic still plagued by interconnected tribal and civil conflict. For the short run the administration's policy of staying officially neutral and hoping for the overthrow of the Lumumba-led leftists seemed to have worked out fairly well. The Kennedy administration, however, would have to contend with persistent strife in the Congo, until finally it had no alternative but to endorse and provide most of the financial support for what amounted to a UN war against the Katanganese secessionists.

In September 1960 various heads of state arrived in New York to address the fifteenth session of the UN General Assembly. Eisenhower spoke first, proposing national self-determination for the Africans and a five-point program of economic and educational assistance to be administered through the UN. The next day Khrushchev, who had hugged Fidel Castro for the photographers and ostentatiously courted the Afro-Asian delegates, told the General Assembly that colonialism must be done away with everywhere. Removing a shoe and banging on the podium for emphasis, Khrushchev charged that Hammarskjold's policies had worked in behalf of colonial interests in the Congo. He went on to demand that the office of Secretary General be abolished in favor of a tripartite executive—*troika* in Russian—consisting of Western, "socialist," and neutralist representatives.

Adamantly opposed by the Western governments, Khrushchev's troika proposal was not even particularly appealing to the Afro-Asian delegates. Even so, the Russian scored some telling propaganda points by his obstreperous attack on Western colonialism. The Eisenhower administration meanwhile persisted in its largely contradictory efforts to win the favor of the new states of Asia and Africa while remaining on good terms with its European allies. Britain and France were able subsequently to build fairly good relations with their former colonial dependencies. Belgium, however, continued to meddle in the Congo in an effort to preserve its economic position, and Portugal, another NATO ally, refused even to consider steps toward giving up its colonies. And for many leaders throughout Africa and Asia, European colonialism would long have potent symbolic uses.

November brought more difficulties for the outgoing administration. On the ninth, the day after the election, the President met with Secretary of the Treasury Anderson, Chairman William McChesney Martin of the Federal Reserve Board, Secretary of Defense Gates, and others to discuss the United States' balance-of-payments deficit, which was growing at the rate of $4 billion a year. Though hampered by the uncooperative actions of the Ford Motor Company in buying up the remaining shares of its British affiliate (see page 109), such administration measures as calling home the families of military personnel and paring maintenance costs at America's hundreds of overseas military bases and installations did stem the gold outflow to some extent. The worsening balance-of-payments situation, however, would be still another problem passed along by Eisenhower to his successor.

That same month CIA training operations for Cuban refugees in Guatemala seemed in jeopardy when a popular revolt broke out against the country's military government. Afraid that Fidel Castro might try to aid the rebels, Eisenhower ordered American air and naval units to patrol the Guatemalan coastline and also to keep a close watch on neighboring Nicaragua, where the dictator Luis Anastasio Somoza claimed to have evidence of Castroite preparations for invading his country from Costa Rica. A few weeks later the Guatemalan revolt petered out, the Nicaraguan situation quieted, and the President ordered the coastal patrols ended.

Meanwhile United States policy toward Cuba continued to operate in the manner of a self-fulfilling prophecy. The more worried and hostile the government in Washington became and the tighter it applied its economic squeeze on the island, the closer Castro and his associates moved toward the Communist countries. After establishing diplomatic relations with the People's Republic of China, Castro bartered Cuban sugar for Soviet-bloc arms and technical assistance. In response the administration cut off almost all exports to Cuba, mined the area around the Guantanamo base, and declared that the United States would never allow the base to be seized. Early in January, when Castro protested that the American embassy in Havana was a center for espionage and demanded that its staff be cut to eleven people, the administration formally severed diplomatic relations with Cuba. A few days later the *New York Times* published a report, complete with map, on the training of anti-Castro elements in Guatemala. With ten days to go in his Presidency, Eisenhower remained silent on the *Times* article because, as he later wrote, "my successor might want some day to assist the refugee forces to move into Cuba." Three months later President Kennedy would give the go-ahead to an ill-fated operation in the Bay of Pigs.

Yet the most immediately pressing situation the administration faced during its last months was not in nearby Cuba, but in faraway Indochina. Since 1958 the forces of Ngo Dinh Diem's government in South Vietnam had steadily lost ground to insurgent elements. Almost entirely indigenous to the South, the insurgents received political support and modest amounts of military aid from Ho Chi Minh's Communist government in North Vietnam. Going along with Diem's claims that his active opponents were all Viet Cong, or Communists, and that South Vietnam was struggling against "aggression" mounted from the North, the Eisenhower administration had pledged itself to finance Diem's efforts to quell all opposition in the South and had sent increasing numbers of military and technical advisers (but no combat troops) to assist him. For the administration the arch-villain was still China, which supposedly was working through Ho's regime in Hanoi to further its insatiable expansionism. Eisenhower's domino theory—that the fall of any portion of Indochina would lead to Communist control over all of Southeast Asia—was fixed more firmly than ever in American thinking. So was the myth of the two nations of North and South Vietnam, one under totalitarian Communism, the other kept "free" only by American protection.

In April 1959, in a portentous but remarkably little-publicized address at Gettysburg College, Eisenhower had strongly reiterated the domino theory and had made his first full public commitment to maintain South Vietnam as a separate national state. The President warned that South Vietnam's "capture by the Communists" would mean not only the end of "freedom" for the twelve million people in the South, but that "The remaining countries in Southeast Asia would be menaced by a great flanking movement. . . . The loss of South Vietnam would set in motion a crumbling process that would, as it progressed, have grave

consequences for us and for our freedom." Although he mentioned "several Communist divisions" north of the 17th parallel,
Eisenhower did not specifically claim that North Vietnamese
troops were operating in the South. He only referred vaguely to
"the dual threat" to South Vietnam—"aggression from without
and subversion within its borders." Nevertheless, the President
was quite definite in his insistence that "our own interests demand
some help from us in sustaining in Vietnam the morale, the economic progress, and the military strength necessary to its continued existence in freedom."

Eisenhower's geopolitical theorizing was dubious, and his
characterization of political conditions in South Vietnam bore
little relation to reality. In fact Diem's government was so
viciously authoritarian and repressive that it was driving great
numbers of South Vietnamese over to the antigovernment forces.
In 1959 Diem instituted a new program of uprooting people in
the rural areas and concentrating them in "strategic hamlets,"
enclosed in barbed wire. Yet not only did the regime have to
contend with cadres of former Vietminh pro-Communists, with
disaffected middle-class liberals, with Buddhists resentful of
Diem's Roman Catholicism, and with rebellious mountain tribesmen; it also had to deal with armed forces that were split into
power-hungry factions. In November 1960 a contingent of South
Vietnamese paratroops tried to overthrow the government, but
Diem still commanded the loyalty of the national police and most
army detachments. An estimated 400 people died in the streets of
Saigon before the rebellion was crushed.

The next month the antigovernment forces, still including
substantial numbers of non-Communists, formed the National
Liberation Front, which quickly became the most powerful
political force in South Vietnam, dominating at least half the
countryside within two years. As Eisenhower left office Diem still
kept his shaky grip on the central government. But the tide of
battle and popular sentiment were clearly running against him.
Since 1954, when the United States began to supplant the French
in Indochina, more than a billion dollars of American tax money
had gone to build up Diem's government and armed forces. Yet
the American goal of a stable, non-Communist national state in

South Vietnam was, if anything, further from realization than it had been six years earlier.

In the winter of 1960–1961 the situation in Laos, the pastoral and jungle kingdom bordering Vietnam, seemed even more critical. There a three-way conflict was under way between the leftist Pathet Lao, permitted to remain intact in northeastern Laos by the 1954 Geneva Accords; the neutralist government of Prime Minister Souvanna Phouma, with its capital at Vientiane; and a rival rightist faction led by Prince Boun Oum and Phoumi Nosavan, which set up its headquarters at the royal capital, Luang Prabang. As Americans read and heard these strange-sounding names, they were naturally confused as to who were the "good guys" in this distant civil war. Already the United States had sent more than $300 million in aid to Laos, mostly military equipment for the Royal Laotian Army, which split its allegiance between Souvanna Phouma and Boun Oum. The Eisenhower administration, still almost as hostile toward neutral-ism as it had been when John Foster Dulles was alive, sided with Boun Oum and Phoumi, who echoed Ngo Dinh Diem's claim to be saving the country from Communism. When a military coup, carried out by leftist elements cooperating with the Pathet Lao, drove Souvanna Phouma from Vientiane on December 13, the Laotian king appointed Boun Oum head of a new provisional government, to which the State Department speedily extended recognition. Phoumi's forces soon recaptured Vientiane, but in the meantime the Soviet Union began flying supplies to the Pathet Lao and its allies, who had launched an offensive and seemed about to cut Laos in half.

On the last day of the year Eisenhower met with General Lyman Lemnitzer, chairman of the Joint Chiefs of Staff, other Pentagon officials, and representatives of the CIA to discuss the turn of events in Laos. "Possibly we had another Lebanon on our hands," Eisenhower recalled in his memoirs. The group agreed that the Seventh Fleet should be redeployed and readied to back up an American intervention. The President knew that little help could be expected from the United States' European allies; the French, in particular, favored Souvanna Phouma's neutralist faction and wanted nothing to do with efforts to save Boun Oum's provisional government. As the meeting adjourned Eisenhower said, "We cannot let Laos fall to the Communists even if we have to fight—with our allies or without them."

Three days later Lemnitzer reported on a plan for American troops to hold Vientiane and Luang Prabang so that the Royal Laotian Army—or at least that portion loyal to Boun Oum— could operate against the Pathet Lao in the countryside. Eisenhower was determined, however, that the United States must not become bogged down in a land war as it had in Korea, and he told his advisers that "if we ever have to resort to force, there's just one thing to do: clear up the problem completely." The American government urged Souvanna Phouma to resign, leave Cambodia, where he had sought refuge, and go to France. But the neutralist leader would not do the United States' bidding, nor would French President de Gaulle, more determined than ever to reassert a role of world leadership for his country, relent in his conviction that a neutral Laos was the only alternative to Pathet Lao domination.

There matters stood at the close of the Eisenhower administration, with the Pathet Lao in control of the eastern half of Laos and with the American-backed rightists offering halfhearted resistance. Unwilling to accept anything short of a militantly anti-Communist government for the narrow, landlocked kingdom, the administration found itself heavily committed to the weakest of the various political factions in Laos, and potentially in direct conflict with the Soviets and Chinese. The Kennedy administration would soon shift American policy to support Souvanna Phouma and a neutralist government as a way of keeping the rest of Laos out of the hands of the Pathet Lao. Even so, the new regime in Washington would remain as convinced as the old that Laos was an area of strategic importance, and as determined to thwart the forces of leftist revolution. Thus during the sixties the United States would become more and more deeply involved in the confused and bloody Laotian civil war, which American policy makers and military leaders saw as part of the larger struggle in Indochina against rapacious North Vietnamese and

Chinese Communism. Ultimately not only Vietnam and Laos, but Cambodia and even Thailand, would become a theater for massive American military intervention.

VIII

Throughout his Presidency Dwight Eisenhower liked to compare himself to George Washington as a national leader above party and faction—as the President of all the people. Well he might, for his popularity with Americans—regardless of party affiliation, socioeconomic status, or even racial background—had proved remarkably durable. A Gallup poll taken just before he left office put his national approval rating still at 59 percent, as compared to Harry Truman's rating of little more than 30 percent in January 1953. Over the years political analysts had expended many gallons of printer's ink trying to explain Eisenhower's phenomenal popular appeal. They generally agreed that for vast numbers of Americans he was a kindly, protective, fatherly figure, one in whose abiding wisdom the country could safely place its trust. Despite the growing criticism of himself and his administration after 1957, in all probability Eisenhower could have been reelected had he been eligible to run in 1960.

Perhaps because he understood the nature of the affection so many of his countrymen still felt for him after eight years of crisis and turmoil, perhaps also because he was more than a little bitter about his successor's charges that his policies had weakened American security, prestige, and economic power, Eisenhower chose, as had President Washington, to say a formal farewell to the nation. On the evening of January 17, 1961, three days before he was to give up the Presidency, he went on the television and radio networks to deliver his farewell address. Only about fifteen minutes long and unusually eloquent, the speech, like Washington's, consisted almost entirely of a series of warnings.[5] Americans,

5. President Truman, on January 15, 1953, had also bid farewell to the American people in a radio-television address. That thirty-minute speech, however, had mostly consisted of Truman's reminiscences about the previous seven years and justifications of his policies.

he predicted, would continue to confront "a hostile ideology—global in scope, atheistic in character, ruthless in purpose, and insidious in method." They must nonetheless resist "the recurring temptation to feel that some spectacular and costly action could become the miraculous solution to current difficulties." Eisenhower cautioned especially against "a huge increase in newer elements of our defense. . . ." Americans must also "avoid the impulse to live only for today, plundering, for our own ease and convenience, the precious resources of tomorrow." Thus the President took his parting shot at those who had insisted that concern for a balanced budget and fiscal restraint should give way to greatly increased expenditures for both military and social welfare purposes.

What made the farewell address one of the most notable presidential documents was Eisenhower's stern, ominous warning about the pervasiveness and power of the American military establishment and its myriad corporate clients. The arms industry in the United States, he pointed out, directly employed 3½ million people. For the first time Americans had seen the "conjunction of an immense military establishment and a large arms industry . . . . The total influence—economic, political, even spiritual—is felt in every city, every State house, every office of the Federal government." While there had been "an imperative need for this development," at the same time the American people "must not fail to comprehend its grave implications." "In the councils of government," the President continued, "we must guard against the acquisition of unwarranted influence, whether sought or unsought, by the military-industrial complex. The potential for the disastrous rise of misplaced power exists and will persist." There was, he suggested, a real possibility that "the weight of this combination" would "endanger our liberties or our democratic processes. We should take nothing for granted."

Intimately related to the massing of industrial and military power was the far-reaching involvement of the federal government in funding scientific research. In a little-noted portion of his speech, Eisenhower referred to the dual threat posed by government's sponsorship of science. "The prospect of domination of the nation's scholars by Federal employment, project allocations, and the power of money is ever present—and is gravely to be regarded." Yet there was also "the equal and opposite danger that public policy could itself become the captive of a scientific-technological elite."

Eisenhower's farewell speech, especially his warning about the looming military-industrial complex, would later appear as one of the most prophetic statements ever made by an American public figure. There was great irony in the fact that such an admonition should come from old soldier Eisenhower, who had approved the expenditure of some $350 billion for war-making purposes during his eight years as President. It was even more ironic that as Army Chief of Staff in 1946, Eisenhower had put down on paper a concise rationale for the very concentration of corporate, scientific, and military talents and influence against which he cautioned Americans fifteen years later. In a memorandum dated April 27, 1946, and sent to the directors and chiefs of the War Department General and Special Staffs, General Eisenhower had argued for the continuation of the close wartime relationship between the Army on one hand and industry, universities, and civilian scientists and engineers on the other. The more use the Army made of civilian resources, "the more energy will we have left to devote to strictly military problems . . . ." Thus civilians should become "organic parts of our military structure . . . ." To that end General Eisenhower ordered the establishment of an Army Directorate of Research and Development, whose responsibility would be "to demonstrate the value [the Army] places upon science and technology and further the integration of civilian and military resources."

Whether Eisenhower recalled this 1946 directive as he prepared his farewell speech is not known. His years in the White House had seen the acceleration and consolidation of tendencies at work since at least 1940 to further interlocking military, corporate, scientific, and technological power in American society. Yet if his administration had done little to counter these tendencies—had indeed furthered them most of the time—it is also the case that Eisenhower revealed more understanding of the transformations the cold war had wrought in American government and economy than any other President. The commonly held belief that Ike knew more about matters involving the military than anybody else had much truth in it.

On January 20, 1961, the oldest President sat looking out over the snow-covered Capitol grounds as the youngest man ever elected to the office announced that "the torch has been passed to a new generation of Americans. . . ." Sacrifice, challenge, a test of national determination and a call for national greatness—those were the prospects the new President spoke of. "Ask not what your country can do for you," he exhorted Americans, "ask what you can do for your country."

Shortly after the inauguration, private citizen Eisenhower and his wife made the eighty-mile trip from Washington to their farm near Gettysburg, Pennsylvania. There General Eisenhower, as he preferred to be called after leaving the Presidency, worked away on his memoirs, published in two volumes in 1963 and 1965, and lived comfortably in retirement until his death in March 1969. While he seldom commented publicly on contemporary issues and events, he could not have been pleased by much that happened under his Democratic successors.

For example, he must have winced at Kennedy's fiscal 1962 military budget, which was nearly 27 percent greater than Eisenhower's for fiscal 1961. Such skyrocketing military outlays—necessitated by the determination of Kennedy and Secretary of Defense Robert McNamara to achieve overwhelming superiority in long-range missiles as well as the capability to fight "brushfire wars" anywhere in the world—were precisely what Eisenhower had stubbornly resisted for eight years. Yet the ex-President also must have gained a certain amount of bitter satisfaction from the Defense Department's acknowledgment, within nine months after he left office, that there was no missile gap—that in fact the United States enjoyed a two-to-one lead over the Soviets in operational ICBMs.

Doubtless Eisenhower disapproved as well of the huge new expenditures on space flight resulting from Kennedy's decision to commit the nation to put an American on the moon by the end of the sixties. Near the end of his Presidency Eisenhower had heard from his Science Advisory Committee that a manned lunar landing was feasible but could cost as much as $38 billion. Urged to approve such a project by a spokesman who likened the lunar mission to the voyage of Columbus, Eisenhower replied, "I'm not about to hock my jewels." In his last budget message he said that "Further testing and experimentation will be necessary to determine whether there are any valid reasons for extending manned space flight beyond the Mercury program."

By the time Eisenhower died the federal government had doubled its costs over what they had been in 1960. Federal deficits, deliberately incurred under President Lyndon Johnson to stimulate private investment and buying power and thereby accelerate economic growth, had reached seemingly unmanageable proportions. Price inflation, bred largely by inflated military costs, was beginning to bite deeply into family income. In Indochina America was pouring tens of billions of dollars annually into the kind of stalemated Asian war Eisenhower had been determined to avoid—and had avoided—after the Korean armistice.

In short, Eisenhower had reason to feel that he had left the country better off than it had been in the years since. Old warrior and cold warrior that he was, he had nonetheless managed to gain the peace and then, sometimes precariously, to keep the peace. His Presidency, coinciding with unprecedented prosperity, had been a time when the American people as a whole seemed content and complacent. The cold war consensus and the nation's undisputed material well-being had worked to vitiate most radical criticism among the minority of Americans—intellectuals and artists—who might have tried to undermine the popular smugness of the period.

Perhaps no President could have pulled public thinking out of the comfortable groove into which it settled after 1953. Certainly Dwight Eisenhower was not one to inspire his countrymen to try for the unattainable. He did, however, serve them with a degree of common sense not generally displayed by other Presidents in the years since World War II. For William V. Shannon in 1958 and for many subsequent interpreters, the Eisenhower Presidency had been a period of stagnation and drift, an interlude in which the American government and the American people postponed coming to grips with their inescapable problems. For others, however, postponement came to look more and more like a good job of holding the line—against the agonies and excesses of the post-Eisenhower years.

Essay on Bibliography

This topically organized bibliographical commentary is intended to be helpful to anyone wishing to dig more deeply into the history of the Eisenhower years. It is not meant to be an exhaustive list of published works pertinent to the period, nor even of everything used in the preparation of this book. Notably missing in the comments that follow is a great deal of contemporaneous material from which I gained a better understanding of the attitudes, ideas, and emotions of the 1950s.

SOURCE COLLECTIONS

The starting point in the way of published source material on the Eisenhower era is *Public Papers of the Presidents: Dwight D. Eisenhower, 1953–1961*, 8 vols. (Washington, D.C.: U. S. Government Printing Office, 1960–1961). Robert L. Branyan and Lawrence H. Larsen, eds., *The Eisenhower Administration, 1953–1961: A Documentary History*, 2 vols. (New York: Random House, Inc., 1971) contains much material from the manuscript resources of the Eisenhower Library at Abilene, Kansas, and also includes useful introductory essays and headnotes. The sections on foreign and military policy, however, consist mostly of gleanings from open printed sources; the bulk of the pertinent archival material is still classified by the Defense Department, the State Department, and other government agencies. The State Department has, however, published a large number of documents in *American Foreign Policy, 1950–1960*, 7 vols. (Washington, D.C.: U. S. Government Printing Office, 1957–1964). The first two volumes are retrospective, covering the years 1950–1955; the remaining five were published serially for the years 1956–1960.

On American involvement in Indochina after World War II, there are three widely varying editions of the much-publicized and politically explosive Pentagon Papers, which came to light in 1970. Forty-three of the original forty-seven typescript volumes in the study ordered by Secretary of Defense Robert McNamara have been printed for the Armed Services Committee of the House of Representatives, as Department of Defense, Office of the Secretary of Defense Task Force, Vietnam, *United States-Vietnam Relations, 1945–1967*, 12 vols. (Washington, D.C.: U. S. Government Printing Office, 1971). Of the twelve published volumes, or "books," numbers 1, 2, 7, 9, and 10 bear directly on the Eisenhower administration. A second version is *The Pentagon Papers: The Defense Department History of United States Decisionmaking in Vietnam. The Senator Gravel Edition*, 5 vols. (Boston: Beacon Press, 1971). Volume five of the Gravel edition combines an index to the previous four volumes with fifteen critical essays, edited by Noam Chomsky and Howard Zinn. A still more drastically abridged version consists of the materials leaked to and published in the *New York Times*, the *Washington Post*, and other newspapers. Published in one volume as Neil Sheehan et al., *The Pentagon Papers as Published by the New York Times* (Chicago: Quadrangle Books, 1971), this edition consists of a narrative summary of documents, some of which are reprinted in full. Two still-useful source collections published early in the American buildup in Indochina are Marvin Gettleman, ed., *Viet Nam: Documents and Opinions on a Major World Crisis* (Greenwich, Conn.: Fawcett Publications, 1965) and Marcus G. Raskin and Bernard B. Fall, eds., *The Viet-Nam Reader* (New York: Random House, Inc., 1965).

An obscure but handy little volume which juxtaposes in chronological order the disarmament proposals offered over the years by the Western powers and the Soviet Union is *A Summary of Disarmament Documents, 1945–1962* (San Francisco: National Lawyers Guild, n.d.). Eric Bentley, ed., *Thirty Years of Treason: Excerpts from Hearings before the House Committee on Un-American Activities* (New York: Viking Press, 1971) provides about as much firsthand exposure as most people would want to the work of that ironically named body. The only other figure in the Eisenhower administration besides the President whose papers have been published is Secretary of the Treasury George Humphrey; see Nathaniel R. Howard, ed., *The Basic Papers of George M. Humphrey as Secretary of the Treasury* (Cleveland: Western Reserve Historical Society, 1965). *The Papers of Adlai E. Stevenson*, 3 vols. to date (Boston: Little, Brown and Company, 1972—), being edited by Walter Johnson, have thus far not reached the presidential campaign of 1952.

GENERAL WORKS

Overall treatments of the post–World War II period include Carl N. Degler, *Affluence and Anxiety: 1945–Present* (Glenview, Ill.: Scott,

Foresman and Company, 1968); Walter Johnson, *1600 Pennsylvania Avenue: Presidents and the People since 1929*, rev. ed. (Boston: Little, Brown and Company, 1963); Eric F. Goldman, *The Crucial Decade and After: America, 1945–1960* (New York: Vintage Books, 1960); Rexford G. Tugwell, *Off Course: From Truman to Nixon* (New York: Frederick A. Praeger, Publishers, 1971); and William E. Leuchtenburg, *A Troubled Feast: American Society since 1945* (Boston: Little, Brown and Company, 1973). Oscar T. Barck, Jr's, *A History of the United States since 1945* (New York: Dell Publishing Company, Inc., 1965), while dryly written, is crammed with an extraordinary amount of factual information. Howard Zinn's *Postwar America, 1945–1971* (Indianapolis: Bobbs-Merrill Company, Inc., 1973) is an original, thought-provoking interpretation, especially strong on social history.

The principal book-length contemporary efforts to survey and understand the Eisenhower administration are Merlo J. Pusey's *Eisenhower the President* (New York: Macmillan Company, 1956), a sympathetic account; Robert J. Donovan's *Eisenhower: The Inside Story* (New York: Harper and Brothers, 1956), a semiofficial narrative of Eisenhower's first term, which utilized internal documents made available by the administration; Richard Rovere's *Affairs of State: The Eisenhower Years* (New York: Farrar, Straus, and Cudahy, 1956), which consists of previously published and generally critical magazine pieces by a leading liberal journalist; and Marquis Childs's *Eisenhower: Captive Hero* (New York: Harcourt, Brace and Company, 1958), an even more unfavorable view. Besides Rovere's and Childs's books, William V. Shannon, "Eisenhower as President," *Commentary*, XXVI (November 1958), 390–398; and Norman A. Graebner, "Eisenhower's Popular Leadership," *Current History*, XXXIX (October 1960), 230–236f., set out the essentials of the liberal case against Eisenhower current in the late fifties and early sixties. Murray Kempton's "The Underestimation of Dwight D. Eisenhower," *Esquire*, LXVIII (September 1967), 108–109ff., reprinted in Robert D. Marcus and David Burner, eds., *America since 1945* (New York: St. Martin's Press, 1972), is one of the central items in Eisenhower's growing rehabilitation among liberal intellectuals. For more balanced views see Richard Rovere, "Eisenhower Revisited: A Political Genius? A Brilliant Man?" *New York Times Magazine*, February 7, 1971, pp. 14–15ff. (reprinted in Barton J. Bernstein and Allen J. Matusow, eds., *Twentieth-Century America: Recent Interpretations*, 2d ed. [New York: Harcourt Brace, Jovanovich, Inc., 1972]) and William Appleman Williams, "Officers and Gentlemen," *New York Review of Books*, XVI (May 6, 1971),

3–8. Herbert S. Parmet's *Eisenhower and the American Crusades* (New York: Macmillan Company, 1972) is a major work, based on extensive research in the Eisenhower Library manuscript collections. The first full-fledged history of the Eisenhower Presidency, this is a book to which I am greatly indebted.

PERSONAL ACCOUNTS AND BIOGRAPHIES

Of course the most important memoirs for the Eisenhower years are Eisenhower's own: *The White House Years*, 2 vols. (Garden City: Doubleday and Company, 1963–1965). While expectedly self-justifying, these volumes are extraordinarily full and useful as presidential memoirs go. Eisenhower's *At Ease: Stories I Tell My Friends* (Garden City: Doubleday and Company, 1967), a loosely structured series of reminiscences, is of some value on his early life. Emmet John Hughes's *The Ordeal of Power: A Political Memoir of the Eisenhower Years* (New York: Atheneum Publishers, 1963) and Arthur Larson's *Eisenhower: The President Nobody Knew* (New York: Charles Scribner's Sons, 1968) are both highly pertinent combinations of history and personal recollection—the former by a major speech writer, the latter by a man who held various high-level posts in the administration. Another key memoir is that of Sherman Adams, Assistant to the President from 1953 to 1958: *Firsthand Report: The Story of the Eisenhower Administration* (New York: Harper and Brothers, 1961).

John Foster Dulles's controversial tenure as Secretary of State has inspired a number of biographies and studies of his diplomacy. The best on both counts is Townsend Hoopes's *The Devil and John Foster Dulles* (Boston: Little, Brown and Company, 1973), a perceptive, readable, eminently balanced work which will be indispensable for many years to come. Until Hoopes's book appeared, the standard study of Dulles was Louis L. Gerson's rather disappointing *John Foster Dulles* (New York: Cooper Square Publishers, 1967), vol. XVII in The American Secretaries of State and Their Diplomacy series edited by Robert H. Ferrell and Samuel Flagg Bemis. Other works which should be consulted include John Robinson Beal's *John Foster Dulles: A Biography* (New York: Harper and Brothers, 1957), a vigorously pro-Dulles contemporary account; Richard Goold-Adams's *The Time of Power: A Reappraisal of John Foster Dulles* (London: Weidenfeld and Nicolson, 1962), a favorable British view; Hans J. Morgenthau's condemnatory "John Foster Dulles," in Norman Graebner, ed., *An Uncertain Tradition: American Secretaries of State in the Twentieth Century* (New York: McGraw-Hill Book Company, 1961); and

Michael Guhin's *John Foster Dulles: A Statesman and His Times* (New York: Columbia University Press, 1972), which has some good insights but is not wholly successful in rehabilitating Dulles. Dulles's sister, Eleanor Lansing Dulles, provides useful information in *John Foster Dulles: The Last Year* (New York: Harcourt, Brace and World, Inc., 1963). Dulles's successor is treated adequately in George B. Noble, *Christian A. Herter* (New York: Cooper Square Publishers, 1970), vol. XVIII in The American Secretaries of State series.

Various other high figures in the Eisenhower administration as well as several leading Republicans in Congress have either written their memoirs or have been the subject of biographies. Far and away the best of the biographies is James T. Patterson's *Mr. Republican: A Biography of Robert A. Taft* (Boston: Houghton Mifflin Company, 1972), a thorough, judicious, and absorbing study of an exceedingly complex, reticent personality. William J. Miller's *Henry Cabot Lodge* (New York: James H. Heineman, Inc., 1967) is not in the same class. Two noteworthy diplomatic memoirs are Robert Murphy's *Diplomat among Warriors* (Garden City: Doubleday and Company, 1964) and Charles E. Bohlen's *Witness to History* (New York: W. W. Norton and Company, Inc., 1973). Allen Dulles, the Director of the Central Intelligence Agency, has set forth his carefully guarded recollections in *The Craft of Intelligence* (New York: Harper and Row, Publishers, 1962). Richard Nixon's *Six Crises* (Garden City: Doubleday and Company, 1962) reveals more about its author than about the six episodes in his political career which he describes. Earl Mazo and Stephen Hess, *Nixon: A Political Portrait* (New York: Harper and Row, Publishers, 1968) is balanced, while Garry Wills's *Nixon Agonistes: The Crisis of the Self-Made Man* (Boston: Houghton Mifflin Company, 1970) is searchingly critical. Two of the Army Chiefs of Staff during the Eisenhower administration have written autobiographies: Matthew B. Ridgway's *Soldier* (New York: Harper and Brothers, 1956) has a tone of anger and dismay; Maxwell Taylor's *Swords and Plowshares* (New York: W. W. Norton and Company, Inc., 1972) is much more guarded on the Army's unhappiness with administration military planning. Of limited value are the memoirs of Lewis L. Strauss, *Men and Decisons* (Garden City: Doubleday and Company, 1962) and Joseph Martin, *My First Fifty Years in Politics* (New York: McGraw-Hill Book Company, 1960). Neil MacNeil's *Dirksen: Portrait of a Public Man* (Cleveland: World Publishing Company, 1970), the biography of a leading conservative Republican senator, adds little to our understanding.

Among accounts by or about Democrats, Harry Truman's *Memoirs*, 2 vols. (Garden City: Doubleday and Company, 1955–1956) is informative on Truman's role in presidential politics in 1952; so, to a lesser extent, are Truman's *Mr. Citizen* (New York: Random House, Inc., 1960) and Margaret Truman's biography of her father, *Harry S. Truman* (New York: William Morrow and Company, 1973). Dean Acheson's memoirs, *Present at the Creation* (New York: W. W. Norton and Company, Inc., 1969), should be consulted for the Korean war and mounting Republican attacks on Truman-Acheson foreign policy. The best biography of Adlai Stevenson is Kenneth S. Davis's *The Politics of Honor: A Biography of Adlai E. Stevenson* (New York: G. P. Putnam's Sons, 1967). Stuart Gerry Brown's *Conscience in Politics: Adlai Stevenson in the 1950's* (Syracuse: Syracuse University Press, 1961) is an admiring discussion of Stevenson's political views. In contrast, Bert Cochran's *Adlai Stevenson: Patrician among Politicians* (New York: Funk and Wagnalls Company, Inc., 1969) relates Stevenson to elitist control of American politics and to cold war liberalism. Walter Johnson's *How We Drafted Stevenson* (New York: Alfred A. Knopf, Inc., 1955) is an account of the group of political amateurs who formed part of the drive to nominate Stevenson for the Presidency in 1952.

An extremely useful political study of Lyndon Johnson is Rowland Evans and Robert Novak, *Lyndon B. Johnson: The Exercise of Power* (New York: New American Library, 1966). Leonard Baker's *The Johnson Eclipse: A President's Vice Presidency* (New York: Macmillan Company, 1966) deals in part with Johnson's career as Senate majority leader. Sam Rayburn, Johnson's close associate and the longtime Speaker of the House, has received adulatory treatment in C. Dwight Dorough's *Mr. Sam* (New York: Random House, Inc., 1962). The first full biography of John F. Kennedy was Victor Lasky's admiring *J. F. K.: The Man and the Myth* (New York: Macmillan Company, 1963), partly superseded by Theodore Sorensen's *Kennedy* (New York: Harper and Row, Publishers, 1965). W. Bruce Gorman's *Kefauver: A Political Biography* (New York: Oxford University Press, 1971) does fairly well with the Tennessee Democratic senator and presidential aspirant. Two remembrances which vary greatly in introspection, candor, and literary quality are Clinton P. Anderson's pedestrian *Outsider in the Senate* (New York: World Publishing Company, 1970) and George F. Kennan's sparkling *Memoirs*, 2 vols. (Boston: Atlantic–Little, Brown and Company, 1967–1972), of which vol. II covers the years 1950–1963. W. Averell Harriman's *America and Russia in a*

Changing World: A Half Century of Personal Observations (Garden City: Doubleday and Company, 1971) is disappointing. Joseph P. Lash's *Eleanor: The Years Alone* (New York: W. W. Norton and Company, Inc., 1972) narrates Eleanor Roosevelt's activities during the 1950s and quotes extensively from her correspondence. Two scientist-administrators associated in various ways with the Eisenhower administration have written their memoirs: James Bryant Conant, *My Several Lives: Memoirs of a Social Inventor* (New York: Harper and Row, Publishers, 1970) and Vannevar Bush, *Pieces of the Action* (New York: William Morrow and Company, 1970). The journalist C. L. Sulzberger had given his recollections, accompanied by extensive quotations from his diaries, in *A Long Row of Candles: Memoirs and Diaries, 1934–1954* (New York: Macmillan Company, 1969) and *The Last of the Giants* (New York: Macmillan Company, 1970).

Joseph R. McCarthy's mercurial but devastating career as an anti-Communist crusader has prompted a vast literature. The best single work on McCarthy is Robert Griffith's extensively researched and gracefully written *The Politics of Fear: Joseph R. McCarthy and the Senate* (Lexington: University Press of Kentucky, 1970). Jack Anderson and Ronald W. May, *McCarthy: The Man, the Senator, the "ISM"* (Boston: Beacon Press, 1952) was the first book-length study of McCarthy; a highly critical account by two journalists, it must be used with caution. Richard Rovere's equally critical but more temperately phrased *Senator Joe McCarthy* (New York: Harcourt, Brace and Company, 1959) is superior to Fred J. Cook's passionate condemnation in *The Nightmare Decade: The Life and Times of Senator Joe Mc-Carthy* (New York: Random House, Inc., 1971) and Reinhard H. Luthin's sketch in *American Demagogues: Twentieth Century* (Boston: Beacon Press, 1954). The major effort to justify McCarthy is William F. Buckley and L. Brent Bozell, *McCarthy and His Enemies* (Chicago: Henry Regnery Company, 1954). Thomas C. Reeves, ed., *McCarthyism* (Hinsdale, Ill.: Dryden Press, 1973); Allen J. Matusow, ed., *Joseph R. McCarthy* (Englewood Cliffs, N.J.: Prentice-Hall, Inc., 1970); and Earl Lathan, ed., *The Meaning of McCarthyism* (Boston: D. C. Heath and Company, 1965) are all handy collections of readings on the Wisconsin senator and the movement he led.

For Martin Luther King, Lerone Bennett, Jr., *What Manner of Man: A Biography of Martin Luther King, Jr.* (Chicago: Johnson Publishing Company, Inc., 1964) still holds up well. A biographical sketch as well as source readings constitute C. Eric Lincoln, ed., *Martin Luther King, Jr.: A Profile* (New York: Hill and Wang, 1970); while

King's widow has set down her recollections as Coretta Scott King, *My Life with Martin Luther King, Jr.* (New York: Holt, Rinehart and Winston, Inc., 1969). Studies of King's views include Walton Hanes, Jr., *The Political Philosophy of Martin Luther King* (Westport, Conn.: Greenwood Press, Inc., 1972) and Warren E. Steinkraus, "Martin Luther King's Personalism," *Journal of the History of Ideas*, XXXIV (January-March 1973), 97–111. King's own account of the events that catapulted him to national fame is *Stride toward Freedom: The Montgomery Boycott* (New York: Harper and Brothers, 1958). The leading black congressman of the 1950s, Adam Clayton Powell, Jr., has published his autobiography as *Adam by Adam* (New York: Dial Press, 1971).

Much can be learned about the Soviet side of the cold war from Adam B. Ulam's huge biography, *Stalin: The Man and the Era* (New York: Viking Press, 1973) and Edward Crankshaw's *Khrushchev: A Career* (New York: Viking Press, 1966). Crankshaw has also edited and vouched for the authenticity of Khrushchev's purported memoirs, *Khrushchev Remembers* (Boston: Little, Brown and Company, 1970).

POLITICS AND GOVERNMENT

For presidential politics in the 1950s see Barton J. Bernstein, "Election of 1952," and Theodore C. Sorenson, "Election of 1960," in Arthur M. Schlesinger, Jr., and Fred L. Israel, eds., *The Coming to Power: Critical Presidential Elections in American History* (New York: Chelsea House, Publishers, 1972), 385–436, 437–457 (the volume as a whole being a distillation of Schlesinger and Israel, eds., *History of American Presidential Elections, 1789–1968*, 4 vols. [New York: Chelsea House, Publishers, 1971]). See also Eugene H. Roseboom's *A History of Presidential Elections from George Washington to Richard M. Nixon* (New York: Macmillan Company, 1970) and Herbert Eaton's popularly written *Presidential Timber: A History of Nominating Conventions, 1868–1960* (New York: Free Press of Glencoe, 1964). The student of history can gain much from such specialized social science studies as Paul T. David et al., eds., *Presidential Nominating Politics in 1952*, 5 vols. (Baltimore: Johns Hopkins University Press, 1954), which is nearly exhaustive; Charles A. H. Thomson, *Television and Presidential Politics: The Experience in 1952 and the Problems Ahead* (Washington: Brookings Institution, 1956); Paul Tillett, ed., *Inside Politics: The National Conventions, 1960* (Dobbs Ferry, N. Y.: Oceana Publications, Inc., 1962); Paul T. David, ed., *The Presidential Election and Transition, 1960–1961* (Washington:

Brookings Institution, 1961); and Heinz Eulau, *Class and Party in the Eisenhower Years: Class Roles and Perspectives in the 1952 and 1956 Elections* (New York: Free Press of Glencoe, 1962). Theodore H. White's, *The Making of the President, 1960* (New York: Atheneum Publishers, 1961) is overdramatized and rather unabashedly pro-Kennedy. A minor classic of American political literature, it is still the best of White's instant histories of recent presidential elections. For the critical Korean issue in the 1952 election, Ronald J. Caridi's *The Korean War and American Politics: The Republican Party as a Case Study* (Philadelphia: University of Pennsylvania Press, 1969) is most helpful; and for the Republicans' persistent use of the Yalta Conference as a political weapon, see Athan Theoharis's *The Yalta Myths: An Issue in U. S. Politics, 1945–1955* (Columbia: University of Missouri Press, 1970).

For Eisenhower's conception of the Presidency and the nature of his leadership, consult Richard E. Neustadt's *Presidential Power: The Politics of Leadership* (New York: John Wiley and Sons, Inc., 1960) and James David Barber's *The Presidential Character: Predicting Performance in the White House* (Englewood Cliffs, N. J.: Prentice-Hall, Inc., 1972), both of which find the thirty-fourth President to be sorely lacking in the qualities effective chief executives should have. Arthur M. Schlesinger, Jr., relates Eisenhower's Presidency to the accumulative growth of executive power in *The Imperial Presidency* (Boston: Houghton Mifflin Company, 1973). The gap between Republican rhetoric about morality in government and actual practice is evident in David A. Frier's *Conflict of Interest in the Eisenhower Administration* (Ames: Iowa State University Press, 1969). John W. Anderson's *Eisenhower, Brownell, and the Congress: The Tangled Origins of the Civil Rights Bill of 1956–1957* (University, Ala.: University of Alabama Press, 1964) deals only with events in 1956. Numan V. Bartley's *The Rise of Massive Resistance: Race and Politics in the South during the 1950's* (Baton Rouge: Louisiana State University Press, 1969) is excellent for white southern reaction to the Supreme Court's 1954 desegregation ruling. Two able specialized accounts are William R. Willoughby, *The St. Lawrence Waterway: A Study in Politics and Diplomacy* (Madison: University of Wisconsin Press, 1961) and Elmo Richardson, *Dams, Parks and Politics: Resource Development and Preservation in the Truman-Eisenhower Era* (Lexington: University Press of Kentucky, 1973).

Apart from the large body of writing on Joe McCarthy, there is also a substantial literature on the post–World War II Communist

phobia and on American Communism itself. An incisive collection of
fresh insights is Robert Griffith and Athan Theoharis, eds., *The Specter:
Original Essays on the Cold War and McCarthyism* (New York: New
Viewpoints, 1974). Earl Latham's *The Communist Controversy in
Washington* (Cambridge: Harvard University Press, 1966) is a solid
study, superior to Walter Goodman's popularized *The Committee: The
Extraordinary Career of the House Committee on Un-American Activi-
ties* (New York: Farrar, Straus and Giroux, Inc., 1968). Allan D.
Harper's *The Politics of Loyalty: The White House and the Communist
Issue, 1946–1952* (Westport, Conn.: Greenwood Press, Inc., 1969) is
excellent on the Truman administration's struggles against charges of
Communism-in-government. For the climate of opinion in which the
Communist phobia grew, see Les K. Adler and Thomas G. Paterson,
"Red Fascism: The Merger of Nazi Germany and Soviet Russia in the
American Image of Totalitarianism, 1930's–1950's," *American His-
torical Review*, LXXV (April 1970), 1046–1064.

Michael Paul Rogin's *The Intellectuals and McCarthy: The Radical
Spectre* (Cambridge: MIT Press, 1967) is a difficult but rewarding
combination of intellectual and quantitative history which effectively
rebuts the thesis, favored by many liberal writers in the fifties and
sixties, that authoritarian tendencies latent in "populism" furnished
the basic drive behind McCarthyism. Athan Theoharis's "The Politics
of Scholarship: Liberals, Anti-Communism, and McCarthyism," in
Griffith and Theoharis, eds., *The Specter*, 262–280, focuses on the
intellectuals themselves. Seymour M. Lipset, one of the leading pro-
ponents of the populism thesis, considerably qualifies it in *The Politics
of Unreason: Right-Wing Extremism in America, 1790–1970* (New
York: Harper and Row, Publishers, 1970), Earl Raab, coauthor.

On the American Communist party in the 1950s, Joseph R. Staro-
bin's fine monograph, *American Communism in Crisis, 1943–1957*
(Cambridge: Harvard University Press, 1972), is basic. But see also
David A. Shannon, *The Decline of American Communism* (New York:
Harcourt, Brace and Company, 1959) and Irving Howe and Lewis
Coser, *The American Communist Party: A Critical History (1919–
1957)* (Boston: Beacon Press, 1957).

FOREIGN AND MILITARY POLICY

Most of what has been written about public events in the Eisenhower
years has had to do with the formulation and execution of American
foreign policy and with the development and expansion of the American military establishment. In turn, the biggest portion of such writing

has been, if not favorable to particular policies, at least in essential agreement with the cold war assumptions which guided the Eisenhower administration. At the risk of grave oversimplification, one can group students of the cold war period into three categories: "traditionalists," who accept the essential elements of the policy rationales offered by the American government; "realists," who, while not challenging the cold war consensus, have criticized American foreign policy as excessively idealistic and as insufficiently cognizant of actual power relations; and "revisionists" (also called "radicals" or "New Leftists"), who have questioned and generally rejected the basic premises of the cold war consensus. Traditionalists tend to view American motives and behavior in world affairs as being high principled and workable were it not for Communist intransigence and aggressiveness. Realists disdain the notion that international relations can be conducted on the basis of high principle; they argue for a more tough-minded approach functioning within a framework of nineteenth-century–style power politics. Revisionists are often, though by no means always, strongly influenced by Marxist and other economic interpretations of history. In any case, they tend to view the United States as being historically an expansionist power, often an aggressive one, and they believe that by more moderate and reasonable behavior in its dealings with the rest of the world America could have avoided the disastrous onset and perpetuation of the cold war. Of course there is much overlap between these three broad and indistinct categories. No effort will be made to categorize each of the items mentioned within this bibliographical section, although descriptive labels will be used when they seem appropriate.

Students of United States diplomatic and military history have published in great quantity on the Eisenhower period. As yet, however, revisionist writers have given major attention to the events of the mid- and late forties in an effort to reevaluate the causes and immediate consequences of Soviet-American conflict. Concerted revisionist examination of world affairs during the Eisenhower Presidency remains to be undertaken. The starting point for surveying revisionist works that encompass the 1950s is William Appleman Williams's *The Tragedy of American Diplomacy*, 2d ed., rev. (New York: Dell Publishing Company, 1962), a book which, when first published in 1959, gained relatively little attention, but which later served as the major scholarly inspiration for the reevaluation of American foreign policy during the sixties. Other key revisionist works covering the Eisenhower period include Walter LaFeber's *America, Russia, and the Cold War, 1945–1966* (New York: John Wiley and Sons, Inc., 1967); Stephen E.

Ambrose's *Rise to Globalism: American Foreign Policy, 1938–1970* (Baltimore: Penguin Books, Inc., 1971); Richard J. Barnet's *Roots of War* (New York: Atheneum Publishers, 1972); Ronald Steel's *Pax Americana* (New York: Viking Press, 1967); David Horowitz's *The Free World Colossus: A Critique of American Foreign Policy and the Cold War*, rev. ed (New York: Hill and Wang, 1971); and Denna F. Fleming's massive *The Cold War and Its Origins, 1917–1960*, 2 vols. (Garden City: Doubleday and Company, 1961). Gabriel and Joyce Kolko, *The Limits of Power: The World and United States Foreign Policy, 1945–1954* (New York: Harper and Row, Publishers, 1972) stresses the continuity between Truman-Acheson and Eisenhower-Dulles cold warriorism. Noam Chomsky's essays in *American Power and the New Mandarins* (New York: Vintage Books, 1969) should not be overlooked.

Among the major realist surveys of cold war policy are John Spanier's *American Foreign Policy since World War II*, 4th ed., rev. (New York: Frederick A. Praeger, Publishers, 1971); Louis J. Halle's *The Cold War as History* (New York: Harper and Row, Publishers, 1967); Seyom Brown's *The Faces of Power: Constancy and Change in United States Foreign Policy from Truman to Johnson* (New York: Columbia University Press, 1968); Michael Donelan's *The Ideas of American Foreign Policy* (London: Chapman and Hall, Ltd., 1963); Walt W. Rostow's *The United States in the World Arena: An Essay in Recent History* (New York: Harper and Brothers, 1960) and *The Diffusion of Power: An Essay in Recent History* (New York: Macmillan Company, 1972); and two excellent books by Adam B. Ulam, *Expansion and Coexistence: The History of Soviet Foreign Policy, 1917–1967* (New York: Frederick A. Praeger, Publishers, 1968) and *The Rivals: America and Russia since World War II* (New York: Viking Press, 1971). Robert E. Osgood et al., *America and the World: From the Truman Doctrine to Vietnam* (Baltimore: Johns Hopkins University Press, 1970) deals with both foreign and domestic factors operating on American policies; while Ernest R. May, "Eisenhower and After," in May, ed., *The Ultimate Decision: The President as Commander-in-Chief* (New York: George Braziller, Inc., 1960), 211–236, is a succinct realist critique of Eisenhower's use of military power.

Examples of works which may be described as traditionalist include Paul Seabury, *The Rise and Decline of the Cold War* (New York: Basic Books, 1967); Desmond Donnelly, *Struggle for the World: The Cold War, 1917–1965* (New York: St. Martin's Press, 1965), a militantly pro–United States overview by a British Labourite member of

Parliament; and Roscoe Drummond and Gaston Coblentz, *Duel at the Brink: John Foster Dulles' Command of American Power* (Garden City: Doubleday and Company, 1960), which justifies American policy while exaggerating Dulles's dominance over it. Selig Adler's *The Isolationist Impulse: Its Twentieth Century Reaction* (New York: Abelard-Schuman, 1957) and Norman A. Graebner's *The New Isolationism: A Study in Politics and Foreign Policy since 1950* (New York: Ronald Press Company, 1956) both confuse predominantly Republican unilateralism in the post–World War II period with a desire to withdraw from the rest of the world. Merriman Smith's *A President's Odyssey* (New York: Harper and Brothers, 1961) gives a leading White House newsman's account of Eisenhower's global travels in 1959–1960.

For American policy in Europe, an interesting place to begin is Anatol Rapoport's *The Big Two: Soviet-American Perceptions of Foreign Policy* (New York: Pegasus, 1971), an effort through content analysis to make sense of rival cold war posturings. Fred Warner Neal, "The Cold War in Europe, 1945–1967," in Nealie Doyle Houghton, ed., *Struggle against History: U. S. Foreign Policy in an Age of Revolution* (New York: Washington Square Press, 1968), 20–40, gives a revisionist analysis of American fears of Soviet aggression on the Continent; while Bennett Kovrig, *The Myth of Liberation: East-Central Europe in U. S. Diplomacy and Politics since 1941* (Baltimore: Johns Hopkins University Press, 1973) trenchantly treats the character and consequences of one of the major illusions of the early Eisenhower period. For Eisenhower's personal contacts with the Soviet leadership, see Elmer Plishcke, "Eisenhower's 'Correspondence Diplomacy' with the Kremlin: Case Study in Summit Diplomatics," *Journal of Politics*, XXX (February 1968), 137–159. The United States' relations with its NATO allies are covered in Robert E. Osgood, *NATO: The Entangling Alliance* (Chicago: University of Chicago Press, 1962); Klaus Knorr, ed., *NATO and American Security* (Princeton: Princeton University Press, 1959); Richard E. Neustadt, *Alliance Politics* (New York: Columbia University Press, 1970); and Lawrence S. Kaplan, "The United States and the Atlantic Community: The First Generation," in John Braeman and David Brody, eds., *Twentieth Century American Foreign Policy* (Columbus: Ohio State University Press, 1971), 294–342. Lionel Gelber, *America in Britain's Place: The Leadership of the West and Anglo-American Unity* (New York: Frederick A. Praeger, Publishers, 1961) is a realist's discussion of the American assumption of the British role in policing the Middle East and other parts of the world. For the on-again-off-again East-West confrontation over Berlin in the late fifties and early sixties, three works are especially valuable: Jean E. Smith, *The Defense of Berlin* (Baltimore: Johns Hopkins University Press, 1963); Jack M. Schick, *The Berlin Crisis, 1958–1962* (Philadelphia: University of Pennsylvania Press, 1971); and Robert M. Slusser, *The Berlin Crisis of 1961* (Baltimore: Johns Hopkins University Press, 1973), which covers a broader span of time than its title indicates.

A good introduction to the functioning of American globalism in the "underdeveloped" countries is Richard J. Barnet's *Intervention and Revolution: The United States in the Third World* (Cleveland: World Publishing Company, 1968). Suggestive for the acrimonious history of the United States' policy toward the People's Republic of China during the fifties is Warren I. Cohen, *America's Response to China: An Interpretative History of Sino-American Relations* (New York: John Wiley and Sons, Inc., 1972). For the focus of recurrent crisis in the western Pacific, see Oliver E. Clubb, "Formosa and the Offshore Islands in American Policy, 1950–1955," *Political Science Quarterly*, LXXIV (December 1959), 517–531. Edwin O. Reischauer, who became United States ambassador to Japan in 1961, analyzes the factors behind the cancellation of Eisenhower's Japanese visit in "The Broken Dialogue with Japan," *Foreign Affairs*, XXXIX (October 1960), 11–26.

The literature on the continual conflict in Indochina and United States intervention is overwhelming. The classic background study is Bernard B. Fall's *The Two Viet-Nams* (New York: Frederick A. Praeger, Publishers, 1963), the contribution of a famous French journalist who later lost his life in South Vietnam. Peter A. Poole's *The United States and Indochina from FDR to Nixon* (Hinsdale, Ill.: Dryden Press, 1973) is a concise, highly critical summary. Probably the best single item on the American role is George M. Kahin and John W. Lewis, *The United States in Vietnam*, rev. ed. (New York: Dial Press, 1969). There are three detailed, scholarly examinations of the tortuous history behind the 1954 Geneva settlement on Indochina: Melvin Gurtov, *The First Vietnam Crisis: Chinese Communist Strategy and United States Involvement, 1953–1954* (New York: Columbia University Press, 1967); Philippe Devillers and Jean Lacoutre, *End of a War: Indochina, 1954* (New York: Frederick A. Praeger, Publishers, 1969); and Robert E. Randle, *Geneva 1954: The Settlement of the Indochina War* (Princeton: Princeton University Press, 1969). For the onset of the second Indochina war after 1955, one of the best accounts is Philippe Devillers, "The Struggle for the Unification of Vietnam," in P. J. Honey, ed., *North Vietnam Today: Profile of a Communist Satellite* (New York: Frederick A. Praeger, Publishers, 1962), 25–47. Also helpful for the deepening American participation in the Indochina conflict are Marvin Kalb and Elie Abel, *Roots of Involvement: The U. S. in Asia, 1784–1971* (New York: W. W. Norton and Company, Inc., 1971); Robert Shaplen, *The Lost Revolution: Twenty Years of Neglected Opportunities in Vietnam and of American Failures to Foster Democracy There* (New York: Harper and Row, Publishers, 1965); Chester L. Cooper, *The Lost Crusade: America in Vietnam* (New York: Dodd, Mead and Company, 1970); and Arthur M. Schlesinger, Jr., *The Bitter Heritage: Vietnam and American Democracy, 1941– 1968*, rev. ed. (Boston: Houghton Mifflin Company, 1968), the last work being an important rethinking of the American role in Indochina by a leading cold war liberal. David Halberstam's *The Best and the Brightest* (New York: Random House, Inc., 1972) focuses on the disastrous turn of events during the Kennedy and Johnson administrations but also provides some useful comparisons with the Eisenhower administration's conduct of Indochina policy.

On the American balancing act in the Middle East during the Eisenhower period, see William R. Polk, *The United States and the Arab World* (Cambridge: Harvard University Press, 1969); John C. Campbell, *Defense of the Middle East: Problems of American Policy*, rev. ed. (New York: Harper and Brothers, 1960); the pertinent sections in the compendious *Political Dynamics in the Middle East* (New York: American Elsevier Publishing Company, Inc., 1972), edited by Paul Y. Hammond and Sidney S. Alexander; and James E. Dougherty, "The Aswan Decision in Perspective," *Political Science Quarterly*, LXXXIV (March 1959), 21–45. Herman Finer's *Dulles over Suez* (Chicago: Quadrangle Books, 1964) is scathingly critical of John Foster Dulles's role during the Suez war of 1956; while Carey B. Joynt, "John Foster Dulles and the Suez Crisis," in Gerald N. Grob, ed., *Statesmen and Statecraft of the Modern West* (Barre, Mass.: Barre Publishers, 1967), 205–250, sees Dulles as the practitioner of rational, skillful diplomacy. Other pertinent items include M. A. Fitzsimmons, "The Suez Crisis and the Containment Policy," *Review of Politics*, XIX (October 1957), 421–445; and O. M. Smolansky, "Moscow and the Suez Crisis, 1956: A Reappraisal," *Political Science Quarterly* LXXX (December 1965), 581–605.

The United States' role in Latin America during the Eisenhower Presidency is well covered in Robert N. Burr's *Our Troubled Hemis-*

phere: Perspectives on United States–Latin American Relations (Washington, D.C.: Brookings Institution, 1967). Also of some use are Donald M. Dozer's *Are We Good Neighbors? Three Decades of Inter-American Relations, 1930–1960* (Gainesville: University of Florida Press, 1959) and J. Lloyd Mecham's *The United States and Inter-American Security, 1889–1960* (Austin: University of Texas Press, 1961). On the American intervention in Guatemala and its aftermath, see John Gillin and K. H. Silvert, "Ambiguities in Guatemala," *Foreign Affairs*, XXXIV (April 1956), 469–482; Frederick B. Pike, "Guatemala, the United States, and Communism in the Americas," *Review of Politics*, XVII (April 1955), 232–261; and Philip B. Taylor, Jr., "The Guatemala Affair: A Critique of United States Foreign Policy," *American Political Science Review*, L (September 1956), 787–806. Theodore Draper's *Castro's Revolution: Myths and Realities* (New York: Frederick A. Praeger, Publishers, 1962) is highly critical of Fidel Castro; while William Appleman Williams's *The United States, Cuba, and Castro* (New York: Monthly Review Press, 1962) presents the case for the Cuban revolution and the Castro regime. For American conduct in relation to the Congo civil war and to sub-Saharan African nationalism as a whole, see Rupert Emerson, "American Policy in Africa," *Foreign Affairs*, XL (January 1962), 303–315.

For the activities of the Central Intelligence Agency, consult David Wise and Thomas B. Ross, *The Invisible Government* (New York: Random House, Inc., 1964) and David Wise, *The Politics of Lying: Government Deception, Secrecy, and Power* (New York: Random House, Inc., 1973). Harry H. Ransom's *Central Intelligence and National Security* (Cambridge: Harvard University Press, 1958) studies the CIA's structure and general operations but is sketchy on particular episodes. For the CIA's greatest embarrassment, see David Wise and Thomas B. Ross, *The U-2 Affair* (New York: Random House, Inc., 1962).

On the Eisenhower administration's uses of foreign military and economic assistance, see David A. Baldwin, *Foreign Aid and American Foreign Policy* (New York: Frederick A. Praeger, Publishers, 1966) and Lucian W. Pye, "Soviet and American Styles in Foreign Aid," *Orbis*, IV (Summer 1960), 159–173. Michael Hudson's *Super Imperialism: The Economic Strategy of American Empire* (New York: Holt, Rinehart and Winston, Inc., 1973) sees the amassing of economic power by the United States government operating through overseas assistance programs, not traditional private capitalism, as increasingly the key to recent American global expansionism.

The literature on issues and developments in the disarmament, arms control, and nuclear test-ban negotiations of the fifties is extensive. The most compendious treatment is Bernard G. Bechhoefer's *Postwar Negotiations for Arms Control* (Washington, D.C.: Brookings Institution, 1961). Chalmers M. Roberts's *The Nuclear Years: The Arms Race and Arms Control, 1945–1970* (New York: Frederick A. Praeger, Publishers, 1970) is a useful summary, as is Richard J. Barnet's *Who Wants Disarmament?* (Boston: Beacon Press, 1960), a revisionist critique of Western approaches. John W. Spanier and Joseph L. Nogee, *The Politics of Disarmament: A Study in Soviet-American Gamesmanship* (New York: Frederick A. Praeger, Publishers, 1962) is an example of the realist tendency to see disarmament negotiations as essentially a contest for cold war propaganda advantage. Joseph P. Morray's *From Yalta to Disarmament: Cold War Debate* (New York: Monthly Review Press, 1961), which also concentrates on rhetoric and propaganda strategy, is nevertheless critical of the United States' position; a more thorough revisionist analysis is Edgar M. Bottome's *The Balance of Terror: A Guide to the Arms Race* (Boston: Beacon Press, 1971). Most informative on Russian military policy and the Soviet side of disarmament negotiations is Lincoln Bloomfield, Walter C. Clemens, Jr., and Franklyn Griffiths, *Khrushchev and the Arms Race: Soviet Interests in Arms Control and Disarmament, 1954–1964* (Cambridge: MIT Press, 1966). More narrowly focused is Joseph L. Nogee's *Soviet Policy toward International Control of Atomic Energy* (Notre Dame: University of Notre Dame Press, 1961).

For the broad background of American military thought and institutional development, Walter Millis, *Arms and Men: A Study in American Military History* (New York: G. P. Putnam's Sons, 1956) is suggestive. Paul Y. Hammond's *Organizing for Defense: The American Military Establishment in the Twentieth Century* (Princeton: Princeton University Press, 1961) is a good institutional history. Arthur I. Waskow, ed., *The Debate over Thermonuclear Strategy* (Boston: D. C. Heath and Company, 1965) contains pertinent readings. Two especially valuable studies of American military policy in the post–World War II years are Samuel P. Huntington, *The Common Defense: Strategic Programs in National Politics* (New York: Columbia University Press, 1961) and Warner R. Schilling, Paul Y. Hammond, and Glenn H. Snyder, *Strategy, Politics, and Defense Budgets* (New York: Columbia University Press, 1962). On the nominally secret Gaither Report, the object of so much controversy during the winter of 1957–

1958, see Morton H. Halperin, "The Gaither Committee and the Policy Process," *World Politics*, XIII (April 1961), 360–384; and on Henry Kissinger's role in preparing the almost equally controversial Rockefeller Brothers Fund study of national security, see I. F. Stone, "The Education of Henry Kissinger," *New York Review of Books*, XIX (October 19, 1972), 12–17, and "The Flowering of Henry Kissinger," ibid. (November 2, 1972), 21–27.

The military-industrial complex described by Eisenhower in his farewell address is treated in Fred J. Cook, *The Warfare State* (New York: Macmillan Company, 1962); Richard J. Barnet, *The Economy of Death* (New York: Atheneum Publishers, 1969); Sidney Lens, *The Military-Industrial Complex* (Philadelphia: Pilgrim Press, 1970); and Seymour Melman, *Pentagon Capitalism: The Political Economy of War* (New York: McGraw-Hill Book Company, 1970). Most enlightening on the alleged disparity between American and Russian missile prowess in the late Eisenhower years are Edgar M. Bottome, *The Missile Gap: A Study of the Formation of Political and Military Policy* (Rutherford, N. J.: Fairleigh Dickinson University Press, 1971) and Roy E. Licklider, "The Missile Gap Controversy," *Political Science Quarterly*, LVIII (December 1970), 600–615. Albert Wohlstetter rejects the thesis that by the late fifties the United States and the USSR had reached a state of mutual deterrence in "The Delicate Balance of Terror," *Foreign Affairs*, XXXVII (January 1959), 211–234. A case study in the political, diplomatic, and technological ramifications of missile development is Michael H. Armacost's *The Politics of Weapons Innovation: The Thor-Jupiter Controversy* (New York: Columbia University Press, 1969). Robert Jungk's *Brighter than a Thousand Suns: A Personal History of the Atomic Scientists*, translated by James Cleugh (New York: Harcourt, Brace and Company, 1958) provides good insights into the controversy over the withdrawal of J. Robert Oppenheimer's security clearance. On the various groups working in behalf of disarmament in the fifties, see Lawrence S. Wittner, *Rebels against War: The American Peace Movement, 1941–1960* (New York: Columbia University Press, 1969).

The origins of the American space program and the history of the United States' first manned space flight effort are detailed in Loyd S. Swenson, Jr., James M. Grimwood, and Charles C. Alexander, *This New Ocean: A History of Project Mercury* (Washington, D.C.: U. S. Government Printing Office, 1966). For the early years of the National Aeronautics and Space Administration, see Robert L. Rosholt, *An Administrative History of NASA, 1958–1963* (Washington, D.C.:

U. S. Government Printing Office, 1966). Constance McLaughlin Green and Milton Lomask, *Vanguard: A History* (Washington, D.C.: U. S. Government Printing Office, 1970) is an able study of America's initial space satellite venture.

THE ECONOMY

The best retrospective item on the nation's economic history during the Eisenhower Presidency is Harold G. Vatter's *The American Economy in the 1950s* (New York: W. W. Norton Company, Inc., 1963). Also valuable is Ralph E. Freeman, ed., *Postwar Economic Trends in the United States* (New York: Harper and Brothers, 1960). Robert Sobel's *The Age of Giant Corporations: A Microeconomic History of American Business, 1914–1970* (Westport, Conn.: Greenwood Press, Inc., 1972) gives an excellent account of the rise and expansion of business conglomerates during the fifties. Robert Heilbroner's *The Limits of American Capitalism* (New York: Harper and Row, Publishers, 1966) and Bernard D. Nossiter's *The Mythmakers: An Essay on Power and Wealth* (Boston: Houghton Mifflin Company, 1964) are both good critical antidotes to the kind of confidence and optimism about the American economic system that characterized such works as John Kenneth Galbraith's *American Capitalism: The Concept of Countervailing Power* (Boston: Houghton Mifflin Company, 1952) and *The Affluent Society* (Boston: Houghton Mifflin Company, 1958); Adolf A. Berle's *The Twentieth Century Capitalist Revolution* (New York: Harcourt, Brace and Company, 1954); and David E. Lilienthal's *Big Business: A New Era* (New York: Harper and Brothers, 1954). On the self-image of American businessmen, see Francis Xavier Sutton et al., *The American Business Creed* (Cambridge: Harvard University Press, 1956). The difficulties of the farm economy are discussed in Ronald L. Mighell's *American Agriculture: Its Structure and Place in the Economy* (New York: John Wiley and Sons, Inc., 1955).

SOCIETY, THOUGHT, CULTURE

A good general treatment of social, intellectual, and cultural trends during the fifties can be found in Nelson Manfred Blake, *A History of American Life and Thought*, 2d ed. (New York: McGraw-Hill Book Company, 1972). On major social changes see Walt W. Rostow, "The Dynamics of American Society," in Freeman, ed., *Postwar Economic Trends in the United States*, 3–29. Max Lerner's *America as a Civilization* (New York: Simon and Schuster, Inc., 1957), which tries to say something about all aspects of American life in the fifties, is diffuse and uninspired; shorter and more incisive is John Brooks's *The Great Leap:*

The Last Twenty-five Years in America (New York: Harper and Row, Publishers, 1966). For a worried contemporary view see Rockefeller Brothers Fund, *Prospect for America: The Rockefeller Panel Reports* (Garden City: Doubleday and Company, 1961). Albert Karson and Perry E. Gianakos, eds., *American Civilization since World War II* (Belmont, Cal.: Wadsworth Publishing Company, Inc., 1968) brings together relevant readings on recent American social and intellectual patterns; while George H. Gallup, *The Gallup Poll*, 3 vols. (New York: Random House, Inc., 1972), of which vols. II–III pertain to the fifties, offers a vast amount of information about American attitudes.

For accelerating urbanization and its many attendant social and economic problems, see Blake McKelvey, *The Emergence of Metropolitan America, 1915–1966* (New Brunswick, N. J.: Rutgers University Press, 1968) and Jane Jacobs, *The Death and Life of Great American Cities* (New York: Vintage Books, 1961). On educational changes in the wake of the Soviet sputniks, see Charles E. Silberman, "The Remaking of American Education," *Fortune*, LXIII (April 1961), 125–130 ff.

Much has been written about the civil rights struggles which followed the Supreme Court's invalidation of racially segregated public education in 1954. The best general accounts are John Hope Franklin's *From Slavery to Freedom*, 4th ed., rev. (New York: Alfred A. Knopf, Inc., 1974); Benjamin Muse's *Ten Years of Prelude: The Story of Integration since the Supreme Court's 1954 Decision* (New York: Viking Press, 1964); Anthony Lewis's *Portrait of a Decade: The Second American Revolution* (New York: Random House, Inc., 1964); Charles E. Silberman's *Crisis in Black and White* (New York: Random House, Inc., 1964); Louis E. Lomax's *The Negro Revolt* (New York: Harper and Row, Publishers, 1962); and Howard Zinn's *SNCC: The New Abolitionists* (Boston: Beacon Press, 1964). August Meier and Elliott Rudwick, *CORE: A Study of the Civil Rights Movement, 1942–1968* (New York: Oxford University Press, 1973) is a solid organizational history of one of the major civil rights groups; the reader edited by Meier and Francis L. Broderick—*Negro Protest Thought in the Twentieth Century* (Indianapolis: Bobbs-Merrill Company, Inc., 1966) —should also be consulted. For the evolution of thought and practice on direct action versus legal strategies, Vincent Harding's "Black Radicalism: The Road from Montgomery," in Alfred E. Young, ed., *Dissent: Explorations in the History of American Radicalism* (DeKalb: Northern Illinois University Press, 1968), 321–354, is informative. For white southern efforts to establish an intellectual basis for resistance to racial desegregation, see I. A. Newby's *Challenge to the Court: Social Scientists and the Defense of Segregation, 1954–1966*, rev. ed. (Baton Rouge: Louisiana State University Press, 1969).

For the history of the Supreme Court under Eisenhower-appointee Chief Justice Earl Warren, the major studies are Paul L. Murphy, *The Constitution in Crisis Times, 1918–1969* (New York: Harper and Row, Publishers, 1972); James D. Weaver, *Warren: The Man, the Court, the Era* (Boston: Little, Brown and Company, 1967); Archibald Cox, *The Warren Court: Constitutional Decisions as an Instrument of Reform* (Cambridge: Harvard University Press, 1968); Richard H. Sayler et al., eds., *The Warren Court: A Critical Analysis* (New York: Chelsea House, Publishers, 1969); and Clifford M. Lytle, *The Warren Court and Its Critics* (Tucson: University of Arizona Press, 1968).

The central item in the vast outpouring of material in the fifties on the nature and significance of popular culture is Bernard Rosenberg and David M. White, eds., *Mass Culture: The Popular Arts in America* (Glencoe, Ill.: Free Press, 1957), whose ambiguous conclusions should be contrasted with those in Rosenberg and White, eds., *Mass Culture Revisited* (New York: Van Nostrand Reinhold Company, 1971). The extremes in the debate over mass culture are represented by Gilbert Seldes's *The Public Arts* (New York: Simon and Schuster, Inc., 1956) and Dwight Macdonald's *Against the American Grain* (New York: Random House, Inc., 1962). Harold Rosenberg's essays on both the traditional arts and popular culture in *The Tradition of the New* (New York: Horizon Press, Inc., 1959) are well worth reading, as are Harold Rosenberg's *The Anxious Object: Art Today and Its Audience* (New York: Horizon Press, Inc., 1964) and Barry Ulanov's *The Two Worlds of American Art: The Private and the Popular* (New York: Macmillan Company, 1965).

On American film-making in the fifties, there is suggestive material in Charles Higham, *Hollywood at Sunset* (New York: Saturday Review Press, 1972) and Ezra Goodman, *The Ffty Year Decline and Fall of Hollywood* (New York: Simon and Schuster, Inc., 1961). For the effects of McCarthyism on the film industry, see Les K. Adler, "The Politics of Culture: Hollywood and the Cold War," in Griffith and Theoharis, eds., *The Specter*, 242–260. Radio and television are well treated in Erik Barnouw's *A History of Broadcasting in the United States*, 3 vols. (New York: Oxford University Press, 1966–1970), vol. III.: *The Image Empire*. Also of interest is John Crosby, "It Was New and We Were Very Innocent," *TV Guide*, XXI (September 22, 1973), 5–8.

Useful studies of literary currents include John W. Aldridge, *In Search of Heresy: American Literature in an Age of Conformity* (New York: McGraw-Hill Book Company, 1956); Ihab Hassan, *Radical Innocence: The Contemporary American Novel* (Princeton: Princeton University Press, 1961); Allen Guttmann, *The Jewish Writer in America: Assimilation and the Crisis of Identity* (New York: Oxford University Press, 1972); Maxwell Geismar, *American Moderns: From Rebellion to Conformity* (New York: Hill and Wang, 1958); and Allan Angoff, *American Writing Today: Its Independence and Vigor* (New York: New York University Press, 1957), originally published in *The Times* (London) *Literary Supplement,* September 17, 1954.

The traditional visual arts during the fifties are covered in Barbara Rose, *American Art since 1900: A Critical History* (New York: Frederick A. Praeger, Publishers, 1967); Sam Hunter, *Modern American Painting and Sculpture* (New York: Dell Publishing Company, 1959); Henry Geldzahler, *American Painting in the 20th Century* (New York: Metropolitan Museum of Art, 1965); John Burchard and Albert Bush-Brown, *The Architecture of America: A Social and Cultural History* (Boston: Little, Brown and Company, 1961); and Oliver Larkin, *Art and Life in America,* 2d ed. (New York: Holt, Rinehart and Winston, Inc., 1960).

Gilbert Chase's *America's Music: From the Pilgrims to the Present Day,* 2d ed., rev. (New York: McGraw-Hill Book Company, 1966) and Wilfred Mellers's, *Music in a New Found Land: Themes and Developments in the History of American Music* (London: Barrie and Rockliff, 1964) give incisive coverage of both formal and popular music. Bill C. Malone's *Country Music U. S. A.: A Fifty Year History* (Austin: University of Texas Press, 1968) is excellent. Irving L. Sablosky's *American Music* (Chicago: University of Chicago Press, 1969) is a handy brief survey; while John T. Howard's *Our American Music: A Comprehensive History from 1620 to the Present,* 4th ed. (New York: Thomas Y. Crowell Company, 1965) lives up to its title.

An overview of recent American political and social thought can be gained from David W. Minar, *Ideas and Politics: The American Experience* (Homewood, Ill.: Dorsey Press, 1964). Ronald Lora's *Conservative Minds in America* (Chicago: Rand McNally and Company, 1971) thoughtfully analyzes the New Conservatism emerging in post–World War II years; while Clinton Rossiter's *Conservatism in America: The Thankless Persuasion,* rev. ed. (New York: Alfred A. Knopf, Inc., 1962) is both a thorough examination of contemporary conservative thinking and also, especially in the original 1955 edition, a defense of the conservative position. Jeffrey Hart's *The American Dissent: A Decade of Modern Conservatism* (Garden City: Doubleday and Company, 1966) less ably argues the conservative case. Both Morton Auerbach's *The Conservative Illusion* (New York: Columbia University Press, 1959) and Gordon Harrison's *Road to the Right: The Tradition and Hope of American Conservatism* (New York: William Morrow and Company, 1954) offer thoroughgoing critiques of recent rightist ideas.

Perhaps the most succinct statement of the New Liberalism is in Daniel Bell's *The End of Ideology: On the Exhaustion of Political Ideas in the Fifties* (New York: Collier Books, 1961). John P. Diggins puts in perspective and insightfully analyzes the New Liberalism of the fifties in *The American Left in the Twentieth Century* (New York: Harcourt Brace Jovanovich, Inc., 1973). Alonzo L. Hamby's fine study, *Beyond the New Deal: Harry S. Truman and American Liberalism* (New York: Columbia University Press, 1973), describes the organizational and ideological foundations of the New Liberalism in the period after 1945 and accounts for the emergence of the dominant "vital center" outlook. Christopher Lasch's *The Agony of the American Left* (New York: Alfred A. Knopf, Inc., 1969) contains a hard-hitting essay on the Committee for Cultural Freedom; Clifton Brock's *Americans for Democratic Action: Its Role in National Politics* (Washington, D.C.: Public Affairs Press, 1962) is a rather narrow institutional history of the New Liberalism's other major organized expression. Marian Morton's *The Terrors of Ideological Politics: Liberal Historians in a Conservative Mood* (Cleveland: Case Western Reserve University Press, 1972) dissects and severely censures the leading "consensus" historians of the 1950s: Arthur Schlesinger, Jr., Daniel Boorstin, Louis Hartz, Edmund Morgan, and Richard Hofstadter. For the intellectual debate triggered by C. Wright Mills's radical analysis, see Norman L. Crockett, ed., *The Power Elite in America* (Boston: D. C. Heath and Company, 1970).

Index

75194